*A Way to See the World*

*Also by Thomas Swick*

Unquiet Days: At Home in Poland

# *A Way to See the World*

From Texas to Transylvania With a Maverick Traveler

Thomas Swick

THE LYONS PRESS
GUILFORD, CONNECTICUT
AN IMPRINT OF THE GLOBE PEQUOT PRESS

First Lyons Press paperback edition, 2005



The Lyons Press is an imprint of The Globe Pequot Press.

A majority of the pieces here appeared in slightly different form in the *South Florida Sun-Sentinel.*

"Back Roads" appeared in slightly different form in *The Oxford American.*

Printed in the United States of America
10 9 8 7 6 5 4 3 2 1

ISBN 1-59228-647-X (paperback)
ISBN 1-59228-170-2 (hardcover)

A previous edition of this work was issued with Library of Congress Control Number: 2004272538.

*To Hania*

*There are people everywhere who form a Fourth World, or a diaspora of their own. They are the lordly ones! They come in all colours. They can be Christians or Hindus or Muslims or Jews or pagans or atheists. They can be young or old, men or women, soldiers or pacifists, rich or poor. They may be patriots, but they are never chauvinists. They share with each other, across all the nations, common values of humour and understanding. When you are among them you know you will not be mocked or resented, because they will not care about your race, your faith, your sex or your nationality, and they suffer fools if not gladly, at least sympathetically. They laugh easily. They are easily grateful. They are never mean. They are not inhibited by fashion, public opinion or political correctness. They are exiles in their own communities, because they are always in a minority, but they form a mighty nation, if they only knew it.*

—Jan Morris, *Trieste and the Meaning of Nowhere*

# CONTENTS

## Part 4: Rio, Meet Waterloo; Where is My America?



## Part 5: Nothing to Declare but My Wonderment

# ACKNOWLEDGMENTS

Robin Doussard, Lisa Shroder, John Dolen, Mark Gauert, Dave Wieczorek, Heather McKinnon, Ben Crandell, Matt Schudel, Greg Carannante. The lines dividing editors, colleagues, and friends blur.

# INTRODUCTION

## *Back Roads*

I am a travel editor in Florida, job and geography conspiring to place me at the apex, simultaneously, of envy and invisibility.

I live in the sun and wander the globe. Every few months I leave a place that's popular for retirement and take what looks suspiciously like a vacation. From the idleness of the superannuated to the mindlessness of the tourist, it is a charmed, unheralded life.

We all know people fortunate enough to make a living doing what they love; I do what everybody loves. In my thirteen years as a travel editor I have met but one person who said, seriously, I'm glad I'm not you. Men and women dream of quitting their jobs and going around the world (it is by far the most common theme of hypothetical lottery winners) only because the idea of getting a job and doing the same is too far-fetched. Travel editor ranks up there, in the pantheon of Elysian careers, with fashion model and ballpark organist. And it gets about as much respect.

Travel exerts a primordial force on the human psyche. Yet, its physical gifts get all the press—the ruins of Pompeii, the canyons of Bryce. The emotional aspects keep it afloat, however, and explain why tourists cheerfully put up with every kind of discomfort and injustice, including that of falling in step behind other tourists. It is not so much their keen determination to see the things for which they left home as it is their uncontained delight in simply being away from home. Travel signifies release: from drudgery, responsibility, the familiar landscape, the quotidian routine. Having a job that frees you from all of these cripples logic; it's an impossible miracle, like growing old in order to stay young.

It is beyond comprehension. When I tell people my profession, the second word often fails to register. "Travel agent?" many will ask, because that is a more familiar, less abstract career. Their offices are on everyday streets, next to banks and drugstores; you can see them behind their windows, sitting at desks under posters of Puerto Vallarta, conferring with clients as if they were adult guidance counselors.

Travel editors are a rarer, more reclusive breed. With the dwindling of newspapers, we now number fewer than a hundred. We reside in large corporate edifices, in the far corners of newsrooms, in tiny cubicles stacked with guidebooks and taped with postcards. We travel, many of us, incognito, our only distinguishing feature, visible even through the weariness of jet lag, is an expression composed of equal parts smugness and guilt. Upon return, we sit alone at our computers and try to conjure up worlds. On Sundays we get sandwiched between the comics and the car ads.

We comprise a unique social group, one of the few that is universally both envied and belittled. (Adolescents being another.) We meet once a year, ostensibly to share ideas, but really because other travel editors are the only people on the planet who will sympathize with our complaints.

Travel keeps us humble—that on-going process of becoming anonymous—and gives us a heightened appreciation of the mundane. If you ever see a man humming down the cookie aisle in the supermarket, there's a good chance that he's a travel editor just back from a long trip.

We are chronically early for parties because we don't want to hear, "She can find her way around Ulan Bator but she gets lost in her own city." We'll even lodge a few nights in the local Days Inn just to deny people the satisfaction of saying we spent our vacation at home. We are the world's greatest dabblers, studying

Russian one month and then, the moment we're back, delving into the history of the Oregon Trail. We are the only writers at the newspaper who not only take their own pictures but also bring back souvenirs. In the course of a year we read more stories on Las Vegas than is medically advisable. We are ignored by the Pulitzers. We go out for lunch.

We rub elbows with a remarkable range of humanity, especially when stuck in the middle seat. We believe in the virtues of happenstance and personal transformation—or at least temporary mood alteration—through a change of scenery. We are eternally torn between arrival and departure. Our ancestral motto? The kindness of strangers.

Peering out of miniscule windows at 30,000 feet, we think about death more than most people do. (We refuse to make our peace with turbulence.) And yet, effortlessly crossing the Equator and the International Date Line, we persist in the illusion that we can fool time.

We inhabit, for all our detailed itineraries and clear destinations, a hazy realm. We are not real travelers, not like those people who actually do quit their jobs and set out from home. In South America, Southeast Asia, even here in the United States, I have met backpackers who made me feel like a charlatan. (Actually, I dislike backpacks, but more on that later.) Travel editors go off for short periods—at most a month, which is not nearly enough time to shed the rhythms and cares of one life and slip under the awkward, tantalizing carapace of another. We try, and we think we succeed—spending longer than an hour over lunch in a sunny piazza—but the very fact that we're aware of a change is proof that there hasn't been any significant one. We worry about work—I know colleagues who actually keep in touch through e-mail—and no traveler worthy of the name ever thought about things back at the office. We are fair-weather vagabonds, corporate wanderers who depend on our papers' largesse for our brief moments of wanderlust.

But we are not real journalists either, though most of us began as such. The people who now tell you about Cancun and Tuscany once covered city council meetings or wrote about bank mergers. It is one of the strangest, least deliberative acts in all of journalism, the anointing of a new travel editor. What usually happens is that the person who has held the job for ages retires (travel editors have, if nothing else, the tenacity of a chosen people) and someone is plucked from the newsroom to be the successor. Traditionally, this is a person who has performed long and faithful service; his or her previous job is unimportant. The travel section may not be the lowest priority at a newspaper—it's pretty much neck and neck with Fashion, Food, and Home & Garden—but the job of travel editor does have the distinction of being, among the four, the only one regarded as requiring absolutely no expertise. Travel possesses no professional vocabulary (as does Fashion) and demands no specialized knowledge (as Food does of the culinary arts, and Home & Garden of horticulture). Fluency in a foreign language is immaterial because, hey, everybody speaks English now anyway. Maps are available for the geographically illiterate. Not only do most people travel, most people also write postcards when they do: ergo, almost everyone has enough experience to become a travel editor.

Assuming the title of travel editor, a journalist goes through a metamorphosis not unlike that of a caterpillar into a butterfly. We no longer plod along in our own narrow beats; we flit about from place to place. With the exception of the foreign correspondent, and a few of the sports writers, we are the only people in the newsroom with frequent flyer miles. We are envied our mobility, but we are no longer accepted as one of the gang; there is something too flighty, too airy about us. We replace the journalist's stock in trade—sources, interviews, scoops—with the even less scientific chance encounters, conversations, trend spotting. We lack seriousness of purpose and, in a chronically superficial profession, depth. In a dilettante's game, we are the ultimate gadabouts. To say you are a travel journalist is to admit to layers of insubstantiality.

We are, in the eyes of some colleagues, just one step above a flack. While they're uncovering, we're promoting. Not outrightly of course, honoring always the sacred division between advertising and editorial; but it just happens that we are among the most positive people on the planet; spoiled perhaps, or maybe just stringent—forced to complain sometimes about the wanting thickness of our towels, or the incompetence of our guides—but persistently upbeat. The time-honored cynicism of the reporter vanishes as soon as we put on the travel editor's hat, partly because it would appear unseemly and partly because it would smack of ingratitude. For how can we not believe in the felicity of the world, having been the recipients of such undeserved good fortune?

And most of us routinely and blatantly commit the cardinal sin of journalism: we write in first person. It is hard not to, though there are still a few papers that flatly prohibit it. Unlike the reporter, who goes out with a specific story to cover—a crash, a missing child—we have no narrative, no reason to be in the place we have come to. (One of the most authentically titled travel books in history is Bruce Chatwin's *What Am I Doing Here.*) We have to find our story and, often, it is whatever happens to us. E. B. White, who began his career as a journalist, once said that he never would have made it in that profession because he always found what he experienced in covering a story more interesting than the story itself—the sign of a born travel writer.

Yet this outsider status is not enough to elevate us into the realm of real writers either. Travel journalism is a contradiction in terms, for the latter's strictures of brevity, clarity, and distance are diametrically opposed to travel writing's leisurely, nuanced, passionate approach. When the two converge, the result is often a story that attempts to wrap a breezy personal account around large chunks of useful information and inevitably ends up in a kind of limbo, possessing neither the authority of diligent reportage nor the atmosphere that comes of evocative prose.

Travel journalism is a hermaphrodite, as unreadable to professional journalists as it is to serious writers. In an interview, I once asked Jonathan Raban if he ever read the Sunday Travel section. "No," he scoffed contemptuously, "I don't want to experience someone's vacation vicariously." He had a point. The trips that give those stories life are generally closer in nature to a mindless vacation (it is rare that the author travels alone) than a journey of discovery, just as the tone usually has more in common with a press release (with its uncritical boosterism) than a work of literature (with its subtle ambiguities). Travel journalism is the media's version of military music.

There are well-known journalists and illustrious travel writers, but there are no famous travel journalists. With each passing day, Lowell Thomas goes from being merely unread to unknown. The award bearing his name, which some travel magazines and newspaper travel sections annually vie for, is—unlike the James Beard Award for excellence in food writing—completely unheard of outside the field. "Lowell Thomas winner" is, fittingly, as much an oxymoron as "travel journalism."

So in the end, we travel but are not really travelers, we write minus the distinction of being called writers, and we feed the voracious appetite of a newspaper without the collegial comfort of belonging as journalists. And, whenever people are reminded of our nebulous existence, we are envied like rock stars.

I am one of the few travel editors who actually set out to do this, or at least one of the few who will admit to it. I grew up in a small town on the northeastern banks of the Delaware River—Phillipsburg, New Jersey—and, because the nearest hospital was in Easton, Pennsylvania, my life began with the crossing of borders.

But I was far from a precocious traveler. My first trips, like many people's, were to grandmother's house: over the river and through the Pennsylvania Dutch farmland in my father's gondola black Buick we'd go. Hex signs dimpled the barns like flattened pinwheels, and the pastures were pillowed with Holsteins, which we counted—burying them of course at the first sign of a cemetery, then starting anew—to see which side would have the most when we pulled into Mechanicsburg.

Mechanicsburg—that storied town, my own private Mayberry! Even today it is difficult for me to recognize as a real grandmother anyone who doesn't live in a place with stout corner churches and red-brick sidewalks and gravelly alleys that all seem to lead to Rakestraw's Ice Cream, whose double-dip cones we always somehow found room for after Grandma's fried chicken and graham cracker pie. Mechanicsburg conditioned me early to expect glad rewards at the end of a long journey.

What added to Mechanicsburg's aura was the fact that it really had only three seasons, all of them golden: Thanksgiving, Christmas, and summer. When I got older—eight, nine—I'd spend a week each July with my grandparents, who would drive over to get me, starting out across their own river, the august Susquehanna. On the return trip one year, my grandfather's Dodge broke down in the fretful hamlet of Ono—my first taste of travel's ironies—and I can still see my little suitcase behind the rear window, rising with everything else atop the garage lift, and the reassuring beam of my grandmother's blissfully untroubled smile.

On rainy days I'd settle on the sofa in the living room, beneath a painting of the old Rockville Bridge, and page through a volume I'd discovered in the glass bookcase: *Around the World in 2,000 Pictures*. Countries were depicted in small, representational, black-and-white photographs, and while the headlines didn't inspire me—"Past and Present Meet in Israel," "Wales Is Land of Coal, Contrast"—the pictures did. South America, I learned, was rich in equestrian statues, while in Thailand the hats of dancers curiously resembled the roofs of temples. Equally wondrous was seeing the Atlantic City boardwalk, which I had walked from end to end, bound between covers with the Temple of Luxor.

Today, I think of travel as anything that extends one's realm of experience or expands one's lexicon of acquired convictions—and occurs beyond the backyard (thus distinguishing it from reading). It is a moment that comes when we are out of our element and allows us to see, or feel, or think, anew. I grow weary of people who declare that travel is dead, who complain about McDonald's in Paris and go off to Namibia in order to avoid being a tourist. It's like saying experience is finite. Yet, if you go to the McDonald's and meet some locals, maybe wangle a tour of the city or an invitation for coffee, then you're more of a traveler than those who fly into Windhoek and book a group safari. A vivid, childhood travel moment for me was visiting the home of a friend who lived, not as I did in a leafy suburban development, but on a narrow street of modest row houses a block back from South Main. As we walked through the living room, his father put down the evening paper and told his younger brother, who was sprawled on the floor struggling with his homework, "Spelling is bullshit." The language, and the sentiment, were so alien to everything I associated with parental guidance and middle-class home life that I felt as if I were in a foreign land. And I was; and it was exhilarating.

My first experience with a wider world, however, came in the sixth grade when I first attended the 1964–65 New York World's Fair. It was a perfectly timed marriage: our nation's pre-'68 self-confidence and my still innocent capacity for wonder. I knew where everything was, and even now as I write this I can still see the layout: the grandiose corporate pavilions forming a fan around the artificial lake at the top (Bell Telephone the keystone, off to the left, the IBM egg, into which moviegoers, seated on a pulleyed grandstand, periodically disappeared); the middle cluster of national and state pavilions, which over the course of five visits I collected like baseball cards; and the ever-popular transportation area at the bottom, Ford (prehistoric audioanimatrons, viewed from gliding convertibles) and General Motors (glittering, impossible metropolises of the future) with a heliport restaurant rising in between, where I imagined all of New York society—Jack Parr, Roger Maris, Kitty Carlisle—dining elegantly at candlelit tables. That doomed city in Queens was the first one I learned by heart, and it was there that I acquired a taste for maps, streets, buildings, and mingling with, what seemed to me then, all the conceivable races of the world.

But my first real "contact" with abroad didn't come until high school, when our family began taking part in what was then called, and perhaps still is, the Experiment in International Living program. For one or two weeks every summer, a foreigner—usually a European male—would suffer through corn on the cob with us, and Saturday afternoon telecasts of Phillies' games, all in the cause of furthering cultural understanding. I eagerly awaited these visits. There was something different, hence infinitely fascinating about these men, who sat in my father's chair not realizing it was his, smoked cigarettes (how could they know he had not long before given them up?) and crossed their legs to show cream-colored socks peeking out between dark trousers and shoes. They moved differently too, with a certain lightness that I assumed came from playing soccer. They were, to a man, miserable at catching things. "Here, Leif, the keys . . . Ooops!"

One morning during my junior year, our Latin teacher announced that the Latin Clubs of New Jersey were sponsoring a ten-day Easter trip to Italy—Naples, Sorrento, Rome—for what seemed to me then the impossible sum of $350. After dinner a few evenings later, as my parents stood at the sink doing the dishes, I nervously mentioned the trip (sensing that this was a pivotal moment in my life; something more than just a way to get back at them for making me study a dead language). After a brief discussion, they agreed to send me.

It was, certainly by today's standards, a late initiation into the mysteries of travel, but I wonder whether had it come any earlier would I have felt them—would I still feel them now—so intensely? The morning of my departure heralded the first true day of spring that year (or so it seems to me now); I came downstairs and stood at the screen door listening to birdsong and looking up at the cloudless blue, which—it now seemed as inevitable as unthinkable—would soon contain me. My mother, who had not yet been abroad herself, bustled about the kitchen, making lunch. My father, in a thrilling completion of the tableau, pulled into the driveway (he had left the office early for the trip to the airport) just as the first chord of the Young Rascals' hit, "It's a Beautiful Morning," played on the radio. It was a moment, perhaps one of my last, of pure, uncomplicated happiness.

If we forget a family trip to Montreal for Expo 67 (and we will), Naples was my first foreign city, and no place on the Continent could have been better chosen to give me that indescribable shock of an unimagined life. I stared out the window of our tour bus at the narrow alleys, billowing laundry, and ancient cafés as we groaned on to museums, churches, and up-to-date ruins. For the entire ten days it was like this: We had flown thousands of miles across an ocean to a place we could look at but we could not touch. I didn't know at the time that this type of tour was actually popular with certain travelers, shielding them from dust and pickpockets and the impromptu, providing a smooth, air-conditioned overview. I gleaned little from the lectures—my sights and mind so fervently concentrated on the passing parade—but I learned how I didn't want to travel.

The other lesson, also unintended, was that in travel, as elsewhere, the *richesse* is in the little things. We, the students, were fascinated with our waiters, who dressed in starched white jackets and went to great lengths to get Kennedy half dollars from us. (One had drilled a small hole at the top of his and now wore it as a medallion.) I was very impressed at ordering a Coke at the hotel bar in Sorrento and receiving the beverage in a tulip-shaped glass with a slice of lemon floating sunnily in the middle. (The simplicity and good sense of a gesture I had never seen, nor contemplated.) We all marveled at the lemons, dotting the yard outside our windows as plentifully as crab apples. And who of that year's itinerant male Latin scholars will ever forget passing in the ruins of Pompeii a group of European schoolgirls (classicists, we could not identify their living language) with trouser cuffs rolled up and exhibiting legs as hairy as our fathers'?

There was a small group from my high school, all of whom complained not just about the tour but about Italy as well. They took to singing, defiantly, "We got-ta get out of this place." Surprisingly, or perhaps not, they all shared Italian backgrounds. I can still hear them singing. Out of weakness, I probably added my own voice, but I still felt something terribly wrong in it. It went beyond the wasting of our parents' savings, the sapping of our teacher's expectations; it betrayed a proud parochialism. They could not see Italy; all they could see was home, and this was not it.

Four years later I decided to give it another try. I was a junior in college, with a vague idea that I wanted to be a writer and a more immediate wish not to spend another summer working on the bridges over the Delaware River. I had pored over brochures of programs offering summer jobs abroad—pictures of slaphappy students in orchards—and imagined that life in a fun crowd might be as wasted as that in a glum one. I decided to fly to London (again with initial backing from my parents) and attempt to find a job on my own.

It sounds so simple now, but I was filled with apprehension. Hours before departure I sat with my family in the den, watching *Casablanca* and wondering who had concocted such an unwanted scenario for me. As the minutes ticked down, it seemed less like an adventure than a sentence. (How different, I couldn't help but think, from the prelude to my last trip.) I had no idea if I would find a job—my roommate's father, an international businessman, had assured me there was no work in London—or even where I was going to sleep the next night.

It turned out to be a hostel in Bloomsbury. Within a week, I found a job—working the pastry counter in the Joseph Lyon's Food Hall at Marble Arch—and a room in the West Kensington apartment of my Nigerian co-worker and her husband. It was straight out of Beckett—a bare bulb hanging over a single bed—and would have sent my old high school buddies packing (a college friend, who came to see me in August, wagged his head in pathetic disbelief). But for me, it was a barebones haven, a symbol of having made my way in the greater (if still English-speaking) world.

I learned that summer not to listen to so-called voices of reason, especially when they say you can't do something you have your heart set on. I also discovered the rewards of self-imposed exile, of releasing yourself from the comfort bonds of the familiar and heading out into the indifferent unknown.

London was the first city I ever lived in, having grown up in a small town and gone off to a suburban college, and it instilled in me a lasting love of cities. In 1973 it was no longer mod and not yet trendy. I walked everywhere—each free day picking a new realm: Mayfair, Fleet Street, Chelsea, the East End—and grew to understand what Charles Lamb had meant when he wrote to Wordsworth, "I often shed tears in the motley Strand from fulness of joy at so much Life." For sustenance, I stopped into sweet shops and stuffed my pockets with colorfully wrapped toffee. When thirsty, I inevitably found the pubs closed. That the buses and the underground ended their day when the night was just starting (an abomination, I thought, in one of the world's great capitals) meant that I eventually returned home on foot, never once looking over my shoulder.

That summer also taught me about the loneliness of travel. A shy American undergraduate and a decorous Old World country do not make a good mix. I was afraid to speak in a place where strangers didn't. In my worst moments, I thought of those happy orchard scenes, and wondered why I had purposefully distanced myself from pleasure. On the plane over, my anxiety rising with each inexorable stage of our descent, I had heard a young couple behind me laughing coquettishly, and the sound had stung me like a rebuke. That was how to travel: confident, carefree, loved. Not as a quivering lonelyheart.

I tried to meet people in pubs, but they weren't like American bars; people arrived in groups, ordered rounds, talked of mutual friends, and then departed as one. There was no room for interlopers, and there were few castaways. Walking into a pub, I'd always get the uneasy feeling that I'd crashed a private party. Yet this gave me early practice in watching other people have fun—a large part of what a travel writer does—and taught me the value of careful observation in the absence of the more difficult, and desirable, participation.

I got so lonely I was happy to go to work. My supervisor, the reedy spinster Miss Lilywhite, by her name alone deepened my allegiance to nonfiction. Behind the counter I was joined at various times by my landlady Ivy, lovely and soft-spoken, and Anne, a tiny widow from Dublin who saw to it that I went home each evening with a couple of leftover Bath buns or scones.

For lunch and tea I would make my way down into the bowels of the building—the food hall occupied the southeastern corner of the Cumberland Hotel—to a cafeteria divided by gender and splattered, like a modernist canvas, with sauce-stained smocks and knockabout accents. The entire Commonwealth was on display: slender waiters from the subcontinent, beefy pastry chefs from the Antipodes, gloomy Hong Kong cooks, African porters, West Indian dishwashers, Malaysian busboys, Irish bellhops, Maltese factotums. For a boy from New Jersey, it was an extraordinary scene. I would sit there and think of how privileged I was, in this most visited of cities, to be witness to something that no tourists saw; how I had penetrated, literally, beneath the surface of the place; how, in short, I had learned to travel.

After graduation I moved to Washington, D. C., and through a friend got a job as a copy editor with an engineering firm that did contract work for the Navy Department. (With friends like that . . .) One day I read an article in *Esquire* magazine explaining how you could live cheaply in France for a year—by becoming a student—and started thinking. It seemed that if I was serious about becoming a travel writer I should speak another language (what did I know?), and I had studied a little French in school. A few weeks later, on my lunch break, I passed a scale model of the *Queen Elizabeth 2* docked in the front window of a travel office on Connecticut Avenue. I knew of course that such grandeur was not meant for copy editors—in fact, that its time was just about up for everyone—but I went in anyway and learned, interestingly, that the ship offered a reduced fare to anyone under the age of twenty-five.

Again, this time with the suspicion that they had created a monster (travel writer being too strange and improbable a beast to imagine), my parents agreed to help me go.

Until now, travel had appealed primarily as an act of disappearance. Like many adolescents, I had been unsure of myself in social situations and assumed that my absence would make a far greater impression than my presence ever did. That instead of humbled in person, I might be glamorized in absentia. Those girls who wouldn't dance with me at the youth center on Fridays would now be forced to consider me strolling through Naples. ("What's become of Waring/Since he gave us all the slip?") I was counting on the triumph of imagination over reality.

Yet now, poring over engineering reports with a sharp red pencil, I saw travel as a vital means of escape.

The bottom deck of the *QE2*, on that October morning in Manhattan, resembled a college dorm during registration week. I met my two cabin mates—one of whom was also headed to Aix-en-Provence—and then went up on deck to watch as the once immovable city began to slide away. Everything passed close and clear (my eyes traveling down the slowly unfolded canyons of cross streets), and I thought that there could be no better way to leave a place—especially one's home, especially for a long time—than in this prolonged and meditative calm.

I was moving closer toward an art of travel (albeit a dying one). There was free seating at lunch and I plopped down at a table across from an elegant dowager. Sipping my vichyssoise—the first intentionally cold soup I had ever eaten—I heard her proclaim that it had been much better on the *Ile de France*. Having nothing to compare it to, I found it excellent. In the evening, one of my cabin mates and I were shown to our table in the dining room, where two attractive young women waited in sleeveless dresses. (Not only was I on an ocean voyage, I was also guaranteed a dinner date for as long as it lasted.) Following dessert we formed a posse to penetrate the first-class realm, and when we did, with little difficulty, we found it deserted, its nocturnal habitants having already descended to our more promising nether world.

During the day the monotony of the sea kept me transfixed. I took strange satisfaction in thinking that while my friends were spending their days gazing at automobiles, billboards, houses of brick, I was surrounded by nothing but ocean, a vast, uncluttered acreage of water. (Not only had I disappeared, but so had the world with me.) It seemed the ideal mode of travel, for you were given a true sense of distance and a chance not only to see and hear but also—in the salt air—feel and taste and smell your progress around the globe.

We were heading east, into a shared and studied past. No other direction had occurred to me. I was a product of the East Coast, born, raised, and educated among the descendants of European immigrants. My family background was Dutch, Welsh, Irish, German—white, Celtic-Saxon Protestant—with no known roots south of Bavaria. I had no Hispanic or Muslim friends; my only contact with Asia, before moving to Washington (and working with a Korean secretary), had been in Chinese restaurants. Europe was not just my mother; she was my world.

In Paris, before heading south, I had one of those fateful moments that the randomness of travel famously bestows on us. Strolling through the Left Bank I stepped into one of the large university bookstores off Boulevard Saint-Michel. In the corner stood a rotating rack of books in English, and as I turned it, my eyes fell on one in particular: a Penguin paperback by Evelyn Waugh titled *When the Going Was Good*. The cover carried a black-and-white photograph of an ancient automobile set in a desolate landscape, atop which an artist had painted the big orange curve of a setting sun. Next to the title were the printed words: "Everything the author wishes to preserve from his pre-war travel books." As an English major, I had read Waugh—*Decline and Fall, A Handful of Dust*—but none of my professors had ever mentioned his travel writing. There is a lot to be said for getting out of college.

I bought the book and took it to Aix where, because I was struggling to learn French, it became about the only written English I allowed myself during the next nine months. It was all I needed. The pleasure, as with all great travel books, was twofold: seeing a previously unimagined life and savoring the language that so wondrously describes it. As in Waugh's novels, the writing was both elegant and spare, restrained and hilarious. There were not just people—itself a welcome change from the endless landscapes of most travelogues—but unforgettable characters. And the eye for absurdity that Waugh brought so successfully to the

English upper classes thrived in travel's vale of displacement, makeshiftness, and impending doom. He made travel writing seem a respectable pursuit.

School finished in the middle of June, and I searched for ways to prolong my stay. For one thing, I had nothing to go back to. And I hadn't really been in France, spending my days with an international crowd whose *lingua franca* outside the classroom was inevitably my own. Language schools are incubators, keeping the young and helpless in a controlled environment until they're verbally competent enough to venture out on their own. It seemed counterproductive, just as I was starting to find my second voice, to head back into the mother tongue.

And as greatly as I wanted to stay in France, I wanted to leave Provence. It had been done: Ford Madox Ford, Cyril Connolly, James Pope-Hennessy, Lawrence Durrell, M. F. K. Fisher. I did not see that the timeless attraction of the name would prove irresistible to lesser writers in a populist age that had forgotten, or simply had no use for, previous masters. And few readers would have been charmed by my year—conjugations, anti-Americanism, cafeteria lentils—in Provence.

There was something about the landscape, too, so lauded by others, that depressed me. The earth was harsh and dry and lacking in shade; it seemed to produce an equally brittle and tearless people. I longed for a large, many-limbed oak, and the soothing sight of cows grazing.

But first I'd try Paris. I stayed almost a month, living in a dorm (*Esquire* was right), and making the rounds of American offices, including, inevitably, the *Herald Tribune,* still in its old location just off the Champs-Élysées on Rue de Berri. Though I had sailed in on an ocean liner, I could not turn back the journalistic clock: no one started out, as Buchwald had done, in Paris anymore.

I had no luck anywhere else; because of the Common Market monopoly, other positions were just as unobtainable. As I wandered disconsolate through the city, I'd see Americans my age, usually in pairs, and appendaged to backpacks—enormous, bright orange bulks on poles that gave them the stiff, awkward posture of astronauts. In a country where I hesitated to speak for fear of betraying my accent, they broadcasted their nationality without uttering a word. It was not so much audacity as ignorance, or innocence. (Though many learned quickly to pass as Canadians.) They looked, even in the city, commendably if incongruously rugged. I suspected that, as travelers, they were as superficial as their parents (*Fodor's* had been replaced by *Let's Go Europe*), but they gave off an aura of well-equipped competence—*that,* I thought not for the first time, is the way to travel—and real immersion. And they were not alone.

With my suitcase, I hitched a ride to Alsace. It was the part of France farthest from Provence (culturally if not geographically) and closest to Germany, the homeland of Claudia, whom I'd wooed in Aix. I never saw Claudia again, but from the highest field in Kutzenhausen, where I baled hay—people with cows to feed being less particular about proper papers—I could see the Black Forest. I felt immeasurably blessed. A visit to an agricultural bureau in Strasbourg, and a call to the first number I found there, had landed me in the half-timbered courtyard (having passed under the garlanded archway) of the 500-year-old Ferme des Fleckensteins. Dany, who ran it with his parents, was a recent dropout from medical school and, as much as he needed a hand, he also yearned for someone to talk to.

It was a blissful summer. I experienced the new and pleasing sensation of having been inserted, willingly, into another life, one far removed from any I had ever inhabited before. Unlike in London and in Aix, where I had remained a passive observer—listening, watching, living on my own terms—here I was inescapably plunged into foreignness. Every morning I awoke under a feather quilt and dressed in front of a picture of Albert Schweitzer. At breakfast there was milk fresh from the cows, followed by a marathon of chores. (The sun shines long in the Alsatian summer.) The novelty of the landscape was amplified by the fact that I was moving through it in another language. Not only was I learning about farm life (a world which had lingered at the edges of my childhood, seen but unknown), I was doing it in French (the third-period terror of my high school days). The combination constituted a startling development. Dany took my spare and halting classroom idiom and, through constant banter and occasional drills, whipped it into shape. He taught me songs—arias from his favorite operas, *chansons* of Brel and Brassens, salacious ditties of medical students—that we belted out from ladders in the cherry orchard. He even taught me a few Alsatian words, so that walking the cows out to evening pasture with throaty cries of "*gaylos oydie*" I marveled anew at who I currently was.

What started as a simple working relationship quickly evolved into a warm friendship, which gave me enormous joy and a sense of accomplishment as well. I had left behind dear friends and family and eventually found new ones, here at the end of a fortuitously dialed number, and months of conscientious study.

Alsace also marked a return, after my brief stint with the lustrous—London, Washington, Provence—to the touristically, if not historically, overshadowed. It was an unglamorous province, especially the northern half where I found myself, and, like my home state, famously caught between two behemoths. That my two months there were more intense and gratifying than the nine months spent in Aix predisposed me, I think, toward unsung places.

The night before my departure, the family presented me with a farewell gift: a beautiful plate painted with a young Alsatian woman in traditional dress standing in front of a Tudor house. I packed it carefully into my suitcase and the next morning, as I walked past the suddenly directionless backpackers in the Strasbourg train station, it felt like a trophy.

My *wanderjahr* was nearly complete. I arrived in London a week before my ship, the *Mikhail Lermontov,* was scheduled to sail, and after finding a room went off to Foyles. The year that began with a book would end with a book. I found a copy of V. S. Pritchett's *Foreign Faces*—an account of a journey around Eastern Europe—and took it back to my hotel where I stopped at the bar and ordered a beer from a pretty Polish barmaid. I insisted she borrow it, since it had just gone, in my mind, from being an unread collection by a favorite author to a promissory note toward another meeting. When it happened, a few days later, Hania confessed that she hadn't had time to look at the chapter on her homeland. (She also worked as a chambermaid at the hotel, a summer break for hard currency from study at the University of Warsaw). I gave her the volume to take back home, first writing my name and address inside, painstakingly, and with hope.

Travel is like math—you begin with the easy stuff and work your way up. Canada was the geographical equivalent of addition, a territorial breeze. Italy, the way I did it, was tutored subtraction. England, with its similar language in an altered setting (ancient buildings, tiny bathrooms) was slightly more challenging multiplication and division. Going to France was like tackling geometry (just in case I had any doubts about the mathematical analogy, the notebook paper was not just lined, it was cross-hatched). Poland, where two years later I found myself after giving up feature writing at the *Trenton Times,* was algebra—still part of a by-now familiar Europe but situated in the little-known eastern half, and with the twisted component of communism added to the equation.

Each new encounter with abroad exceeded in length and intensity the one that had preceded it. I had gone from a ten-day excursion to three months to a year to an indefinite stay; just as I had gone from tourist to summer hire to student-worker to family man. In the fall of 1980, Hania and I had married, and like all good Polish newlyweds we shared an apartment, in our case with an aunt and cousin. To help support us, I got a job teaching at a private English school. Travel, in the space of only a couple of years, had moved from a lark to a life—a hard and satisfyingly invigorating one. I was experiencing a place few Americans had seen, precisely at a time when—because of the rise of Solidarity—it was capturing their attention. The journal that I had kept since college became a diary.

I was also seeing beyond the stereotypes (one of travel's most vaunted attributes). Warsaw was gray and bleak (the journalists' all-purpose shorthand for Eastern Europe) only in the most superficial sense, in its outer shell of overcast skies, socialist housing, empty supermarkets. Yet once inside the cramped apartments of those dilapidated blocks you often encountered a liveliness of spirit and an intensity of discussion, a true and—the secret of its incandescence—defiant *joie de vivre* that made the Frenchman proudly announcing the year of his wine a pathetic character. Even out on the lusterless downtown streets—Nowy Świat, Marszalkowska—I found more beautiful women per block than in Paris or New York, and not just the blue-eyed, golden-haired *Polonaise* of legend, endlessly repeated, but sloe-eyed sirens and raven-haired girls with high Tartar cheekbones. (Years later I would read Paul Theroux's *Riding the Iron Rooster* and feel vindication in the scene in which he sits next to a passenger who "reminded me that young Polish women are madly attractive, with clear skin and large, limpid eyes and lovely hair.")

My students, contradicting the joke makers, were bright, knowledgeable (even, especially, about the outside world), and cultured, passing around with reverence a just-published collection of Norwid's poems, and coming to class on Friday nights, when I, at a similar age, would have been awash in beer and football games. It was in Poland that I first felt the thrill of original discovery, and the urge—no, the need—to share it.

In October of 1982, I sailed on the *Stefan Batory,* one last taste of the sea before the throes of unemployment. Fourteen days from Gdynia to Montreal, it had all the resonance of my previous voyages, with an added historical note: immigrants. Hania, a somewhat reluctant one, joined me in Philadelphia a few months later, and for the next few years I worked at unengaging jobs while, in my free time, writing about Poland. I envisioned a book: not a study of a peaceful revolution and an internal occupation (the few books on Poland that existed in English were almost all either political or historical) but an impressionistic portrait of a short-changed people.

There seems to be a logical progression to many people's lives—the right college, the connected friends, the high-powered job—that I was sure had eluded me. I had been too footloose, too dismissive of the rules. It took me five years to get back into newspapers; the fact that I had left to spend two and a half years in another country, one that for much of that time had occupied their front pages, was viewed as a detriment (the broad cosmopolitanism of American journalism). Though I wouldn't have wanted to be a reporter, or even a foreign correspondent; what I was hoping for was a much less common and exalted thing, a bright balloon that floats high into the sky and causes a single heart to sink.

Then one spring day in 1989 I saw in the back of *Editor & Publisher* magazine that the *Fort Lauderdale Sun-Sentinel* was looking for a travel editor. I sent, as requested, a letter stating my philosophy of what a travel section should be. It began by saying that it shouldn't be like any that currently existed. The travel writing that appeared in Sunday newspapers was pedestrian, clichéd, soulless. It revealed nothing of the real life of a place; it was focused on the tourist and it was stuck in the past. It had no personal voice (the stories all sounded as if they'd been written by the same person) or point of view (there was almost never anything negative).

A good travel section, I argued, should inspire people not just to travel but also to read, through characters, dialogue, humor, insights, fresh observations, original language. It should entertain and enlighten, and teach about the world. I was sure I'd never get a response, but the prize was so unattainable that it didn't seem worth an exercise in diplomacy. Someone had asked for my opinion on something I felt strongly about, and I had given it. That alone was therapeutic.

A few weeks later I got a call; a short time after that I flew down for an interview. The taxi driver asked if I'd like the scenic route, and drove to my hotel along the beach, pointing out the bar made famous by the movie *Where the Boys Are.* (He claimed that it was also where the wet T-shirt contest had originated, which I later learned was an instance of well-meant albeit misguided civic pride.) The visit seemed to go well, though in retrospect my callowness alarms me. I knew nothing about budgets, so didn't ask about them; nor did I learn anything about production schedules or the relationship of the travel editor with the advertising department. When the two young women conducting the interview wondered if I had any questions I asked, unable to come up with anything else, what magazines they read.

My dream now seemed almost within reach, and still I hesitated. It had presented itself with strings attached—a jejune address, an Animal House heritage. Before boarding my flight, I called an old friend from the *Trenton Times,* then living in Miami, and sought his advice. "Well," he said, in his usual, unmincing way, "if you wanna go on cruises with a bunch of old geezers." At the airport in Newark I saw a thoughtful young man in glasses, wearing a trench coat and carrying a briefcase, and realized with a shock that I hadn't seen anyone remotely like him in the past twenty-four hours.

In the end, the perfection of the job won out over the imperfections of the place.

★ ★ ★

Driving down I-95 that August, I did not see the synchronicity, the poetic justice of becoming a travel editor in Florida. Of course there were obvious parallels: a rosy job in a sunny place whose whole *raison d'être* seemed based on the theme of my purview. Mr. Travel in Vacationland, I was going both ways on Easy Street. But I was also heading toward the job I had pined for in a land I had rarely given a thought to. And I did not yet see how in that dichotomy lay the seed of similarity: My new profession and my latest home were also joined, perhaps most absolutely, through their marginality.

You need only look at a map. Geographically, Florida does not fit naturally into the contours of the rest of the country; it sticks out awkwardly, come to think of it, like a thumb, left to soak in salt water and never retrieved.

Its landscape and climate—increasingly flat and miasmal as one heads south—are equally unique, found nowhere else in the United States. In winter, cold fronts and massive storm systems sweep across the land from the Great Lakes to Okefenokee, leaving the vast majority of Florida untouched. Being here then is like living in an embassy compound in a despotic country—you watch the slow torture of others from the climatic equivalent of diplomatic immunity. (Until hurricane season, the anarchic revolution.)

Historically as well, Florida seems a world apart from the rest of the country. It contains our oldest city, although it is so little known that it turns up regularly as a question on quiz shows. (St. Augustine, for $300.) This oversight is sometimes attributed to the Anglo bias of our history textbooks, but it is more realistically connected to the fact that St. Augustine, unlike the newer cities of Boston and Philadelphia, did not enjoy strong, continuous growth, but instead—due to climate, and more importantly, its distance from the emerging American mainstream—suffered a dramatic decline, in population as well as in worldly significance.

After a grandiose start, Florida fell into a torpor from which some might argue it has never emerged. Most of the state was not comfortably livable until the twentieth-century advancements of air-conditioning and pesticides.

The Florida that I was headed toward was near the muggy bottom, one of the more recently inhabited patches. While people speak of Florida as a single entity, there are really two Floridas (at least two principal ones), and they differ more dramatically than do the two Dakotas or Carolinas. That they don't separate must be partly out of respect for semantics, for North Florida is unmistakably the South—with its pick-ups, boiled P-nuts, and drawl—while South Florida—gold chains, delis, and lip—is irrefutably the North.

It is the North with most of the life sucked out of it. The great urban engines that churn night and day up there—ambition, curiosity, dedication, hunger—corrode in our humid, soporific air. People say that we have no history, but unfortunately we do: It is a history of unproductiveness. South Florida has always been a place you come to after you've completed important business—made a fortune, passed your exams, raised the children, closed a deal—somewhere else. Here, achievement is rewarded but not inspired. It was for the idle rich that Henry Flagler, the father of modern Florida, built his railroad and his grand hotels; for randy college students that Gregg Newell popularized Spring Break; for northern retirees that Irwin Levy started Century Village, for vacationing families that Walt Disney turned Orlando (psychologically if not geographically South Florida) into a metastasizing theme park—the four men creating a lasting legacy of luxury, debauchery, decrepitude, and childishness.

There are those who claim that South Florida is changing, that people now come here for work (as I did), not just to escape (as everyone thinks I did). And it's true. Children, though still banned in some precincts, grow up here, and quite of few of them turn out well (though often moving North in the process).

Corporate headquarters compete for land with hospitals, banks, churches, and schools, which are forever sprouting new limbs of mobile classrooms to house the swarms. We have fine restaurants in strip malls (good for keeping tourists off the scent) and symphony concerts in modern halls (though a few music lovers notoriously leave early to beat the traffic). "Some of us live here," reads a local bumper sticker, and you can't help but notice, driving along I-95 with its reflective glass offices (all the better to reiterate the idea), the semblance of a serious life.

But the vacation/retirement mentality lingers; like sand after a trip to the beach, it infiltrates everywhere. Climate is still the main attraction—ask ten people what they like most about living in South Florida and nine will answer, "the weather"—and a place known primarily for its physical comforts inevitably attracts a less than rigorous settler. The standard uniform of the South Floridian is still a T-shirt and shorts, and it is impossible to take a man seriously when he's bared his legs. On those rare mornings when I chance upon neighbors in the elevator, I feel like a relic in my shirt and tie, even though I'm twenty years younger than the kids in their play clothes.

Ours is still an external culture built on water and sunshine. On weekends people do not make hot cups of tea and curl up with a book; they go out fishing, kayaking, rollerblading, biking, swimming, sunbathing. Our profusion of beaches guarantees a twelve-month supply of inert bodies and minds. For the proper aesthetic presentation of the former, there are countless gyms; in South Florida, a bicep is a terrible thing to waste.

Behaviorally, there is an attitude of entitlement here as strong as at any five-star resort. It is what caused a man to call the paper a few years back and ask me to find out what time his wife's plane was due into West Palm Beach. He was an older resident, as many of them are, and their malaise is a result of a dual marginality: They are shunted aside in an overlooked place. Not only are they burdened with endless time on their hands, they feel that, having paid their dues up North, everything down here should now go their way. And in many respects it does: The sun shines, the car starts, the driveway never needs shoveling. But as soon as something goes slightly awry—an unnaturally long line at Publix, getting put on hold by their spouse's air carrier—they're unable to cope. And yet, with their Old World ties and staunch passion for learning, our seniors are often the most interesting and stimulating people around.

There is a lack of civility that shocks people when they first move here (especially those who come expecting the South). A certain distance, even adverseness, is to some extent understandable in a community made up of strangers and transients, but in South Florida it all too frequently takes an aggressive form. In the course of a day it is rare not to hear at least one grasping voice or rude remark. At any given time, probably a quarter of the people on the roadways have no job to go to, and yet I have never lived anywhere where drivers are quicker to the horn when the light turns green. We have the least laid-back beach culture in the world, with the possible exception of Israel, and they deal with bombs. A native who visits almost any other part of the country is immediately impressed by how friendly people are. The true symbol of South Florida is not the palm tree, or even the wet T-shirt, but the concrete lawn pyramid, placed in a row at the edge of the yard so no one will park there.

Miami is a little different, for it is a real city (though one unnavigable without a car). People dress as though they were not on constant holiday—the result, partly, of the sophisticated segment of the Latin population—and there is an occasional sweetness, usually provided by their other half. But it has not lived up to its billing, in the late 1980s, as the "city of the future." Since then, the downtown skyline has barely changed, while less on-the-cusp places such as Raleigh and Houston have reared up in glittering palisades. The construction boom in Miami—perpetuating the sybaritic stereotype—has been in waterfront condos.

The city has developed some excellent institutions, and a certain notoriety in architecture and design. But the colleges and universities have not garnered national renown, except in one case for football, and they do not confer an intellectual climate onto the rest of the community as good schools do in places such as Providence, Austin, and Berkeley. I have vivid memories of a sunny Saturday in winter, coming back from my favorite bookstore in Coral Gables and stopping in South Beach for a drink at a café. I was wearing a sport coat and I carried my new purchases about a block until I was struck by how utterly out-of-place I looked. I high-tailed it back to the car and headed home to read in my neonless apartment.

For most Americans, South Florida is a place that is visited for the tonic reasons of beach vacations or family visits (everybody, not just Cubans, has somebody living in South Florida); it is not somewhere where real life goes on. I have friends up North who in my thirteen years here have never visited, out of principle. The same thinking occurs to residents who move away; a colleague who left the paper to take a job in New York said that as soon as she arrived it was as if her life here had never happened. For her, South Florida had become the geographical opposite of the leg the amputee still feels pain in: It was a physical reality that had dissolved into nothingness.

Yet foolishly or heroically, South Florida continues to believe in its glorious, pertinent existence. In a world that rarely gives it a glance (and then does so with a mixture of bemusement and horror), it still thinks of itself as one of the more blessed and irresistible players. It takes itself seriously even though nobody else does. It is the perfect place for a travel editor.

# PART ONE

## *What in the World Is So Great About Travel?*

Leaving home.

The atlas, with its impossibly rich offering of places to go. (Beside which the choices of career and life partner seem painfully limited.)

The travel section of the local bookstore, a paperback Candyland of color and promise.

The picture (in the guide you buy) of the beautiful girl in traditional dress that will not be replicated even remotely by anything you see when you get to her country but will linger in your mind longer than most of what you do run across.

Telling friends where you're headed.

Their expressions.

The novel you always meant to read that's set in the place you're finally visiting.

The plane tickets, miniature flying carpets stitched with cabalistic coding and wearing the airline's colors winsomely on their stiff jacket. (And now technology's going to deprive us of this?)

Airports, which, while striving lately for the normalcy of a mall, still provide dramas of euphoria and grief. Where else but in these way stations of travelers (and in hospitals) can you find side-by-side the dual extremes of prologue and conclusion?

Flying, the most bad-mouthed miracle of modern times. How many of us travel so much that we can justifiably take for granted the four-course meal conjured from a two-inch slit in a metal pushcart at 30,000 feet? The Gabriel-like view down on passing clouds? Pour a glass of Bordeaux (damn the jet lag) and consider yourself the lucky soul you are.

Touchdown.

The *thwump* of the immigration official's stamp.

Foreign air, inhaled through still-alert nostrils.

The hotel, in the heart of a maze (every new place is a maze) with a bedroom all made up and waiting for you (yet another in a seemingly endless series of miracles), clean sheets and fresh towels and a view that, even if bleak, contains nothing familiar.

New streets, new shops, new faces, new façades, new customs, new concepts—the everlasting thrill of the novel.

The taste of things never before tasted.

The feeling—after all you have heard about globalization, Americanization, the shrinking planet—that you are in another world.

Hearing a foreign phrase escape from your lips.

The slight slippage you then feel, into a new persona.

The ache in your legs from walking so much.

Cafés, where you linger with people who are not on vacation but somehow also have time (and make you wonder with regards to home: Where's globalization when we need it?).

Sitting on park benches.

Markets, where you are plunged headlong into the needed nutrition of the everyday.

Non-green money.

Newsstands layered with unintelligible headlines and indistinguishable cover girls.

The *International Herald Tribune.*

Music (suddenly moved from "world" to "local") in which every note seems a perfect evocation of place.

The Americans you stop to chat with (reveling in your command of the language, your grasp of idioms) and discover to be as beguiled by everything as you are.

Finding just the right postcards, and then affixing to them heartbreakingly beautiful stamps.

The thickset man in the sweet shop who drops a few extra samples into your bag (wordlessly elevating you from lowly tourist to honored guest).

The dancer in the late-night café whose sinuous movements tell you more than any museum was able to.

Going to sleep with absolutely no idea of what tomorrow will bring.

The names—Jinsook and Azim and Slava—that chummily join Dan and Bob and Pam in your address book.

The way that, in learning about another country, you inevitably learn about your own.

The thought, on certain iridescent evenings, of loved ones far away.

Coming home.

# 1

# *The Longest Day*

If you define "day" the way most people do, as the period between when you get up in the morning and when you next go to bed, then this was—by far—my most protracted.

4:50 A.M. Friday: The radio alarm goes off. WTMI is still broadcasting its nighttime jazz.

I shower, shave, and stuff my toiletries and sport coat into my already packed bag. After checking the windows, the oven, the lights, my passport, my ticket, my zipper, I head downstairs to wait in the lobby for SuperShuttle.

It arrives at 5:45. On the street, the driver—unusual in my experience with the company—heads in the wrong direction. I think: I have to get to Asia today and I'm having trouble getting onto Davie Boulevard.

I direct the driver to I-95. We exit at Ives Dairy Road to pick up a passenger at Turnberry Isle. Along Biscayne Boulevard young women with bare legs jog in the darkness. Do their mothers know they're out here?

An island woman joins me in the shuttle. "Going to Boston?" she asks. Flattered, I think, that I look Bostonian, I say "No, Los Angeles." "You've got a day ahead of you," she says. "And then Hong Kong," I add. "You've got a life!" I so enjoy the double meaning of this reply that I hold back my destination. For what would she say to that?

★ ★ ★

The sun is up by the time we reach Miami. At the airport I perform my good luck ritual—drinking a cup of pina colada juice—and head to the American Airlines counter. A large man directing traffic in front sleepily asks to see my ticket.

"Vietnam?" he says, with wakened interest, and directs me to the appropriate counter.

8:13 A.M.: Takeoff. Once in the air, the pinstriped man beside me opens his briefcase and goes to work. I dislike him immediately. Then, noticing that the seats in front are vacant, he moves. He seems a very decent fellow. I slip off my loafers, curl across both seats, and make a feeble attempt to sleep through the Heartland.

My neighbor returns somewhere over Arizona. He's a securities lawyer from Miami on his way to meetings in Los Angeles. Conscious of the Twenty-Minute Rule—for instance, a Harvard graduate will casually drop that fact within twenty minutes of talking to a stranger—I nonetheless tell him I'm going to Vietnam.

"Your first time I hope?" I say yes.

He tells me about his grandfather, who lived in Burma and built airport runways throughout the East. I begin to feel less like The Great World Traveler.

Descending into L.A., we gaze out the window at the fingered mountains. The lakes on top look like puddles in the sun. Then the smog moves in. The dusty film, as we glide above it, gives the downtown a submerged look, like a city at the bottom of a waterless sea. Its grid of low brown squares rises, in the distance, into grim brown towers. There is no color, no movement, no sign of life in a landscape seemingly as barren as Nevada. You wonder not how people can live down there, but if.

Then, breaking through the lid of smog, like diving beneath the water's surface, we see the living city—the matchbox cars, the pincushion Forum—that becomes lovingly magnified as we surge toward earth.

"Have a good trip," my neighbor says. "I'll look forward to reading your articles." Not even out of the country yet and the expectations are already building.

10:45 A.M. (West Coast time): No baggage to claim. I step outside into the cool poisonous air and take the shuttle to the international terminal. I'm delighted to see that I've grown at least three inches in the course of the morning. Then I realize that I am surrounded by Asians. Men as compact as their briefcases, in suits as black as their hair, crisscross under a mockingly high ceiling. Check-in counters are for Japan Airlines, China Eastern, Garuda Indonesia, Nippon Air.

I present myself at Cathay Pacific. The agent asks for my Vietnam visa, gives it a cursory look, and then hands it back. The destination obviously doesn't carry the weight here that it did in Miami.

In the bookstore, a young man calls to his wife: "Honey, you want Ayn Rand or Anne Rice?" "Anne Tyler," she says.

The cafeteria upstairs offers the usual airport fare: burgers, barbeque chicken, breaded fish, udon soup. I go with the soup—may as well start now—and eat it delicately with chopsticks and spoon. I've still got a long way to go in this shirt.

At Gate 102 our plane's nose nearly kisses the window. Something about its green and white design gives it an old-fashioned look, and it suddenly occurs to me that I like that look in probably everything except the aircraft I'm flying in.

The cabin fills—mostly Asians—but the seat between me and the bearded Caucasian by the window remains empty. I've always suspected airlines match passengers by gender; now I wonder if they add race, or perhaps language, into the equation.

The screen at the bulkhead delivers the grim statistics. Distance to destination: 7,243 miles. Time to destination: 14:03. Estimated arrival time: 6:39 P.M. Local time at origin: 1:34 P.M. Local time at destination: 4:34 A.M.

Minutes before we push back from the gate, after everyone has been seated, all the overhead compartment doors have been shut, a man comes huffing down the aisle. He too wears a beard. His shirt is mapped with sweat; its tail hangs out. If he weighs less than 300 pounds it is only because he is not very tall. He aims himself, of course, at the seat next to me. My suspicions are confirmed.

"Don't mind if I squeeze in here, do ya, mite? Nime's Walker, Ian Walker. Bloody lucky to mike this pline. My flight from Dallas-Fort Worth got in fifteen minutes ago and I mide a run for it. G'dye, Shirley," he greets the head flight attendant. Unlike me, she seems delighted to see him.

"They're a grite crew here. I fly 'em all the time. Grite, grite service."

I find myself doing something I never imagined myself doing: missing a securities lawyer.

"So how long are you intending to sty in beautiful downtown Saigon?"

Airborne only a couple of hours—two down, twelve to go—and the Aussie is restless. His condescension merely makes Saigon seem all the more appealing.

Around 7 P.M. (I'm not sure whose time) the flight attendants come around with dinner. Obeying all the rules for avoiding jet lag, I decline wine but get it anyway: a ruby flow down my chest and back. (It is, I find out later, a 1990 California cabernet sauvignon.)

The flight attendant who caused the spill—a striking young woman with shiny black hair, cerise lips, soaring cheekbones, and perfect skin—is mortified. Immediately she dashes off for towels. I picture myself at midnight walking into the lobby of my Saigon hotel wearing what looks like a bloodstained shirt. Ian says, grinning, "I guess I shouldn't have prized the service so much." I forgive him; there are not many times when the man in the middle gets to gloat.

The attendant returns and starts rubbing me down—front and back—with wet towels. It is extremely pleasant. A kind of Oriental massage and Chinese laundry rolled into one. Then, because my shirt is now damp, she undoes the buttons and places warm towels against my body so I don't catch a chill. We could go down now; at least I'd die happy.

Her supervisor appears shortly afterwards, with apologies and a form for me to fill out and mail in with the dry cleaning charges. Ian says, "Shirley, could you turn the thermostat down a bit? It's about twenty-three degrees in here now and it needs to be around twenty-one."

We enter a kind of limbo. For the first time ever, my watch face is meaningless. Meaningless. The shades are all pulled, so there's no indication of day or night. No announcement, either, when we cross the International Date Line. Have we crossed it? What day is it now?

I can't remember which movie this is either—second or third. I do know it's Chinese. A dismal mixture of gunfire and martial arts. What trash these people produce. Then I remember the American fare that preceded it.

Listlessly, time passes. I read. I try to sleep. I eat when they feed me. I duck when they pour the wine. I joust with Ian's elbow on the armrest. I think of the poet Philip Larkin who said: "I wouldn't mind seeing China if I could come back the same day."

Noodles arrive. A tall circular carton of ramen pressed in broth. I take up my chopsticks and slurp with gusto. It's nice not having to worry about stains.

I doze fitfully, fearful that I'll wake up with a hairy antipodean head on my shoulder. When I open my eyes, *The*

*Simpsons* are on the screen. The more your landscape changes, the more it stays the same.

And then, an hour after we were supposed to, we begin our descent into Hong Kong. It is 7:13 local time, the exact time it is on my watch, which I haven't moved since leaving Fort Lauderdale, where it's now Saturday morning not Saturday evening.

"If you've never flown into Kai Tak before," Ian says knowing I haven't, testing to see if I recognize the name of the airport, "you're in for a thrill." We take the less dramatic approach—in from the sea, rather than over the mountain—but it is still a sight. Orangey lights of high-rises fill the windows. It's like landing on a runway along the West Side Highway.

"Have a grite time," Ian says loudly, "in beautiful downtown Saigon."

Kai Tak is a burst of animation after fifteen hours of collective inertia. Saturday night at the crossroads of Asia. I scan the magazine racks and wander the duty free shops with the wistful eyes of a man anticipating a socialist republic.

The collective waiting by the gate has the patented look of socialism: grimmer, shabbier, less radiant than the rest of the world into which, temporarily, they have unfairly been thrown. Of course, who am I to talk? Though my wine stains are now extremely faint.

The fair-haired man in the polo shirt stands out. I introduce myself. He is from California, hoping to sell his water distribution equipment in Saigon. It is his first trip, but a partner, who's been there a month, is meeting him at the airport. As always, I envy the man who's being met at the airport.

He wonders about me. I say I'm coming to write stories. It sounds so slight compared to the efficacious transport of potable water. My ego has been in a tailspin ever since I said good-bye to the woman on the shuttle. Yes, I have a life. But does it have a purpose? Maybe I'm just tired.

The fact that Cathay Pacific is the airline of Hong Kong doesn't guarantee its planes a jetway at Kai Tak. We have to take a bus out to ours and, stepping off, I feel for the first time in my life the air of Asia. The sweep of lights and the rumble of engines, the glittering backdrop of skyscrapers and mountains, give our boarding an undeserved glamour.

10:27 P.M.: We're told that the members of tonight's crew come from Hong Kong, Malaysia, Thailand, India, and the Philippines. The passengers, who take up less than half the plane, are mostly Vietnamese.

The next in a seemingly endless succession of dinners consists of delicious fried noodles with Singapore-style chicken and stir-fried Chinese broccoli. Immediately after eating, I set to work on the four forms we've been handed.

The *Giay khai suc khoe hanh khach nhap* (passenger's health declaration on arrival) asks, among other things, if I am currently experiencing diarrhea or fever. It goes on to inquire whether I am traveling with either *thuc an* (food) or *tro cot* (body ash). Number three simply asks: "Is there international vaccination book?" I assume this is a trick question and leave it blank.

But the real puzzler appears on the next form. It asks my occupation. And all the old anxiety before communist officialdom returns in an instant. I break out in a sweat. (They'll think it's fever.)

My problem is that I'm entering the country on a tourist visa. So I can't write "journalist" and hope to convince them this is simply a vacation. I vacillate between "writer" and "travel writer" and give some thought to "economist."

I settle on "travel writer" and spend the remainder of the flight carrying on an imaginary debate in my head concerning the fundamental nature of my work, i.e.: If I'm writing about a country I'm experiencing as a tourist, what does that make me? Philosophical discourse proves difficult for a man who has been up for twenty-nine hours.

11:22 P.M.: We hit the runway at Tan Son Nhat. The airport is dark and quiet and riddled with ghosts. At the bottom of the portable stairs—no jetways here—wait a soldier with a rifle and a woman in an *ao dai,* the traditional dress. The air is sticky and still.

We trickle into an empty arrivals hall. Three young military men in too-large hats sit behind three wooden podiums. The two foreigners in front of me are sent off to a corner where a photographer sits; obviously they didn't read the section in the guidebook about bringing extra pictures. I step up.

The officer on the left says something to my man that makes him giggle. I have never seen an immigration officer giggle before. All ruthlessness instantly drains from him.

Still, he takes his time. I wonder if I mistakenly gave him the dry cleaning form. Then he wields his stamp (making one of the sweetest sounds a traveler can hear), returns two papers, and motions me past. My eloquent defense of the writer as tourist goes unspoken.

I am the first one through. Smugly, I tote my carry-on bag past the still empty luggage area. Customs, too, is a cinch.

Outside, a small cluster of people waits expectantly in the darkness. None of them is happy to see me. I walk over to one of two taxis and give the name of my hotel. A young man puts my bag into his trunk and we set off. Out of the window I catch a glimpse of the words "*Tan Son Nhat*" glowing in blue atop the terminal. And the capering accent marks, the hushed hour, my groaning fatigue all add to the exquisite strangeness of the moment. I am in Vietnam.

We pass a few motorbikes, girls in skirts sitting sidesaddle on the back. We are the only car. It is almost midnight. I notice a movie theater that's playing, as if for me, *The Longest Day.*

I can almost taste the cool sheets, the foreign pillow, when the muffler falls off. I've come this far and now . . . The driver stops, no need to pull over, and gets out for a look. Unable to reattach it, he rips it off and stuffs it in the trunk. We thunder onto a wide boulevard and swing around an empty circle. My hotel, the Rex, is boarded up.

No, that's not the entrance. It's there on the side. The great glass doors swing open. And now my surroundings—the bright lobby, the hatted bellboy—take on the contours of a dream that, finally, I am about to have.

# 2

## *Women on a Train*

I had a good feeling about this journey as soon as I arrived at the station in Annecy.

There was no cause for cheerfulness. It was 10:30 at night and most happy people were safely at home, if not already in bed. I stood alone in the chill autumn air of a foreign city, sharing a platform with the usual straggle of serial killers who frequent nighttime terminals. At home you pay little attention to drifters; abroad, they grate with their foreign clothes, haircuts, postures. Like garbage dumps, they're erased from the travel brochure pictures. They give you the shivers. And I had been thinking: seductive, mysterious strangers. Such is, admittedly, the not-always-false image of overnight trains.

The 10:35 was a commuter, taking me to Chambéry to catch the midnight train to Genoa. It arrived on time but stopped every few miles—with that prolonged, hollow, heartrending screech—so passengers could stare out into the unrelieved blackness. I knew I'd miss my connection.

After more than an hour, the lights of Chambéry filtered into view. We passed under the great iron roof of the station and I grabbed my bag and stepped onto the platform. There was no other train in sight.

Ascending from the underground tunnel, I found a conductor being shadowed by a backpack. I asked him about the midnight train. "It's been canceled. A strike in Italy. The next one leaves at 2:48." The backpack swung around to reveal a comely teenager.

"Where are you going?" she asked in an accent I took to be Italian.

"Genoa. And you?"

"Pisa."

We walked across the street to the Café de la Gare. The café resembled a stage set: five weary travelers seated at three circular tables, four drunken locals leaning against a chromium bar, a golden light spilling out into the dark street. As we entered, a bearded, breathless man asked us if the Paris subway was on strike. I said I didn't think so.

"But you don't know?" he asked sharply.

I said no, I couldn't say for sure.

"Then you're not *au courant,*" he said dismissively and walked away.

We took a table against the side wall, under a large mirror. I walked to the bar to buy us two teas. The bearded man again approached.

"Excuse me, sir. Do you know if the Paris subway is on strike?"

I told him I still didn't have a clue.

"Then," he said triumphantly, "you're not *au courant.*"

He moved to the man next to me. "Excuse me, sir, do you know if the Paris subway is on strike?" The man said he didn't and was informed he was not *au courant.*

The bartender was so amused he forgot to put the teabags in our water. I walked back and placed the steaming cups on the marble table. A wavy strand of thin brown hair, like a side lock, fell between the girl's left eye and ear. She casually brushed it back. This sequence was to continue for the next two and a half hours.

"I'm looking forward to seeing your country," I said. "Eventually."

"Argentina?"

"No, Italy. Aren't you Italian?"

"No, I'm from Buenos Aires."

She had left home four months earlier after graduating from high school. "I thought traveling around the world would be the better education for me than the university." Her parents did not agree. But what could they do? She spent the first three months with her brother and his wife in Stockholm. Both were actors. They made up what must be a very small contingent of Argentinean actors on the Swedish stage.

Giselle ("my mother wanted me to be the ballet star, so she named me for her favorite ballet") didn't like Sweden, especially Swedish men. "They're calm all week and then drunk on the weekends." But it gave her a chance to learn English, which—hard to believe—she did not speak when she left Argentina. "It's not yet very good," she said.

"I wouldn't say that. You speak better than Gabriela Sabatini."

"Oh, thanks," she said sarcastically, then added in a husky voice: "I blay at Wimbiddledon."

"How does she sound in Spanish?" I asked.

"Just as bad. All she does is hit tennis balls. She's not intelligent. Not like Vilas. He writes poetry, songs. He's into singing now."

"How's his singing?"

"Terrible."

Giselle had been traveling with a young Mexican she met in Germany. I asked if he had taught her the Mexican expression: "Ego is the little Argentinean we all carry inside of us." She looked hurt. I changed the subject to books.

"I like Carlos Castaneda. And Marquez. I read *One Hundred Years of Solitude* three times. The first time, when I finish, I start reading it again, immediately. And Borges—when I started to read him I didn't really understand but I knew he was great . . ." She caught herself. "My Argentinean ego," she apologized.

A waiter came around, shoving chairs atop tables with a meaningful clatter. We picked up our bags and headed out into the street. We were the only sign of life. Inside the dusky station, we found a wall not overgrown with the outstretched limbs of sleeping travelers and took seats on the soiled floor next to it.

"The station in Bern was the most terrible," Giselle said. "All night there was drug people wandering in and out. It was like a bad dream."

"Don't you get tired of traveling?" I asked. It was one o'clock and we had almost two hours before the next train. My stomach growled and my eyelids fell. I wished I could rustle out of bed, and set on this floor, all the people who have said they would love to have my job.

"No," Giselle said. "Because I don't want to go back. It's crazy in Argentina now.

"You would not believe my high school. In class, while the teacher teaches, one girl is knitting, another is reading a comic book, in the back, a boy and a girl are making out."

"Still, you must miss your home. Your own room. Your own bed." The cold, hard floor was making me obsess about beds.

"I miss only my dog."

"What kind of dog?"

"Like Benji, only prettier. Oh," she said sheepishly, "my ego again."

By two o'clock, we were deep into family history. Her grandfather had been a Polish Jew by the name of Bursztyn—"it means amber in Polish." She complained about her looks, her narrow, elongated face, ignoring its smooth complexion, its liquid, curious eyes. "I look like something, how do you say, out of space?"

"Extraterrestrial. No," I corrected her, "more like a Modigliani."

* * *

Our train arrived at 2:48. Waiting to board, we were joined by two young women speaking French.

The smaller of the two was also the more intriguing, with a smooth olive complexion and curly, almost kinky black hair pulled into a tight ponytail. She wore a loose sport jacket over a low-slung silk blouse and tight corduroy pants: all as black as her hair. A pair of small, gold, wire-rim glasses with lozenge-shaped frames added to her charm. Although she seemed more southern Mediterranean, she had that look of certain French women that combines, without apology, the sultry and the studious.

"*Ils disent qu'il n'y a pas de couchettes*" (They say there are no couchettes), the other woman said. "But that we can have an empty first-class compartment."

We entered the first one we came to, Giselle and I taking seats by the window, our French companions seats by the corridor. The train started to move. The woman next to Giselle stood up and, fiddling with her seat, made it slide down into a horizontal position. The unexpectedness of the movement made us all giggle.

The intriguing woman did the same with hers. "It's three o'clock in the morning," she said in a shockingly clear American accent, "and I'm fighting with a king-size bed." Soon all the seats were aligned into one continuous mattress, with us atop it, giddy with fatigue. We curled up chastely into sleeping positions, one person's shoes abutting another's nose. Someone switched off the light.

"There's the moon," I said in French, and everyone laughed again in its generous glow, so bright that I could see, peeking out from under the black corduroy pants, a pair of brown-and-white argyle socks.

I lay in the moonlight marveling at the progression of this journey and wondering who this woman sleeping next to me was. She had appeared out of nowhere, an apparition with Levantine features and an American accent speaking fluent French. And now she was lost in impenetrable slumber.

It is difficult to sleep when you have the vague impression you're already dreaming. I eventually nodded off, though, just in time to hear the compartment door slide open and a prosaic conductor, less respectful of sleep than I, cry for *billets.*

Four drowsy heads rose in unison. Slow-motion hands stretched out with tickets. (The apparition, I learned, was going to Naples.) We were told we did not belong in a first-class compartment. In a variety of languages, we said that we did. The conductor retreated, as if into a dream.

Shortly after came an intrusion for *passaports* (the apparition's was French), then one for *bigliettos,* timed perfectly to coincide with my next loss of consciousness. We were told, for the first time in Italian, we did not belong in a first-class compartment. We argued our case with groggy indifference, and then dozed off before hearing the response.

When I next opened my eyes, it was to rows of fast-moving cypresses shrouded in mist. Morning in Liguria. Without regard for my personal curiosity, the train was heading inexorably toward Genoa. I would never know who this young woman was. I pulled my bag down, pushed my seat up, and stepped delicately over six female legs.

"Where are we?" Giselle asked, rubbing her eyes. "Genoa," I said and wished her well.

Out in the corridor, I stood by the window and waited for my stop. The compartment door slid open and the nameless, mysterious woman emerged. Time was running out. I skipped the niceties of asking how she had slept.

She lived in Paris, she said in English, but went to Lyon twice a week for graduate school. International business. She was on her way to Capri—having visited it for the first time a week ago, she'd been so enchanted that she decided to return. For the weekend.

I asked her where she had learned her English. We entered a tunnel.

"In Washington, D.C. My grandfather was the Swedish ambassador when I was a girl, so I went to grade school there."

"Swedish?" I asked, surprised. We emerged into the light.

"Yes," she said, smiling. "My mother's Swedish. My father's Lebanese." Her name, she said, was Ayla.

The train eased into the station. We said good-bye.

And I stepped onto the platform of another new city—tired, alone, but *au courant.*

# 3

# *Man's Destiny*

"Well, would you take a look at that," I said to my wife as we drove through Miami. "Somebody's put a funnel atop the Fontainebleau."

Then I remembered we were not on the Beach; we were headed to the port. Some smaller funnels suggested that the hotel really was a vessel. Not just any vessel, of course, but the Carnival *Destiny*—the largest cruise ship in the world. I had my ticket in my book bag.

"Have fun," Hania said, dropping me in front of the terminal.

"Tomorrow," I reminded her, "is a 'fun day at sea.'"

I trudged through check-in, across the gangway, and into a nine-story Rotunda with four glass elevators outlined in Tivoli lights. On a raised platform behind the bar, a quartet played Vivaldi.

I continued down to the lowest passenger deck and the cheapest cabin, where inside lay the threat of a roommate. As I opened the door, a presence rose from the bed. In the darkness I could make out only a stream of flowing hair. "Somebody's made a mistake," I thought. But then as the figure fell to the floor on hands and knees, the glow from the television caught a prophet's beard. It took him a few seconds to crawl to the door.

"Hiya," he whispered, standing up and pulling me back into the corridor. "I'm Norman from Oklahoma City. Nice to meet ya. I'm videotaping the TV and didn't want to get in the way."

⋆ ⋆ ⋆

Norman was short and round and wore a tightly stretched, canary yellow Carnival T-shirt printed with nautical flags, the majority of them shrouded by his salt-and-pepper beard and mane. "Wait here a minute—I'll turn it off and give ya my ten-cent tour." As the door closed, I reminded myself: My wife just dropped me off for a weeklong cruise; my parents didn't just drop me off for my first semester.

Norman, who looked like no one I'd ever seen on a cruise ship, had sailed on the maiden voyage of the *Destiny* the week before; this was his ninth maiden voyage on a Carnival ship, his thirtieth cruise. "Do ya think this one could count as a maiden voyage?" he asked, seriously, as he led me down the corridor. "I mean, it's the first time she's been to the western Caribbean."

We climbed three flights of stairs. "You're really gonna like this," he said, and we entered a large theater with a steep, horseshoe-shaped balcony. "This is the Palladium. Amazing, isn't it? They have ten-watt water-cooled lasers." He climbed onstage and discovered a door leading behind the curtain. I stared dutifully at a system of pulleys. "They can pick up whole sets," he said.

Back outside, we paused at the Rotunda. "Ya see how part of the ceiling is dropped? Joe Farcus did that and I'm not sure it's totally successful. On other ships it would all be open. There are supposed to be clouds in it, but they're hard to make out."

He opened the door to the outside. "They have a promenade that doesn't go anywhere. But beautiful deck chairs. Thick pads. Very comfortable."

He climbed the Rotunda stairs to the Galleria Shopping Mall. "There seem to be fewer shops on this ship. But I like this idea"—he pointed to the tuxedo rental.

Down the Promenade Deck, past the Millionaire's Club Casino and the Cappuccino Bar ("didn't seem too popular last cruise") to the Point After. "Look at that video wall. Have ya ever seen so many monitors in a disco? I think they said they've got 535."

A curved flight of steps led down from the dance floor. "This is a strange room. Joe's idea was that it would be for people who didn't want to be involved in the disco but didn't want to be cut off from it either."

Then into the Apollo Piano Bar. "Look," Norman said, walking to a table and picking up a microphone from an opening in the center. "For singing along. They can also spotlight any table in the room." From the Down Beat Lounge—"great jazz singer in the evening"—we walked over to the Criterion Lounge.

"I personally think they ought to move the Late Night Show out of here to the Palladium, where the sight lines are better. One of the serious omissions on this ship is a place for ballroom dancing. Cruise ships are the last bastion of ballroom dancing." It seemed an odd cause for a guy like Norman.

On the Lido Deck, I was proudly shown the twenty-four-hour pizzeria, the Chinese kitchen, the burger grill (Norman grabbed two) and was then led out onto a vast tract crammed with deck chairs, pools, whirlpools, a glass-roofed bandstand, and a 200-foot spiral waterslide.

"Up there," Norman said, pointing to the base of the winged funnel and moving close enough that I could make out burger crumbs in his beard, "is the topless bathing area. It was officially initiated last week by a woman who publishes a swinger's magazine out of Michigan. She had the date of her cruise posted on the Internet for months. Now, if women can go topless, does that mean men can go bottomless? I've got a thong that's about as bare as you can get. I'm gonna wear it this cruise and see if I get any reaction."

"I'd like to change my cabin."

"That's not possible," the man behind the purser's desk said.

"Why? Is the ship full?"

"For the next seven months." He smiled smugly.

I wandered, listless, and returned a few hours later to petition a young woman named Elizabeth.

"I'd like to change my cabin."

"Is something wrong?"

"I've got a cabin mate."

"What's the matter, isn't he your type?"

I gave the briefest physical description of Norman. She knew him instantly. Her eyes softened with sympathy. She suggested I check back tomorrow, after everyone had settled in.

We pushed away from the pier a little before sunset and a little after the first official playing of the "Macarena." Far below, along the banks of the channel, camera bulbs flashed and tiny figures waved; causeway traffic slowed to a crawl. We were an attraction, one of the few in the world that consists of locals staring at tourists. South Beach drifted past like a miniature village on a moated platform. Then the sea enwrapped us, and the largest cruise ship in the world became just another speck in its dark immensity.

At dinner, my table was occupied by a thin-lipped couple from Georgia and their head-lolling teenage son. They sat at one end—it was set for eight—I at the other. In silence, I ate my gazpacho and curried vegetables.

The show began at 10:30. "Welcome to Carnival's *Destiny!*" cruise director John Heald cried from the Palladium stage. He wore a double-breasted navy blazer with a red handkerchief in the pocket and spoke with an English accent.

"The largest, newest, most expensive cruise ship in the world! One hundred thousand tons of fun! Right now we've got 3,097 passengers on board—the most people ever to sail on a cruise ship! Ladies and gentlemen, you are part of history!!!" I was the only one who didn't applaud.

Eight people were called up on stage, stooges for games and that moribund mixture of sexual, ethnic, and scatological humor. "Take HER hand, not mine, you idiot. This is a fun ship, not a ferry boat!" (Howls from the audience.) Cruise ships are also the last bastions of political incorrectness.

I retreated to the Down Beat, where I listened to jazz and sought solace from the bartender. "Ivana," I asked, "where are you from?"

"Croatia. Far away from here." And her dreamy smile suggested she meant more than in the geographical sense.

Norman's snoring woke me around 2:00 A.M. My immediate feeling, other than discomfort at the frigid temperature in the cabin, was relief that a) he was asleep, and b) I now had a legitimate (and non-incriminating) case for transfer.

I knew from the female purser's response that the ship probably wasn't full, and I decided that, if refused a change, I would threaten to sleep in the Rotunda.

So began my fun day at sea.

I walked out onto one of the dead-end promenades and slept on one of the very comfortable deck chairs. A little past noon I strolled up to the buffet in the Sun & Sea Restaurant and sat down with three attractive young women in bikinis. (Let somebody else endure an unwanted presence.)

"Tom? Hi, nice to meet you. I'm Leigh and this is Kathy and this is Lisa. There are twenty-one of us. We all met last year on the *Sensation* and made a date to meet on the *Destiny.*"

"How do you like it?"

"Love it. It's the best of the Carnival ships. The food's much better and there's more cabin space. You know, the important things."

"My cabin's smaller," said Lisa.

"Really? But everybody's so nice. We staked out places near the bandstand, and we already know all the musicians. Three of the guys in our group have one of the penthouses, and we have a party up there every night before dinner. They came on board with twenty-one bottles of champagne in their luggage. You should come up some evening—it's room 7198. But you'll hear it before you see it."

"Leigh, we're missing out on good tanning time."

"OK, Tom, nice meeting you. See you up at the party."

That afternoon, high in the Palladium balcony, Norman sat videotaping the cruise director's port talk. Outside, I struck up a conversation with an exotic-looking woman named Carmelita.

"I'm here with a group of law enforcement people from Sacramento," she said. "Most are in SWAT teams and undercover narcotics. They're pretty wild."

I left her and wandered past the purser's desk, but Elizabeth wasn't there. I strolled down to the infirmary on the crew deck and found, posted on a bulletin board, a list of crewmembers' names and nationalities. In addition to the usual Latin Americans, Indonesians, Filipinos, there were a good number of Croatians, Hungarians, Romanians (especially in the bars), and a high percentage of Indians in the kitchen.

Back at the purser's desk, I saw Elizabeth and took my place in line.

"Do you remember me?" I asked after a short wait.

"Oh yes. Let me go check."

She came back shortly.

"Yes, there's an empty cabin—2191. Here's your new key."

Packed in minutes, I carried my bags up one deck. Never had a room looked so beautiful.

Later I ran into Norman in the Rotunda as he was passing an elderly man with uncombed white hair playing solitaire at the bar.

"Norman, I found another cabin."

"Really? Why'd ya do that?"

"Well," I tried to be delicate. "You snore."

"Oh, sorry."

Because of the number of passengers, the captain's cocktail party was held in all the bars on the Promenade Deck, with the captain stationed in the hallway opposite the disco. To his right stretched a line of men in tuxedoes and women in sequined gowns, waiting for him to grace their pictures.

At dinner, a writer for *Vogue* replaced the Georgia family. "I have a place in South Beach," Viva said. "Last week I came back from Paris and I sat down and looked out the window and saw this ship sailing by. And I said to myself 'I'm going on that ship.'"

Astonishing how quickly the traveler's fortunes change.

"This is wonderful," she said. "I've never been on a cruise before. My friends all said: 'Oh, Viva, you've become one of those divorced women who goes on cruises.' But I love this ship. I spent all morning out on deck with a hilarious crowd from South Carolina. They were all lit by ten o'clock. And the casino is divine. Before five o'clock you can play twenty-five-cent roulette."

"What about the food?"

"Eh. I lived in France for a year. But this Caesar is tasty."

Around midnight—after the Paris Review and the late-night adult comedy show (Al Ernst on men's health problems)—Carmelita sat with her friends Eddie and Dozer in the disco. During the dance contest, a deputy's date did a lap dance on him.

"She's a stripper," Carmelita whispered to me. "Everyone's really embarrassed by her."

Tuesday morning, getting off on Cozumel, I ran into a Polish couple from New Jersey. "There are about twenty of us," they told me. The *Destiny* was turning into a kind of Noah's Ark for collectives—the party group, the police group, the Polish group. Many of them spent their one day in Mexico with hundreds of fellow passengers at Carlos and Charlie's, an upstairs bar on the Malecón.

After buying a few Christmas presents, I returned to the ship for dinner. My table was empty save for a pretty young woman in a black dress who was translating the menu into French for a bald man who could have been, but obviously wasn't, her father.

"I'm Claudine," the woman introduced herself. "And this is Pierre."

I recognized Pierre from the casino.

"I've won $900 already," he said casually in Quebecois French. "And we paid only $1,200 for the cabin. People on this ship don't know how to play blackjack."

"He's very good," said Claudine proudly. "Hotels in Las Vegas fly him in as their guest."

"So you like the ship."

"It's a good deal," Pierre said smiling. "But the food is so-so. And look," he reached over his plate. "This is a fifty-dollar bottle of wine. We shouldn't have to pour it ourselves. Monsieur?"

We sailed a little after midnight, again to the tune of the "Macarena," which I had never really liked. I realized, however, that it was reducing the number of times I had to listen to "Hot, Hot, Hot."

Up on the Lido Deck, a couple staggered away from the dance party to make out quietly on the side. Tired of bending, the gangling young man lifted his new paramour onto the railing, where she rocked drunkenly in his rubbery arms twelve stories above a marble black sea.

I walked over to them.

"Howdy," the young man said, slowly extricating his mouth and trying to act casual.

"Get down from there," I ordered. "It's dangerous."

Then I headed off to my empty cabin. As I turned the corner, he was fumblingly lifting her back up.

"Ninety-nine percent of them are the friendliest, funniest people you'll ever want to meet. Super, super people. But one per cent will spoil your day by hassling."

It was John Heald, our cruise director, on Jamaicans. It was Wednesday morning somewhere south of the Yucatan Channel.

"And please DO NOT buy any drugs," Heald continued. "Last year Carnival had 400 passengers arrested for purchasing drugs in Jamaica."

Outside, a young Japanese woman stood at the railing looking down into the Rotunda. The elderly man with uncombed white hair was again playing solitaire at the bar. In the shop across the way, a woman with a camera zeroed in on a young man buying a Snickers bar.

"I get things ready for group of one thousand Japanese people who sail next week," Takako, the Japanese woman said. "They do not speak English, so I very busy all day translating bulletins, menus, things like that."

I wondered how they'd like the food.

"Japanese have different tastes," she said with traditional delicacy. "It a bit better than other Carnival ships. Kind of like Denny's."

Then she looked at her watch. "Have to go. Time for lunch meeting."

In the afternoon, the usual sea of bodies blanketed the Lido Deck. It rose up from the bandstand in ten gradual, chaise-longued levels, a gently rolling jigsaw puzzle of furniture and flesh. Leigh from the party group danced languorously by the pool with a hurricane glass in her hand. She was the picture of cruising contentment. There may have been another, my ex-cabin mate Norman sunning in his thong up on the topless deck, but I didn't go see it.

At dinner my table for eight was empty. In seven cruises, I had never had such a mercurial table: one night laconic Georgians, then Viva the fashion maven, followed by a couple of high-rolling French Canadians. Ken the maitre d' appeared—an Irish Rhett Butler, with slicked-back hair and a pencil-thin mustache.

"Come with me, sir."

He led me down the stairs to the dining room's lower level, pirouetting around serving carts and swerving past waiters and ducking under trays (Scorsese would have filmed it beautifully) and deposited me into an empty chair in the middle of an animated party gladdened by a beautiful young Indian woman with a small diamond embedded in her left nostril. Viva presided happily in the center. (She flashed me a conspiratorial smile as I unfolded my napkin.) In four days I had gone from a shared cabin and deadbeat diners to an empty cabin and exotic tablemates. And I hadn't even been up to the penthouse party.

"I met the chef this afternoon," Viva said, leaning across the table. "He took me all over the galley."

Thursday morning a grumbly crowd filled the corridors waiting for the tender to take them to Grand Cayman.

"We go on Royal Caribbean," sniffed a sixtyish woman abutting my right elbow. "Ten times better than this."

"Look how much more you pay with them," answered a sixtyish man abutting my left shoulder. "This is the line we take when we bring the kids. By ourselves, we usually go on Holland America.

"The first day I went to the purser's desk and asked about table tennis," he continued. "They told me there weren't any tables. Well, that shot me down for about an hour. Then I found the ice cream machines."

"We miss bridge, too," his wife said. "On most ships you get loads of people playing bridge. Here only eight people showed up."

"I got stuck in an elevator yesterday," her husband said. "There was one woman who was pretty hysterical. I guess she'd been stuck in one earlier in the day. They finally had to pull us out."

"A dollar fifty for a soda," the elbow woman whined. "That gets me. It's like they're trying to suck every penny out of you."

"That bottle of water in the cabin that they try to sell you," the shoulder man agreed. "That's pretty tacky."

The Polish couple I'd met in Cozumel appeared, pushing their way in the opposite direction.

"A man fell trying to get into the tender," said Basia, the wife. "It was very terrible. They had to pull him up out of the water. Somebody said he was a baseball player."

After forty-five minutes we finally got on the tender for the short ride to the capital. Walking by a bank I saw the solitaire player. Almost out of a sense of obligation, I introduced myself. If not for Norman, I figured, he would have been my cabin mate.

"Nice to meet you. I'm Buffy from Baton Rouge."

Buffy was in his usual tan suit, white shirt, and thickly knotted red tie. The tie was crisscrossed by several camera straps and studded, together with his lapels, with souvenir pins gathered on his travels. Prominent among them was the LSU tiger.

"You weren't interested in any of the ship excursions?" I asked.

"No. I've been here about fourteen times."

"Really?"

"I'm seventy-three years old," he said. "This is my ninety-sixth cruise."

Norman, I thought, thirty years hence.

Back on board, I sat in the shade with a pale, thirtyish woman with thick black hair.

"I loved the *Fascination,*" she said. "This ship is trying to be more sophisticated, but it lost some of its whimsy and hasn't replaced it with anything.

"And I don't get a sense of it being so big, in the sense that there are all that many more restaurants and clubs and places to go."

Amy worked in marketing in Manhattan, though she was gradually starting a career as a comic.

"I've been getting some material here—from the perspective of someone who's a little scared of sailing. The menu, for instance. Do you really want to be on a ship and hear about iceberg lettuce? And the lip-sync contest. I mean, if my lips are syncing, what's the rest of me doing?"

On my way back to my cabin, a woman wearing an anxious expression joined me in the glass elevator. I wondered if she was the one who got stuck. "I'm so afraid," she said, looking up to the railing opposite, "that somebody is going to jump from there."

An hour later I knocked tentatively on the door of penthouse 7198.

"Tom? You're Leigh's friend, right? Nice to meet you. Come on in. I'm Roger. This is Phil and this is Weasel." Leigh and Kathy waved from the corner.

"Are you from Boston, too?" I asked Roger.

"No, sir. I'm from Chicago. Union sheet metal worker. We met Leigh and her friends last year on the *Sensation* and we just hit it off. They're good people."

I had penetrated the notorious Carnival party sanctum and it was resembling a scene from *High Society.*

"Here," said Phil, handing me a glass and looking a bit like Cary Grant in a T-shirt. "Let me pour you some champagne."

On my way down to the dining room I ran into Takako and three of her translators. "Can't talk," she said. "Time for dinner meeting."

During the appetizer—tough chicken satay (Oriental night)—Ken appeared and told us that the passenger involved in the tender accident was Eddie Matthews. He had suffered fractures of the pelvis and had been flown by air ambulance back to Miami. "An older gentleman. A fine player, was he?"

"A Hall-of-Famer," I said. "Played third base for the Braves when they were in Milwaukee."

"Tis a real shame."

Cindy, a newlywed, said that she'd run into passengers from another ship who told her that one of their excursion groups had been robbed at gunpoint the previous day in Jamaica.

After dinner, Buffy stood in the Rotunda holding two typewritten pages.

"It's a story I wrote about getting on the wrong ship once. I wanted to read it in the talent show but your cruise director John Heald wouldn't let me. Instead he stands up there and makes jokes about sex," he pronounced the word with gravelly distaste. "And going to the bathroom. I'm planning to write a letter to the cruise company."

Before the show, Heald announced that word had just come from Jamaica that, in honor of the *Destiny's* first visit to the country, there would be free rum and beer for us all day on the pier. (Super, super people.) Then three passengers performed—out of a total of 3,097—all of them singers. They were followed by an "improvised" audience participation skit, choreographed by Heald, of predictable script and in dubious taste. The audience howled.

Later in the disco, Leigh and Weasel and Kathy and friends talked near the bar. Carmelita sat with her Sacramento SWAT team crowd. I told them about the Jamaican mugging. Freddy and Dozer practically licked their lips in anticipation.

"That explains," said Freddy sagely, "the free rum and beer."

We docked in Ocho Rios early Friday morning. Colorful booths of distillers lined the otherwise sorry pier and representatives from resorts handed out brochures. A military band, regal in fusty yellow uniforms, greeted us with marches.

It was too early even for Red Stripe. I took a taxi into town and spent the morning at markets. At the recommendation of a vendor, I walked to the Jerk Center for lunch. Taking a seat at a picnic table in the grass, I was approached by a young woman in revealing tight shorts—one of about a dozen painted ladies lingering in the wings.

"Is this place always like this?" I asked, stabbing a piece of pork.

"No. It's because de ship is in town." (In honor of the *Destiny.*)

"But there's nobody else here from the ship."

"Dey fom de ship," she nodded to my left, and looking over my shoulder, I saw a huddle of hungry-eyed crew.

About 3,096 passengers—I learned back at the dock—climbed Dunn's River Falls. All had an exceptionally good time. Nobody got robbed. Everyone was now celebrating with free rum and beer. We sailed at 3:30, leaving a pier of empty paper cups.

As I sat down for dinner Ken appeared and informed me I was expected at the captain's table. Viva, of course, was already there. I shot her a hostile glance (she obviously had blown my cover) and took a seat between the first engineer (the captain apparently had better things to do) and an executive from Hawaiian Pools.

"We have about 140 of our people on board," he told me. So: the party group, the police group, the Polish group, and now the pool group.

A few hours later, Buffy—eternally nonaligned—sat playing solitaire at the bar in the Down Beat. I introduced him to the Croatian bartender; he seemed so lonely.

"What is it," Ivana asked with interest, "that you like so much about cruising?"

"The people," he said.

★ ★ ★

Saturday—our last day—I stopped by the purser's desk and requested the official passenger figure. The young man checked on the computer and said 2,666. I had been wondering how 3,096 people had fit into Dunn's River Falls.

For the last dinner, our Colombian waiter appeared in straw boater, bow tie, and red-and-white striped vest. After the meal he gathered with his colleagues—a boatered company of Latins, Asians, and West Indians—and sang "God Bless America."

Late at night, a weary young woman named Vivien sat at the bar in the Down Beat.

"I've been doing the sound for the film team," she said. "I've only been on for the last two weeks, but they've been on since the ship left Trieste. They're making a documentary for British TV."

"Tell me," I said, "the skit they do on talent night—it's rehearsed, right?"

"I think so. Did 'Mary' run into Heald and knock him down?"

"Yes."

"Yes, it's the same."

The director entered, with some of his crew, and Vivien introduced me.

"Oh, right," the director's assistant said. "You're Weasel's friend."

From Norman's roommate to Weasel's friend. It had been an eventful seven days.

"They're good kids," he said in a patronizing way. "They work hard and they want to make the most of their one-week holiday. The company sells them this dream of a luxury cruise and they think they're getting it."

I took one last look in the disco. It was around one in the morning and only a few couples bobbed on the dance floor. Weasel stood off to the side in his coat and tie.

"Last night at dinner," he said, "I was trying to eat and they were sticking the camera in my face. They came in the cabin and filmed me getting dressed. I said, 'Hey I can't brush my teeth with you standing there.'

"They asked me what I did and what I thought of the ship and why I came on board. They tried to get me to say that I came on to meet girls, but I wouldn't play along.

"Annie over there, for instance," he pointed to a petite woman in a red dress. "We like each other. But I'm not going to sleep with her because I know she wouldn't respect me and I wouldn't respect myself. We're just good friends."

At that sentiment, I headed down to bed. When I awoke the largest cruise ship in the world was making a 180-degree turn in the roseate glow of a Miami winter morning. And I knew that all the people who had agreeably crowded my week would now disappear back into their real lives.

# PART TWO

## *Crashing the Sesquicentennial*

Where have the years gone? Why, it seems like only yesterday we were traipsing through the mangrove swamps.

Forget it; it won't wash. At least not here in the south, which, as everyone knows, is not the South. Had a people ever been less deserving of a Sesquicentennial than we were?

Florida turned 150 a few years ago, yet so many of us—below St. Augustine at least—go back no further than twenty years. Some go back every summer. The furlough state.

Our own histories are elsewhere—in Brooklyn, Rockford, Port-au-Prince; our lives have not paralleled that of Florida, they have detoured, wintered, or dead-ended here. Our hearts are often far away. We even watch the weather forecasts for other states.

So we were lackluster Sesquicentennialists. It was a party that we wandered into late and inadvertently, without a present and without a wish. We hardly knew the birthday boy.

Many places—countries, states, sometimes even cities (Dublin, Chicago)—have sharp divisions between north and south. But in Florida each geographical region curiously takes on the personality of the other. It is only on the question of age that we revert to North American form: The "north" is old; the "south" is young.

One hundred fifty years ago there was only the north, a thin, sparsely inhabited strip on the belly of the United States. The southern leg, except for Key West, was a sticky, unwanted wilderness.

In 1845, Henry Flagler, the father of modern Florida, was working in a general store in Republic, Ohio—at a salary of eighty dollars a year. He had, David Leon Chandler writes in his biography, "a knack for salesmanship, and his reputation spread to other parts of northwestern Ohio." It would be another forty-nine years before he would run his railroad down from St. Augustine and begin the phenomenal popularization of the peninsula that continues to grow almost beyond its capacity.

So that was the north's anniversary, not ours. Not only have we been here a shorter time, so has, in a sense, Florida. Florida became a state before it became a place. (The opposite of, say, New Mexico.) And becoming a place is a longer process—it took, in this case, disposable incomes, northern recessions, foreign dictatorships and air-conditioning.

Today South Florida is the ultimate postmodern promised land. We are a microcosm of the country, with our salad of immigrants—Colombians and Jamaicans replacing Italians and Irish. But then we go beyond that easy comparison by attracting misfits, sailors, hitmen, playboys, and true blue Americans in lime green slacks. We are perhaps the first region in history to draw both huddled masses yearning to breathe free and plaid foursomes looking to play golf.

So many people leaving so many pasts, to come to a place without a history.

This is no land for Sesquicentennials; hardly a land for "Hi, how's the family?" How can we be moved by anniversaries when the ramp we use today to get on I-95 replaced the old one constructed last year?

There is no trace of yesterday here, let alone last century. Everything is new—the malls where we shop, the malls where we eat, the malls where we go to see movies. Travel north, really north, and the first things you notice—with shocking disapproval—are the rusting guardrails and dusty crabgrass.

Newness is in our veins. Every time we visit South Beach we see new restaurants, new hotels, new boutiques, new people. It has gotten so out of hand that one of our few legitimate institutions, Joe's Stone Crab, advertises itself with the eloquent denial: "Not new. Not improved." In Fort Lauderdale even the beachfront is new, and frequented by a shirtless sexagenarian on in-line skates.

There was a new stamp to commemorate the Sesquicentennial—an exquisitely garish painting of a green, open-jawed alligator emerging from a purple swamp under an orange sky. The word "Florida" was written in red in a circus billboard script, and the year 1845 was superimposed on the swamp. It would have graced a letter beautifully, if only we weren't all addicted to e-mail.

The up-to-dateness of the place nearly suffocates until one day you drive along some residential street and see a woman in a bright flowered dress and a lopsided hat. She carries a faded black umbrella (open of course) and, despite her bulk, walks with a graceful island languor. Her story is as old as the pilgrims' and her antiquated presence on this bright, sidewalkless, South Florida street lifts your heart.

The celebration, for us, is not in anniversaries, but in the ongoing saga.

# 4

## *Love on the Key*

It begins, as all the best games do, with a ball. Pliable, lime-yellow, fuzzy—it is the loveliest ball in all of sports. The cricket ball, with its coat of cherry red belted by golden stitching, looks like a Christmas-tree ornament, but it's hard as steel. The old-fashioned soccer ball, with its bovine patches, also packs a punch. By contrast, the tennis ball is a cuddly sphere of universal goodness. It slips cozily (if itchily) under the backside of a female server's panties, and can be gripped, without potential disaster, by infant fingers. (See what they do with the prettily dimpled golf ball.) Even dogs find it irresistible.

"What do tennis players want?" reads the front of a popular T-shirt. "New balls," reads the back. The greatest advance in the game in the last fifteen years has not been graphite rackets, or wider frames, or elongated handles, but transparent tubes which let you look in at the three virgin globes in their lemony column. A vertical jackpot. A downy trinity. Buying new tennis balls is like purchasing a fresh loaf of bread; the only way it could be improved upon would be if a tiny heater were installed in the tube so that the balls were warm when you took them out.

But not even the crunch of a heel broken off a baguette can match the sound of a tube of new tennis balls being cracked. In an admirable feat of engineering, the packagers managed to dispense with the metal container but saved the sound of its opening, which was a bit like salvaging the song of the dodo. It works on the same principle as does the opening of a can of cashews, or Miller Lite, but it produces an altogether different *PSHHhh:* plusher, giddier, richer in expectation. And with the sound comes the release of pressurized air—that inanimate sigh—redolent of wool, rubber bands, and summer afternoons.

It seems almost a shame to hit the things, but hit them you must. Luckily, the space in which you do this has its own aesthetic pleasures: a rectangle of green charted with two identical plots of straight white lines that regularly meet but never cross, creating an exercise book of mirrored Ts that echo the trinity of the balls and produce an unwavering print, a cheerful symmetry in the midst of an anarchic city block or at the edge of an overgrown park. And in the middle of that print, rescuing the sport from the unwatchability of a board game, stretches a low, sagging, surrealistic net.

The net is as out of place in this one-dimensional, right-angled world as is the clock in the Dali desert. But time has given it, like the clock, like the Eiffel Tower, an aura of indispensability. A tennis court without a net is not just pathetic (infinitely sadder, and more inutile, than the netless basketball rim); it is a philosophical abstraction, an argument missing a crux.

The net is to a tennis court what the rock is to a Zen garden: a necessary focal point. (When the court is clay, you also get the raking around it.) Only tennis players appreciate the court's tranquil purity, its metaphysical stamp, and not all of *them:* Those men, for instance (it's almost never women, as they're evidently the more spiritual sex), who curse and toss their rackets. Would you throw a tantrum in a temple?

It seems almost a shame to clutter this perfect space with your own imperfections, but that's what it's there for. There was a time, up until about twenty years ago, when the tools brought to the tennis court enhanced its elegance: slim-handled, melon-shaped racquets made of wood that looked hand-carved. They had the homely humanity of snowshoes. Even the word—"racquet"—had a graceful, unhurried quality, taking three letters to make the sound of two. "Racket"—meaning also clamor, and a vowel away from a type of weaponry—is much better suited to the modern game.

Players now carry their rackets over their shoulders in sinister, oversized vinyl cases. A foursome walking onto a court looks like a squad of hit men heading to a job. Then they unzip and pull out stick candy with strings, the frames blinding with flashes of magenta and apricot. Their sneakers bulge with bubbles of air. Somewhere, by law, is sewn a swoosh.

But out on the court, all the ugliness fades; the Grand Guignol vanishes in the eternal beauty of the game, which starts—as seems fitting—at love. With the very first point the ritualistic dance begins, as the server performs a micro-pirouette, arms—the first followed automatically by the racketed second—reaching as if for a piece of sky, and, failing to grab it, propelling the legs into a compensatory, terrestrial pounce. The ball, if this awkwardly graceful motion succeeded, has already landed in its box on the other side of the net and is about to sail back, simultaneous with the over-the-top salute of the opponent's follow-through. From this, if two equally talented players are at it, emanates an air show of elaborately boomeranged fuzz.

A ball hit with a force that should send it over the fence mysteriously dips after clearing the net and neatly lands a foot inside the baseline. It is returned with a backhand slice that causes it not only to lose its forward momentum—stopping practically dead on its bounce—but also to skip to the side. This is then scooped up with a rakish flip of the racket and more topspin abracadabra. A few long-range missiles follow, nearly grazing the net at impossible angles, until a drop shot—like a bad pun—silences the rally. But not for long. Poorly disguised, it is not only reached, it is sent back deep and . . . right to the punster, who, caught by surprise, turns it into a high arcing lob, a brief solar eclipse, a hanging, perfectly formed fruit to be plucked.

★ ★ ★

Florida has long been renowned for sport fishing, and more recently college football dynasties, but in tennis it finds its apotheosis, and not simply because the ball resembles an exotic type of fuzzy citrus. It is here that the top players make their homes (a wide choice of gated leisure communities) and here where those wishing to dethrone them come to train. The flatness of the place is perfect for the laying down of courts (the same quality that deprives the golf courses of drama), and the subtropical climate allows for year-round play. (A beautiful sight, as I drive home from work in the winter, is the steady flight of balls under lights in the park.) Before the advent of insecticides, a flicked tennis racket was an ideal defense against mosquitoes.

Probably the most famous person ever to come out of Fort Lauderdale, where I now live, was Chris Evert. Driving guests around town, desperate for a historical landmark, a worldly reference, I always come upon Holiday Park with relief, for here (I announce) is where she learned to play the game. Up until a few years ago you could still see her father Jimmy stringing rackets in the shop, or standing patiently on one of the courts, swallowed in a cloud of flailing children.

At Holiday Park, as at many tennis centers, you get a few men playing at being champions—that learned swagger and solemnity of the tour compressed into a suburban Saturday. But the rest of us play for health and amusement and the brief pleasure that comes from a ball landing exactly where you intended it to, the meaningless satisfaction of a deft physical act.

Once a year we get to watch the pros on Key Biscayne. At its start, the March tournament was known as the Lipton (conjuring summery images of ice-cold pitchers of tea) while the new sponsor, Nasdaq-100, suggests something else entirely. But the location—on an island backdropped by the Miami skyline—assures the sport its eternal aloofness.

I go down every year, driving across the causeway, past the families bivouacked on the ribbon of beach, the wind-surfers playing happily without rackets. I take the turn-off to the same makeshift parking lot, a vast dusty field, and board a bus that's large and frigid enough to go cross-country. It drops us off a couple miles down the road, and we walk—a beshorted, soft-soled company—across the street to the fountained entrance.

The first years I was caught up only in the tennis. I liked catching the practice sessions, seeing stars out of costume, in sweats or spandex, joking, mumbling, hitting like robots. For matches I prowled the high-numbered courts, watching at intimately close quarters players I'd never heard of before. It didn't matter. There was the same impossible power and speed, which seemed to shrink the court to about half its normal size, and the same concentrated grinding out of a living, the endlessly repeated process punctuated only by the *pong* of ball on racket, occasional grunts, and the staccato squeak of restless sneakers.

The few times I entered the stadium, I was struck by the heroic simplicity of the game. Of the armed sports, only tennis achieves the epic, face-to-face grandeur of an old-fashioned shoot-out. Tennis players carry their weapons not as part of a greater whole, but as the sole extension of themselves. Hockey players wielding sticks are like an angry mob of peasants, while baseball players, with their heavy bats (and over-the-counter drugs), resemble cavemen. Golfers are often borderline couch potatoes with canes. By contrast, the tennis player, standing alone in the sun with a tightly strung racket, is Gary Cooper at high noon.

The fact that tennis players wear less than the others strangely adds to their stature. They cannot hide behind helmets or pads, though some of the men try, with pulled-down caps and voluminous shorts. It's interesting that, as the men have been adding clothing, their female counterparts—in halters and backless dresses—have been taking it off. (The explanation, in part, for the growing popularity of the women's game?) And despite the asymmetry of an oversized playing arm—Popeye on one side, Olive Oyl on the other—the revealed physiques are often works of wonder. It is very easy to imagine Michelangelo's *David* holding a Wilson Hammer over his left shoulder.

The unadorned bluntness of the sport gives the participants their romantic appeal. Tennis players are like nineteenth-century Russian poets who have been dragged out to duel before they've completely finished dressing. The difference being that the tennis duel goes on and on. For televised matches, even the most ardent fans have learned pretty much how to time things—varnishing a table, stirring a bouillabaisse, reading a travel story—in order to catch the last game of every set. Television needs a script and a cast, neither of which are adequately supplied by the chummy commentators in the booth. The same with film: What was the last good tennis movie you saw? On radio, tennis would sound like a dripping faucet.

Then a few years ago I noticed another interesting aspect of the sport: a universality that exceeds even soccer's. Checking the electronic schedule in the middle of Crandon Park that first Saturday, I realized that it resembled a departures board at an international airport that, for some strange reason, was displaying surnames instead of destinations: Van Roost. Likhovtseva. Dragomir. Li. Enqvist. Costa. Philippoussis. Campbell. Prieto. Vinck. Appelmans. Halard-Decugis. Sawamatsu. Brandi. In that septet of singles matches (only a small sampling of the long day's duels) you had, I figured, the representation of at least a dozen countries and possibly five continents. The world was spread out on hardcourt before me.

I headed over to the Slavic lands. Jana Novotna from the Czech Republic was playing Magdalena Grzybowska from Poland. Grzybowska, at nineteen, looked like an Anna Kournikova for adults, with her golden ponytail and regal mien. "*Spokojnie,*

*Magda,*" the man on my left shouted, urging her to calm down after an errant forehand sailed off toward Gdynia.

The Czech was pouncing so I slipped across the border into Slovakia, where Henrietta Nagyova was playing a German who should have been invited for her name alone: Meike Babel.

Dollops of Slovak floated down the stands. (Players' retinues often nest in a corner of the last row.) The dark-haired man next to me looked hawkishly Eastern European.

"Hungary," he said. (Another flat land.) "We don't have many good tennis players. Only Seles."

"She's from the former Yugoslavia," I said.

"Ah, but the family's Hungarian. They speak Hungarian at home. I know."

At the conclusion of the match he handed me his business card. It read: Hun Realty.

Tennis globalism was beautifully captured a little while later when Jonas Bjorkman of Sweden met Leander Paes of India. It would be difficult to think of two more diverse countries, yet there on the same court, in vaguely similar outfits (Bjorkman's decidedly baggier) and with almost identical weaponry, the two men stood separated only by a net. During one of the changeovers—as if underscoring the benign exoticism of the meeting—a large iguana scurried across the court.

When I returned on Wednesday, the field had dwindled but the international aspect remained. Tim Henman of Great Britain practiced on Court One while his opponent for the day, the Brazilian Gustav Kuerten, loped onto a neighboring court with a man wearing a cap patterned with a blue globe orbited by green and yellow triangles. Nearby, a Ukrainian hit with Kournikova's doubles partner, a young woman from Latvia—two former citizens of the Soviet Union peacefully rallying under apolitical palms.

At lunch I joined a table of Germans just as they were about to bite into their hamburgers, and then struck up a conversation with a vacationing tennis instructor from Prague. In front of the stadium, a small band of what looked like sneakered revolutionaries paraded around the Chilean flag.

Late in the afternoon, waiting for the start of the Kournikova doubles match on the grandstand court, a stadium announcer who looked like my high school gym teacher took the microphone and frankly admitted: "I don't know how to pronounce these names. Does anyone here speak Japanese?"

A young woman diffidently raised her hand.

"Come down here," the man said. "I want you to introduce them and everyone else to get up and greet them with a standing ovation. We'll give them the warmest welcome they've ever received."

The woman—born in Okinawa, now living in Miami—practiced a little nervously. Then, finally, Anna Kournikova and Larisa Neiland appeared in the wings.

"Wait," the gym teacher said. "Let the Japanese women out first." And they politely, if cluelessly, stepped aside for Naoko Kijimuta and Nana Miyagi, who walked onto the court to a stream of fluent Japanese followed by a great roar of applause. They looked at each other in shocked bemusement.

Kournikova didn't budge. "We want Russian!" she demanded, smiling, obviously in a good mood after defeating Lindsay Davenport.

"Does anybody here speak Russian?" the gym teacher now asked. And sure enough, a young blonde in a gray pantsuit ran down and, taking the microphone, filled the grandstand with hearty sibilants.

A few minutes later, the wordless debate began.

# 5

## *Into the Panhandle*

The place seems too drawly to be the Sunshine State, but too liquidy to be the South. Even before you cross the Suwannee River you see the boiled P-Nut vendors, the American-made pick-up trucks, the houses not much bigger than the motorboats parked in their yards, the signs pointing the way to "Rabbits and Cane Juice." In your future are places with names like Panacea, Niceville, Sopchoppy. As darkness descends, the pairs of orange road reflectors, coming up one after the other, resemble an unbroken line of alligator eyes.

Long past the river I felt the presence of water somewhere off to my left. Panacea looked the exact opposite of curative (i.e., dead), so I pushed on, stopping for dinner at a place down the road called Angelo's. It sat at the edge of a dark body of water. Inside, I found fat-bottomed waitresses, all of them squeezed into identical khaki shorts. They were better advertisements for the house cuisine than the culinary awards posted by the cash register.

I ordered broiled red snapper and cheese grits and received not one but two large fishes on a plate garnished with hush puppies and a small plastic cup of garlic butter for dipping. The sauce gave to the fish, like the cheese to the grits, a novel and indescribable richness.

I knew as soon as I'd finished that I'd have no trouble making the fifty miles to Apalachicola. An hour later, rolling into town off the Apalachicola Bay Bridge, my car became the one moving object in a world of perfect stillness. Just on the outskirts, in a motel office smelling of curry, I paid an Indian receptionist for a room.

"She's got cuts and scratches but not a broken bone in her body. Now tell me the good Lord didn't take care of that."

It was the next morning, and Linda Page—"executive director of the Chamber of Commerce and master of nothing"—was gabbing on the telephone. She sat at a desk in the antique hallway of Raney House, a handsome Greek Revival structure on Market Street. There was an open bottle of Pepsi-Cola to her right. Outside, though it was nearly mid-morning, the town barely stirred.

"Well, the orster men are out gathering orsters," she explained. "In the morning, the coffee drinkers meet at the Riverfront restaurant. Later you'll find a lot of people—the deliverymen and telephone workers—at the Seafood Reef 'cause they have a lunch special of meat and potatoes. People here love seafood but we usually fry it, and there's only so much fried seafood you can eat.

"Then there's a group of old guys who sit every day in Battery Park. They get together to cuss and discuss. Everybody calls them 'the green bitch crew.'"

"Why green?"

"Because that's the color of the bitch they sit on."

Apalachicola is a town enclosed, if not lulled to sleep by, water. It is to oysters what Tarpon Springs is to sponges—a small, coastal community that lives, and dies, on the harvest of the sea.

The bay has long been favored for its delicate balance of salt and fresh water, and the optimal temperatures for supporting the species. Years ago, the bay was responsible for 90 percent of Florida's oysters, but in 1985, hurricanes wreaked havoc on many of the beds.

Most of the oyster businesses are housed in simple, flat-roofed buildings on the outskirts of town. They have the half-hearted air of trailer parks, stretched along U.S. 98 as it runs past one of the many inlets. The parking lots in front are gauzed with the dust of loose earth and crushed shells.

Among the businesses is D. W. Wilson Seafood, run by D. W. Wilson. I found him sitting in his small, cramped office beside an open bottle of Coca-Cola. He wore a hat with the words "D. W. Wilson Seafood—Apalachicola, Fla." printed across the front.

"There's been oystering here ever since man was here," he said. "When white men came, they found piles of oyster shells around Indian camps. My great-granddaddy was in the business, my granddaddy. That was the catching end of it. I can remember as a child sitting in a stall while my mother shucked oysters. I went into the service and came back here in 1970, worked on the water for a few years and then went into business."

There are, Wilson said, twenty-three miles of oyster beds throughout the bay system, with "hundreds and hundreds of bars—we call them 'bars.' And they are coming back, though there are still restrictions. No boat is allowed more than fifteen sixty-pound bags per day, and all must stop at an inspection station on their way in. (Here the oysters are measured by an agent from the Department of Natural Resources to make sure that they are at least three inches in length.) Boats are allowed out only five days a week.

Wilson Seafood, like most of the other companies, depends on independent oystermen for its supply. They visit the beds in small wooden two-man boats, raking the oysters up with old-fashioned tongs. It is a gruff, scavenging, elemental labor. In the late afternoon, not far from Wilson's place, you can see the boats putter up to the inspection station. The boaters, even the women, have a coarse, sunburned, unwashed look; the men often sport dirty blond beards and long stringy hair—not so much out of a sense of fashion, you suspect, as of indifference. It is illuminating, having watched the consumption of oysters in elegant restaurants, to see its somewhat humbler origins, to discover the connection, however distant, between the bibbed society lady and the tonged oysterman.

At lunchtime, all was still quiet downtown. Dogs dozed in the middle of the street, and egrets scoured the high school football field. In the Long Dream Gallery, someone had posted an editorial from the *Apalachicola Times:*

> Apalachicola is the east coast version of what Monterey was in its heyday, an isolated outpost of American true grit that lives in every sense, by and from the sea. . . . In Apalachicola, our businesses still close up shop on Wednesday afternoon; our kids still call us Mr. Jim and Miss Betty; our people still make handmade cast nets . . .

Over at Boss Oyster, the help was having fun with tourists.

"A couple came in the other day," one of them said. "Wanted me to direct them to Thomas Edison's house, Henry Ford's house, and Firestone's house."

"Did you tell them," the man at the bar asked, "to go up two blocks and take a right?"

It was the homeboy's one sure stab at global superiority. And yet, when a German family entered a few minutes later, the young man waiting on them did so in German. "I still haven't forgotten what I learned in the Army," he said proudly returning to the bar.

Boss Oyster was squeezed between the warehouses of the shrimp docks. The houses were originally built for cotton; in the late 1800s, Apalachicola was the third-largest cotton port in the United States. Today, like much of the coastal Panhandle,

Apalachicola also makes a living from shrimp, and you can watch the great metal buckets swing from the docked boats to dump waterfalls of pink-and-gray crustaceans into tubs.

A few blocks away from the restaurant, Gorrie Square had the languid air of an August afternoon. Its white Victorian houses were girdled by porches, and the columns of Trinity Episcopal Church were speckled with the shadows of Spanish moss. The only car in sight sat in front of the Gorrie Museum.

Dr. Gorrie is, along with oysters, Apalachicola's claim to fame: a dedicated doctor who, trying to create a cooling system for his yellow fever patients, accidentally stumbled on an ice-making machine. The machine—now in the Smithsonian—went unrecognized in Gorrie's lifetime, though the principles that went into its construction made possible the development, years later, of refrigeration and air-conditioning systems. While less acclaimed than Henry Flagler, Gorrie was more responsible for Florida's current configuration. Flagler simply made it possible for people to get here; Gorrie's efforts made it bearable for them to stay.

In the evening I stopped into the bar of the old Gibson Inn, where a biology teacher from Kentucky was sipping a glass of Chablis.

"The thing that gets me about Florida," she said, "is how visible the food chain is. Pelicans eating fish, people eating fish, alligators eating chickens. I go to bed at night and can almost hear the munching."

The next morning, I continued west on U.S. 98. Past Port St. Joe, with its paper and chemical plants, the road hugged the gulf, and new apartments and townhouses hugged the road until I came to the sad culmination of this coastal development: Panama City.

In the morning light, it looked like a town with a hangover. A few addicted joggers ran sluggishly past the even less animated animal figures in the miniature golf courses. Other tourists, in college sweatshirts, listlessly packed their car trunks. In the cracks between hotels, you could glimpse narrow wedges of turquoise sea, like shoots of green on an asphalt playground.

West of this clutter, the scenery once again turned rural maritime. Veering off 98, onto County Road 30-A, I drove the stretch of beaches that have been named among the most beautiful in the country. The one at Grayton Beach State Recreation Area is often cited as the *ne plus ultra*. And, on a clear spring morning, it did look lovely, its white sand dunes, like frozen waves, dotted with sea oats.

I came into Seaside like somebody stumbling onto a classical music station on a radio full of country. In front of me rose an immaculate cluster of gleaming new houses, their cupolas and towers punctuating the sky. Weathervanes, depicting whales and pelicans, sprouted atop corrugated metal roofs. Strolling about, I found screened porches appendaged to the fronts of houses, whose walls were painted the color of butter mints. There were red brick streets and white picket fences and sandy back alleys. Everything was neat, quaint, felicitous, prim, with a brightness that dazzled in the southern sun. The place had the idyllic air of a miniature village, one that had been removed from its electric train set and dropped by the sea for humans to live in.

Seaside, designed by the celebrated Miami architectural team of Andres Duany and Elizabeth Plater-Zyberk, is one of the most acclaimed planned towns of the past few decades. Its novelty is its nod to the past: the willful (if not forced) return to alleys and porches and streets that encourage walking. "The newest idea in planning," Duany once told a conference of Florida apartment developers, "is the nineteenth-century town."

Since its beginnings in 1981, Seaside has been written about in countless magazines and architectural journals. *Time* magazine proclaimed that it "could be the most astounding design achievement of its era, and . . . the most influential." The list of its architectural awards runs for more than a page and it has won the admiration of the Prince of Wales.

The story of the town's genesis has already taken on the aura of myth. Robert Davis, a sixties' radical turned successful developer, inherited eighty choice beachfront acres from his businessman grandfather. Davis, who grew up in Birmingham, Alabama, had fond memories of childhood vacations in the Florida Panhandle. And he had become distressed by what he saw as the large-scale spoiling of the coast by characterless resorts and inhuman condominiums. With his wife, and sometimes Duany, he drove around the South in a red Bonneville convertible, examining small towns and formulating an idea of the one he wanted to build. He then asked Duany, and his wife Plater-Zyberk, to work on a design.

Since then Duany and Plater-Zyberk have gone on to other projects; Davis has remained at Seaside, working out of a second-floor office and coolly overseeing the evolution of his dream.

Having read the articles and seen the pictures, visitors to Seaside are struck by at least three things: One, there are actual inhabitants. (Photographs focus almost exclusively on the architecture.) Two, they are uniformly white and well-to-do. And three, they are dressed in the unmistakable attire of people of leisure.

Davis claims that he is not disturbed by this; that he always saw Seaside as a resort town. "I tried to create a beach place with houses that might stay in the same family for generations," he said when I interviewed him. "And I think we're going to see that. It has already become a popular place for family reunions."

Seaside's amenities are those of an impossibly upscale small town. The post office, situated on the town green, is a precious Greek Revival–style building. The shops are boutiques, the restaurants trendy. Bud & Alley's quotes A. J. Liebling in its promotional blurb. The food market, though run by a mom-and-pop store couple, is touted in the literature as "Seaside's answer to Balducci's," and includes in its inventory grapeseed oil and lemon-pepper pasta. Sundog Books is surely the finest bookstore in the Panhandle.

Despite its candied Cape Cod feel, Seaside's real models are the picturesque villages of the Italian Riviera. "People on holiday in Italy generally go to holiday towns," Davis told the *Seaside Times,* ". . . holiday towns like Portofino and Forte Di Marmi combine relaxed elegance with liveliness, exuberance, and the messy vitality that makes real towns more fun than resorts."

The distinction, however, between Portofino and Seaside is that Portofino began not as a popular resort but as a poor fishing village. And so it has, for all its fashionableness, more in common with Apalachicola than it does with Seaside. Seaside grew from nothing, and has no reason for being, other than that which one man gave it. In fact, it is everything Apalachicola isn't: contrived, idle, and rich.

Seaside is an experiment, and exudes the clinical sterility of the laboratory. The features that at first glance give the place charm—the porches, the small yards, the low picket fences—are not whimsical touches but mandatory elements of a building code devised by Davis. All houses must have porches, and they can sit only so far back from the sidewalks.

The intentions behind the code are unquestionably noble: to encourage neighborly exchanges, a sense of community. But they smack of behaviorism; sometimes the town seems less a Portofino than a Walden Two. And anyone who cherishes the insubordinate nature of the human spirit cannot help but cheer quietly at night when passing empty porches lit by the glow from living room TVs.

When I left the next morning, it was with an odd sense of relief. Entering DeFuniak Springs, about twenty-five miles north, I saw a place that seemed to be everything Seaside wanted to be. Large, prosperous homes surrounded a circular lake, on the banks of which sat a Hollywood vision of a small-town library. (A plaque outside stated that it was the oldest continuously operated library, in its original building, in the United States.) You could see why Chautauqua had chosen the town for its winter sessions.

On the other side of the railroad tracks, four old-timers sat on a bench.

"You're looking at 360 years of wisdom," Louie said. "I'm 39 but Harry here's 100."

"I'm going to get up," Harry said smiling, "and knock you flat."

"Now gentlemen," A. W. interrupted, "am I wrong in telling this young man that Florida State University started in this town?"

Across the street stood a gazebo labeled "The Opinion Place."

"That's where we sit in the summer," Howard said. "But it's too cold to sit there now."

Driving out of town, I passed a billboard for the Lutheran church: "New Location, Old Message—Behind Wal-Mart."

Next came Niceville—"'Nice' folks, 'Nice' town, Have a 'Nice' time"—and Destin, "World's Luckiest Fishing Village." (Although it looked more like the Home of the World's Luckiest Land Developers.)

Pensacola, hosting a weekend jazz festival, seemed a pleasant city. I arrived too late for lunch at Hopkins Boarding House, so I wandered around the side streets running off Seville Square. The houses were small with decorative balconies. One posted a painting of female fingers, with the heading: "Gulf Coast Institute of Nail Technology."

At Trader Jon's, seven Marines formed a tan and blue circle at the bar. A squadron of model airplanes, suspended from the ceiling, dive-bombed their heads. Photographs of generals and majors, framed and signed, cluttered the walls. One picture stood out from the others: a portrait of an impish, potato-nosed man in a Navy sweater and a USS *Lexington* cap. It was Trader Jon, painted by Jeff McNelly.

I considered getting a room for the night, but the lure of the highway proved too strong. I got back in the car and drove to Tallahassee.

There is only one thing worse than a seat of government, and that is a seat of government on a Sunday. In the morning I headed down to Wakulla Springs, location for some of the Tarzan movies and *The Creature from the Black Lagoon*. In the lobby of the handsome lodge, I saw my first Panhandle alligator. The plaque read:

*Old Joe—Legendary Reptile*
*Established homestead at Wakulla Springs prior to any construction in the area. Estimate age around 200 years. Wt. 650 lbs.; length 11'2". Lived at Wakulla Springs on sand bar across from swimming area. Was murdered by assailant unknown on Sunday night Aug. 1, 1966. Had never molested man, woman, child or pets.*

Having paid my respects to Jon and Joe, I headed off to Julia Mae's, the seafood roadhouse in Carrabelle, the town with "the world's smallest police station." (It's in a phone booth.) Waitresses bustled out of the kitchen carrying huge plates of fried food for families famished by church. I'd had about enough of fried, and went for the broiled grouper. Hush puppies arrived regardless. I wrapped them up for the long drive home.

# PART THREE

## *Helpful Advice for the Bookish Traveler*

The decline of reading is often safely attributed by those in the writing trade—journalists, for instance—to the simple fact that people no longer have the time to read. (Sure, that's it, it couldn't be that we're boring.) Even if this is partially true, it ignores the more important point that there are now large numbers of people who find it infinitely less taxing to watch images on a screen than to decipher markings on a page.

Which of course brings us to travel. (Doesn't everything?) Among travel's many virtues is the fact that it now constitutes one of the few occasions in our lives when we find ourselves both saddled with large chunks of free time and detached from demanding home entertainment systems. Sadly, however, this is changing. It is now possible to sit at your gate and watch CNN before boarding your plane, only to find your own mini-TV embedded in the seat in front of you. The airline industry, having enraged smokers, is now pandering to video addicts.

Still, there are moments during every journey when you have to fall back on your own resources. These aren't just on long nights in the Hindu Kush either; they can come while waiting in line at Disney World. In either situation: What do you do to pass the time?

I believe I can help. Travel writers around the country have various monikers: There's the "Practical Traveler," "Fearless Traveler," "Savvy Traveler," "Mature Traveler." Well, call me the "Bookish Traveler," if only because it sounds better than the "Impractical, Fearful, Unsavvy, Immature Traveler."

Here's how I do it. First, I always arrive early for my flight, even these days, because it gives me time to read the paper before I board. As you set out to see the world, it's good to know what's happening in it, and coach seats were never designed for the turning of newspaper pages. If it's a slow news day I can finish the *Times* just as those requiring assistance are summoned; if it's a

Sunday, I slip the magazine and the book review into my book bag for reading on the plane.

A book bag is de rigueur for the bookish traveler. Mine, a weathered leather satchel, carries my notebook in its front pocket (equipped with a nifty little divot for three Papermate Flexgrip Ultra Fine pens); ticket, passport, address book, and house key in a zippered compartment; and, in the main cavity, two or three books slumming with a magazine.

Magazines make for ideal airplane reading—topical, compact, light (usually both in weight and subject matter, though, as a rule, the heftier the periodical the airier the writing). And I always carry my own, rather than subject myself to the stringently inoffensive blandness of the in-flights. Occasionally I'll leave behind a *Harper's* or a London *Spectator* for the next lucky passenger who, undoubtedly, is a national laptop solitaire champion.

On long flights I finish my magazine well before arrival and then delve into my books. Like the plane, I breach a higher altitude.

But let's not get carried away. One is usually a guidebook, which entertains me for a while with fine descriptions of the many diseases that await. As gripping as these are, however, they never compete with the sweep of a novel.

Here's my rule regarding fiction: Going, I read something pertaining to my destination: *Death Comes for the Archbishop,* say, for New Mexico; *Time for a Tiger* for Malaysia; *The Quiet American* for Vietnam. There are people, I know, who read nothing but trashy novels while traveling, but my belief is that they do to the brain what junk food (their edible equivalent) does to the arteries.

Then, coming back, I read something that is as far removed as possible from where I've just been. The trip is over, the place I've long obsessed about has disappeared below the clouds. I am, gloriously, free of it.

I sometimes spend one of the last days of a trip looking for a book for the return flight. (Browsing in bookstores is not only the bookish traveler's prerogative, it's his duty.) A few years ago in Jerusalem I came across a thick paperback that seemed not only the right size but also the perfect antidote to the approaching ten hours on El Al after two weeks in Israel preceded by a months-long diet of everything from the Old Testament to Saul Bellow. *The Stories of John Cheever.*

# 6

# *City of Writers*

> *Russia has always been a curiously unpleasant country, despite her great literature.*
>
> —Vladimir Nabokov

It felt strange, as I headed out of the courtyard and up the street, to be walking in the city of Vladimir Nabokov—"the world's most gaunt and enigmatic" he called St. Petersburg—but odder still was the suspicion that I had become a misplaced character from one of his novels.

Namely, Franz, who, in *King, Queen, Nave,* spends his first waking hours in Berlin in an exquisite blur having stepped on his glasses the night before. Mine were intact, but beaded with tightly bunched drops of drizzle, like miniature carbuncles, which, combined with the wooziness of jet lag (my Lufthansa plane had splashed down only an hour or so earlier), left me feeling like a drunkard gazing through a crystal into a dream.

I was able to make out, underfoot, a rolling sea of black macadam (sidewalks of tar on Nevsky Prospekt!) and, up above, strung across the storied avenue, the melting Cyrillic of banal banners. "Plausible street corners" appeared, after long intervals, as did the more convincing bridges. I knew from maps that I had three to cross before I got anywhere near Vlad's old hood.

He left it, never to return, in 1917, several days into the Bolshevik Revolution. ("The Soviet era was a dull week old.") In his brilliant memoir, *Speak, Memory,* there appears a black-and-white photograph, "taken in 1955 by an obliging American tourist," of the family house "of pink granite with frescoes and other Italianate ornaments, in St. Petersburg, now Leningrad, 47 Morskaya, now Hertzen Street."

I crossed St. Isaac's Square, the cathedral a wavering vessel at the top, and found with double joy a resurrected Morskaya Street. A few doors down on the right dripped the leaves of the linden trees I recognized from the photograph; by the entrance hung a plaque etched with a name I deciphered as Nabokov's. The museum, as I expected, was closed; it was enough, these first hours, to stand outside and squint.

Returning two days later, I admired the walnut ceiling in the empty dining room, examined a photo exhibit of the Nabokov's in Switzerland, and wandered through a few more furnitureless chambers. The bare-bones homage to one of history's most thematically complex, stylistically ornate, linguistically rich writers felt like a hoax. Leaving the museum, I hesitated at the foot of the marble staircase before stealthily making my way to the top, the radiant beauty of the stained glass window taking my mind off the mundane trespassing.

The second floor had held the parents' bedrooms; now it housed the offices of the *Nevsky Times.* Barging into one, I asked if there was anyone who spoke English, and was told to have a seat. Five minutes later, a short, energetic woman appeared and introduced herself as Alla Yunosheva, managing editor. She apologized for her English; she had not used it much, she said, since the year she had spent at the *St. Petersburg Times* in St. Petersburg, Florida.

Her *Times* was a little more than ten years old, and it had lived at 47 Morskaya an even shorter length of time. "It was a funeral office," Alla said. (This after a life as the Danish mission and a school of architecture.) "There were maps of cemeteries on the wall."

She took me upstairs to Nabokov's bedroom, where the institutional lighting echoed, I imagined, the "sullen, harsh, jaundiced tinge" that made his eyes "smart" at 8 A.M. And the reporter tapping at her terminal in the corner was engaged in an updated, upright version of the budding writer's morning routine: "Leaning my singing ear on my hand and propping my elbow on the pillow, I would force myself to prepare ten pages of unfinished homework."

Back on the second floor we entered the mother's boudoir, similarly wired, and stood at the oriel overlooking Morskaya. "This is where Nabokov saw his first dead person," Alla said, and immediately I remembered the passage from the memoir: "He was being carried away on a stretcher, and from one dangling leg an ill-shod comrade kept trying to pull off the boot . . ."

But on this afternoon the street was tranquil, washed in the undying light of the brief northern summer.

The following afternoon I met Svetlana, the friend of a friend in Florida, who had graciously offered to show me her city. Almost immediately, she kept with the theme.

"This is where Saigon used to be," she said, pointing past the hoarding at the corner of Vladimirsky Avenue and Nevsky Prospekt. The first floor was gutted; the terra-cotta-colored building was being transformed into a luxury hotel; Western businessmen would soon be dealing where Petersburg bohemia had plotted. For in the 1960s and 1970s, Saigon (the name more political than culinary) had been the gathering place for writers and artists, a kind of poor and more engaged man's Elaine's. I wondered if the hotel would at least put a plaque: "On this site the Nobel Prize winning poet Joseph Brodsky drank countless cups of coffee."

"He'd come here, or go to friends' apartments," Svetlana said. "The intelligentsia. They'd sit around somebody's kitchen and eat *vinegret*. It's a salad of boiled beetroot, potatoes, carrots, onions, and pickled cucumbers dressed with vinaigrette sauce. And they'd drink vodka and smoke cigarettes and discuss."

A romantic image not likely to be replicated by financial consultants. But St. Petersburg has had its share of creative types—not only Nabokov but Pushkin, Dostoyevsky, Blok, Akhmatova, Zoshchenko, Rimsky-Korsakov; all of their houses and apartments, as well as those of the less famous, now turned into museums that must make this city the world's leader in posthumous nurturing. Compensation for its poor showing in providing the other kind? Maybe it's time to give bankers a shot.

"You know," I said to Svetlana, "everything we read in the States about Russia is negative."

"But that's always been the case, hasn't it?" She allowed herself a weary half-smile. She had short blond hair, heavy glasses, and a steady expression, which I had not yet seen in my short time in Russia, of bemused tolerance. She taught English to medical students and was a single mother.

"The situation is not as bad as some people are saying. It's true that there are people who don't get paid. There's no money for research. People go abroad: South Korea, Poland, France, Canada, the U.S. Engineers can't find work. Now it's bankers who prosper. The nicest buildings are banks.

"St. Petersburg and Moscow are not representative of all of Russia," she continued. "Moscow now looks very good. You go there and think: What a rich country! St. Petersburg has always been poorer—an academic, cultural, research city." Earlier, someone had boasted to me: "Most of the people you meet here have been to university. There are I don't know how many universities. People read."

"There was a cover story in a magazine before I left," I said. "The title was, 'Is Russia Finished?'"

"I hope not . . .," Svetlana said, with something close to hurt, "for all it has in terms of culture, history . . ."

* * *

We stepped onto the Anichkov Bridge. To the right, the curve of the houses vaguely echoed a smaller Île de la Cité as seen from Île Saint-Louis. "What distinguished Petersburg from other European cities," Alexander Herzen wrote, "is the fact that it looks like all of them." The agitated horses decorating each side of the bridge called to mind D. Arkin's theory, as interpreted by Svetlana Boym, in her book *The Future of Nostalgia,* that St. Petersburg—created in 1703 by Peter the Great as his country's "window on the West"—was "'Satanic Russia' in opposition to 'Holy Russia'" and that "each equestrian monument of Petersburg symbolizes one of the Horsemen of the Apocalypse." There was the nagging urge to look underneath each of the steeds, remembering the story that the sculptor, frustrated by meddling from Nicholas I, carved his likeness into the groin of one. ("They were recently restored," Svetlana said, "and the report from the restoration crew was that no such image exists.") And, of course, we were crossing the Fontanka, the river immortalized in the song about the little finch:

*Puffed-up Siskin, where have you been?*
*I drank some vodka on the Fontanka River*
*I drank a glass, and then one more*
*And my head began to quiver.*

Before we reached the other side, the thought hit me: If one bridge triggers this many associations for a moderately literate foreigner, what does this city do to the average Russian—or Petersburger, who has pages of personal footnotes heaped onto all of the historical and cultural ones?

We turned past the portrait artists into Ostrovskovo Square, with its towering statue of Catherine the Great. "This is where people of sexual minorities gather," said Svetlana. Then we made our way around the Aleksandriinsky Theater to the Vaganova School of Choreography, which gave us more names to consider: Pavlova, Nijinsky, Nureyev, Barishnikov. Passing the National Library I tossed an old has-been into the pot.

"Lenin studied here," I said.

"And others," Svetlana quickly added, in a tone not meant to boast but to eclipse.

On Malaya Sadovaya Street, Svetlana introduced me to the two cats—Mashka and Elisey—peering down in stone from opposite second-floor perches. And under the linden trees on Klenovaya Street she recited the opening lines of Pushkin's *Ruslin and Liudmila.*

For lunch we found a place free of any literary or historical allusions. "There are a lot of new restaurants," Svetlana said, "which is good." Against a wall papered with a blown-up photograph of palm trees, Svetlana ate her salad (not *vinegret*) and I my *bliny.* Because of the décor, perhaps, we talked of Florida. I said I liked waking up to sunshine, but was often frustrated writing in a place where so few people read. It made my home, I realized, sound like the exact opposite of St. Petersburg, which someone had told me gets fifty-three days of sun a year. And I pondered, not for the first time, the relationship between climate and bookishness.

Climbing the steps of the Equerries' Church, Svetlana pulled a kerchief out of her purse and had it tied around her head by the time we reached the top. I had never been in a second-floor church. It looked more Lutheran than Orthodox, with its mostly unadorned walls (the legacy of seventy years of official state atheism), and an unlikely place for Pushkin's funeral. A young man stood just inside the entrance, bowing from the waist and touching the floor. A priest, his white curls overflowing his collar, sat on the windowsill, impassively hearing an old woman's confession. Svetlana lit a candle and placed it before a darkened icon.

"He's one of my favorite saints," she said.

Outside I asked: "You're religious then?"

"I believe there is something. I was baptized secretly by my grandmother, without my parents' knowledge. They were not Party members, and we celebrated the holidays. At Easter we always had eggs. But if you went to church it was observed."

We walked along the Moyka River to the apartment of Pushkin, the hero of Nabokov. The statue in the courtyard was ringed with children.

"He was very short," said Svetlana, examining the likeness, "but very attractive to women. He had many lovers. He had charisma." She could have been describing Brodsky.

Another brief bridge and a short walk to Palace Square. A giant Samsung advertisement filled one side.

"That's inexcusable," I said.

"I think so . . .," Svetlana said, and then caught herself. "But before, for special occasions, there would be pictures of Party leaders there. This is better."

We trudged beside the Winter Palace, two worthless entities in the wake of a monumental extravagance. I drank in the endless succession of pilasters, the vast inventory of roof-top urns, and said to Svetlana:

"You can understand, knowing what life for the peasants was like, why there was a revolution."

She looked nonplussed.

"The incredible inequality," I said.

"There is always inequality. Even in nature."

"But here it was enormous."

"I don't like revolution," she said finally. "Reform, yes. Revolution, no."

Across the Neva River crouched the Peter and Paul Fortress (its defensive walls, I would find a few days later, softened by sunbathers along the banks). On the island below it, two lighthouses stood windowless, but exotically plump and ornate. Svetlana pointed to a pale green façade a little farther south.

"That's the school of linguistics where Lydia and I studied," she said, referring to our Florida friend. Back at the New Hermitage building, she had shown me the atlantes whose toes they would rub for good luck in exams. "In the winter we would walk across on the ice. Because the bridges are so far apart, it was faster."

We passed the Bronze Horseman (see Pushkin's poem) and St. Isaac's Cathedral (its great columns still pocked from the Siege of Leningrad but no longer serving as the gateway to the Museum of Atheism). Looking in the direction of Morskaya Street, I recounted my visit to Nabokov's house.

"I read his wonderful memoir," she said.

Then, as you always seem to in St. Petersburg, we found ourselves back on Nevsky Prospekt. Svetlana sliced through the crowds with unruffled ease.

"There's the university," she said, crossing the Moyka, "that my son graduated from yesterday."

"Did you go to the ceremony?"

"They didn't have one. I gave him a mountain bike as a present." I wondered how long an English teacher had to save for a specialty bicycle.

"What's he doing for the summer?"

"He started his training at the Gallup Institute today."

A little later she pointed across the street. "In that church there was a swimming pool during Soviet times." A few yards on: "And that one was a storage facility for a comedy theater."

We passed a small band of Communists occupying the sidewalk with loser looks and pictures of Stalin. Then we skirted the fresh concrete replacing the asphalt in front of the new "Fabergé egg" boutique.

It was a long walk back to the Neva and the Monument to the Victims of Totalitarian Oppression. Designed by émigré artist Mikhail Chemiakin, it consisted of two small sphinxes, each with a face that was half human/half skeleton. They stared at each other from atop pedestals engraved with literary quotations—Akhmatova, Solzhenitsyn, Brodsky, et al.—directly across the river from the infamous Kresty Prison. A chill wind rattled in off the river.

It was a short walk down Liteyny Prospekt to the KGB headquarters, a large but otherwise self-effacing building, its shabby exterior putting it in a brotherhood with most of its neighbors, most of the city.

"I was offered a job with the KGB after graduation," Svetlana said calmly. "They'd often ask students of English. I spent a lot of time trying to come up with a good excuse, that my interest"—she started to laugh—"was really in technical English. They would tell you about all the privileges they could give you."

I asked about trust back then.

"People spoke honestly in private, at home with friends. Though sometimes friends could be informers. I knew someone who typed writings of Solzhenitsyn and distributed them. A friend reported him. He got out—he went to Italy first, then the United States. He came back a few years ago."

"Have many people returned?"

"I think he's the only one," she said laughing again.

Brodsky's address, conveniently, was just down the street from the KGB, in an apartment house that handsomely filled its part of the block. The tireless Svetlana led me along its length, and pointed to the balcony she believed to have been his, or rather his parents' and the other families' with whom they shared living space. Behind those walls, at the end of World War II, a young Joseph Brodsky ate his first American corned beef.

"Its flavor was less memorable than the cans themselves," he wrote in the collection of essays, *On Grief and Reason.* "Tall, square-shaped, with an opening key attached to the side, they heralded different mechanical principles, a different sensibility altogether. That key . . . was a revelation to a Russian child: We knew only knives."

Two decades later he would be put on trail for "parasitism" and sent into internal exile, before eventually being expelled from the country.

Down one of the back streets and into a shop, its shelves crowded with ceramic showpieces in a soothing design of blue and white. They were made, Svetlana said, in the village of Gzhel, not far from Moscow, which had been producing such treasures for more than 600 years. Among the plates and vases and statuary stood a small figure: a woman bundled against the cold and intently reading a newspaper. Stuck to her striped skirt was a well-swaddled child. Svetlana opened her purse; I turned my back as she scavenged for rubles. Then, after the shop assistant handed the figure to her, she presented it to me:

"So you'll always have readers."

# 7

## *Thurber Country*

*Columbus is a town in which almost anything is likely to happen and in which almost everything has.*

—from *My Life and Hard Times*

He was kidding. Columbus is a town in which almost nothing has happened and very little is likely to. It rises quietly and a little apologetically out of the flat farmland of central Ohio, dedicated to government and dreaming of football. A city of legislators and hefty linemen.

Even the things that people think happened in Columbus didn't really. Americans with merely a passing knowledge of James Thurber—literature by hearsay—still believe there was a night when the bed actually did fall on father, a day when the dam truly did break. Some can still see his drawings of this non-event, the woman who climbed the "These Are My Jewels" statue in the Statehouse yard, the dignified Dr. H. R. Mallory—"you remember Dr. Mallory, the man with the white beard who looks like Robert Browning?" —running madly and shouting "It's got us!"

The Columbus of today—with its requisite glass towers, its Kinkos and Marriotts—looks on the surface like any American city. "You won't find Thurber there," a Columbusite cautioned me about the City Center mall. Yet what fun he would have—this man whose first book was titled *Is Sex Necessary?*—with Victoria's Secret.

*The night I was born, December 8, 1894, Cesar Franck's D-Minor Symphony had its world premier in Paris. Fifty percent of the audience cheered at the end and the others booed, tore up the auditorium seats, and fenced the other side with walking sticks. The piece is now known as "The Keystone of Modern Symphonic Music." At 147 Parsons Avenue that night the score was 4-1 in favor of me.*

—from a letter to John O'Hara

The house on Parsons Avenue—"an eastern boundary of polite, middle-class living"—no longer stands; it was torn down several years ago to make way for Interstate 70. Driving through this neighborhood that became a highway, you can't help but think of the Thurber cartoon of the house that turns into a woman.

During Thurber's youth, the family moved frequently about the east side of Columbus. Among the houses still standing is 77 Jefferson Avenue, which inspired the well-loved and poorly remembered stories in *My Life and Hard Times.*

It was here that the bed didn't fall on father (it fell on James) and here that the ghost got in and prompted Mrs. Thurber, who believed there were burglars, to alert the neighbors by throwing a shoe through their window. "Mother suddenly made as if to throw another shoe, not because there was further need of it but, as she later explained, because the thrill of heaving a shoe through a window glass had enormously taken her fancy."

Today this residence makes up part of a lone row of restored brick houses that stand out starkly in the open spaces just off Broad Street. "What have you done with Dr. Millmoss?" an indignant woman asks a hippopotamus standing in the grass by a pipe, a shoe, and a hat (in *Men, Women and Dogs*). "What have you done," you want to ask it on Jefferson Avenue, "with the rest of the neighborhood?"

But there is no hippopotamus, only a unicorn, in the ellipse across the street. "Did you see as you came in . . . ?" volunteer guide Martha Wood asked me as I stood in the dining room. "There's a unicorn in the garden," she continued, with a throaty, satisfied laugh, before saying softly, "and he lived happily ever after.

"This is the room where the electricity leaked," she explained quite sanely. "These are the stairs the ghost came down." On the second floor we pored over mementos, family pictures, original drawings. Then we entered "Jamie's" room, the one he had lain awake in that night trying to think of the name Perth Amboy.

" . . . I thought of every other town in the country, as well as such words and names and phrases as terra cotta, Walla-Walla, bill of lading, vice versa, hoity-toity, Pall Mall, Bodley Head, Schumann-Heink, etc., without even coming close to Perth Amboy. I suppose terra cotta was the closest I came, although it was not very close." Finally he went into his father's room, shook him and said, "Listen. Name some towns in New Jersey quick!"

Back downstairs in the kitchen-turned-office, I piled my pickings from the adjoining gift shop. "Used to be around here," Martha said, "you never knew if the cash box was going to be in the oven or the refrigerator."

> *Ohio State University lies in a region of literacy and slurred enunciation, literary tradition and careless diction, vivid vocabulary and flat pronunciation.*
>
> —from *The Thurber Album*

There are prettier campuses, but not many as large. Even the buildings impress with their size; you stroll the outstretched lanes thinking not, as at Princeton or Harvard, of the generations of scholars who have walked here before you, but of the accumulated multitudes. Gigantic Ohio State.

Though it is easy to think of Thurber. Buildings are all identified by signs out front, so walking by Dreese Lab you imagine him inside, still peering dolefully through his microscope. "Students to right of me and to left of me and in front of me were seeing cells; what's more they were quietly drawing pictures of them in their notebooks. Of course, I didn't see anything."

A weathered stone edifice reminds you of military drill. "At eleven o'clock each morning thousands of freshmen and sophomores used to deploy over campus, moodily creeping up on the old chemistry building."

You locate journalism and, taking the stairs to the second floor, find the offices of the *Lantern,* the student paper for which Thurber wrote. Down the hill sits the football stadium, the opening of which Thurber covered for the *Evening Dispatch.*

"A wonderful structure," he wrote to his college friend Elliott Nugent, "set down in the pastoral back eighty of OSU like a modernized Greek temple or a Roman Coliseum born of mirage."

In the early 1900s, football terminology had already infiltrated even the College of Arts. "There is no forward passing in learning," one of Thurber's professors once said: "you have to cover the ground the hard way."

The brothers at Thurber's old Phi Kappa Psi are, today, mostly jocks. Still, they take new pledges through the Jefferson Avenue house and do work around the grounds. One of the three who lives in the writer's old room (The Thurber Dome) told me he'd read a Thurber story in English class but he couldn't remember the title. As he sat in front of his computer, searching his memory, I was reminded of Bolenciecwcz, the football player in "University Days" who struggles to name a means of transportation.

"The Catbird Seat?" I suggested, acting more helpful than Professor Bassum, who says to the tackle, "*Chuf*fa chuffa, *chuf*fa chuffa."

"No," he said. I could now see clearly the drawing that accompanies the story, and the caption under it: *Bolenciecwcz Was Trying to Think.*

"The Secret Life of Walter Mitty?" I said.

"Yeah!" the student brightened. "That was it."

> *Before going to France, I worked on the* Columbus Evening Dispatch, *a fat and amiable newspaper, whose city editor seldom knew where I was and got so that he didn't care.*
>
> —from *Memoirs of a Drudge*

Downtown the old-fashioned letters glow nightly over the *Dispatch* building: "Ohio's Greatest Home Newspaper." A startlingly qualified boast. *Columbus Monthly* magazine once described the *Dispatch* as "a place where anonymity is prized, celebrity shunned."

Thurber began at the *Dispatch* in 1920, working under city editor Norman 'Gus' Kuehner. "'If you've got any idea of going to New York to become another Oscar Hammerstein,' he would growl [at all new reporters], 'quit now. This is no place for you.' . . . To him the name 'Oscar Hammerstein' was derogatory, like Phi Beta Kappa." Thurber, who not only went to New York but also joined the *New Yorker,* later received a letter from Kuehner containing "the names of half a dozen Oscars, or former Columbus newspapermen who had come to New York to work."

Is there today, I wondered, an editor at the *Dispatch* who growls: "If you've got any idea of going to New York to become another Katie Couric . . ."?

> *Nobody from Columbus has ever made a first-rate wanderer in the Conradian tradition. Some of them have been fairly good at disappearing for a few days to turn up in a hotel in*

> *Louisville with a bad headache and no recollection of how they got there, but they always scurry back to their wives with some cock-and-bull story of having lost their memory or having gone away to attend the annual convention of the Fraternal Order of the Eagles.*
>
> —from *My Life and Hard Times*

Among the many delights contained in this book—an American masterpiece as perfect in its way as *The Great Gatsby*—are two of the finest travel cartoons ever published.

Thurber was not much of a traveler. He lived in France twice, working first as a clerk in the American embassy and later as a reporter for the *Chicago Tribune.* But this was as far afield as he was to get. Returning to the States in 1926, he settled in New York, started at *The New Yorker* and then, in fine *New Yorker* tradition, bought a house in Connecticut. There were some extended trips to Bermuda, but for the most part Thurber lived the sedentary life of a writer with failing eyesight and devoted dogs.

So not much of a traveler and, some people would say, not much of a draftsman either. The story has now become legend of how Thurber would dash off drawings between tortured bouts of writing and then toss them into the wastebasket, only to have them retrieved by his friend and office-mate E. B. White.

The drawings themselves are an intriguing paradox: childlike lines—Dorothy Parker said that all of Thurber's people "have the outer semblance of unbaked cookies"—conveying an adult angst. After they began appearing in the *New Yorker,* mothers inevitably started submitting their children's works. Thurber sent them a standard reply: "Your son can certainly draw as well as I can. The only trouble is he hasn't been through as much."

What he had been through is pricelessly depicted, through words and drawings, in *My Life and Hard Times.* While most of the stories take place in Columbus, in the last chapter—"A Note at the End"—Thurber recalls a trip to the West Indies.

> *Instead of being followed by the whispers of men and the glances of women, I was followed by bead salesmen and native women with postcards. Nor did any dark girl, looking at all like Tondelayo in "White Cargo," come forward and offer to go to pieces with me. They tried to sell me baskets.*

It is this last sentence that appears beneath his drawing of a market woman seated by a palm tree. The tree alone is remarkable, its droopy fronds prefiguring—the book was published in 1933—a Rastafarian coiffure. You can almost feel in the wavering lines the pleasure of an Ohioan, whose uncle "died of the chestnut blight of '66," drawing a palm.

But it is the woman who makes the drawing. She is laughing and pointing derisively at something that has moved outside our view. And in her doughy gesture is contained a sad and rarely mentioned truth of travel: that no matter how distant and exotic the place we visit, we can never escape our mundane selves. Whenever I suffer humiliation on a trip (an experience that occurs with depressing frequency) six words run helplessly through my mind: "They tried to sell me baskets."

The second drawing also relates to the text, but can stand alone as a kind of elegy on the loneliness of travel. The caption, more like a title, reads: "A hotel room in Louisville." A man perches on the edge of a chair holding a sock in one hand and his head in the other. His elbow, by virtue of a daftly elongated arm, rests on the footboard of an unmade bed. He probably is from Columbus and has a bad headache, but for anyone who has ever awakened from a dream of home in a foreign city he is Everytraveler.

> *If I have any beliefs at all about immortality, it is that certain dogs I have known will go to Heaven and very, very few persons will be there. I am pretty sure that Heaven will be densely populated with bloodhounds, for one thing.*
>
> —from *People Have More Fun Than Anybody*

The map of Green Lawn Cemetery calls it "The Resting Place of Those Who Shaped Columbus's Past & Present." Columbus's Greatest Home Cemetery. It is a bucolic expanse south of downtown, a kind of woods with tombs; former newspaperman Bob Ryder, a non-Oscar remembered in *The Thurber Album,* used to come here with his wife for bird watching.

The Thurber family corner sits near a pond in the center of the park. Each modest granite slab, set low in the ground, is engraved with a name and the relevant years. James's stone also has chiseled on it, between the 1894 and the 1961, the drooped flower from the last page of his book *The Last Flower.*

Epilogue: On Monday morning, before leaving Columbus, I returned to the Ohio State campus to read letters and manuscripts in the Thurber Reading Room. (It had been closed over the weekend.) Arriving before the room opened, I logged onto a computer downstairs.

"Connecting to Oscar," the screen read. Ohio State Catalog for Automated Retrieval. It gave me the feeling of a séance. Then, after I had indicated I wanted to search for an author, I received an example of how to type in my entry:

> *Thurber, James*
> *(last name first)*

# 8

# *Cows in Normandy*

We must have been an hour outside Paris when I looked up from my book and saw the farm. It gave me that fine shock of recognition you get when entering a place you've seen only in photographs. The buildings were half-timbered, the brown and white cows haughty, the trees billowy with apple blossoms. The sky was gray. There was no need for a billboard saying, "Welcome to Normandy."

I had just been reading about cows in *Normandy Revisited* by A. J. Liebling, the great *New Yorker* writer. Liebling's attachment to the province went way back: He had first become acquainted with what is known as Lower Normandy—the western departments of Calvados and Manche—in the fall of 1926, before beginning studies at the Sorbonne. When, as the *New Yorker*'s war correspondent eighteen years later, he learned that the Allied invasion would take place in this region, he felt "as if on the eve of an expedition to free the North from a Confederate army of occupation, I had been told that we would land on the southern shore of Long Island and drive inland toward Belmont Park."

In 1955 he returned to Normandy and wrote the book that I was now rereading on the Paris-Caen train. I was into my favorite chapter, "Madame Hamel's Cows," in which Liebling revisits the farm in Vouilly that had served as the press corps' headquarters in the period between D-Day and the liberation of Saint-Lô. "For five weeks in 1944," he wrote, "the Château had been one of the news centers of the world."

Madame Hamel, looking "a proper chatelaine, though she made no claim to nobility," had welcomed the journalists onto her estate. The living room was turned into a pressroom, and the correspondents slept in tents pitched in the pasture in front of the château. Liebling with his fluent French and savoir-faire, quickly, got on a first-name basis with the cows, including L'Anglaise (from the Channel Islands) and La Nitouche, "who pretended a maidenly aversion to the bull."

Like many who visit Normandy, I wanted to plod across beaches, peer through pillboxes, mourn in cemeteries. But I also wanted to find Madame Hamel's cows.

## The City

The train pulled into Caen (say "con" but hold the "n" in your nose) in mid-afternoon. A row of buses stood outside the station—this was a month before the fiftieth anniversary—each large window decorated at the bottom with a small band of flags—French, American, Canadian, British, Belgian, Dutch, Norwegian, and Polish. Above each band was printed, in English: "Welcome to Our Liberators."

Bookstores (Caen, a university town, has more of these per block than American cities have drugstores) displayed numerous tomes on the war, D-Day, the Battle of Normandy, and the destruction of the city. Special newspaper supplements—often with a soiled G.I. and a smiling Norman kid on the cover—filled their racks.

The window at Roland Chocolatier on Rue Écuyère featured Les Cartouches (The Cartridges), pastries shaped like artillery shells and stuffed with chocolate. They reminded me of the Christmas I spent in France when I saw an entire nativity scene made out of favorite foodstuffs. The colorful boxes bore a frighteningly sanitized version of D-Day landings.

The war was even on the evening news. Watching TV in my hotel room, I heard that some veteran American paratroopers were planning to commemorate the anniversary by jumping again in the vicinity of Sainte-Mère-Église, the town made famous by John Steele when his parachute got caught on the church steeple. The only problem was that French authorities had not given them permission.

## The Restaurant

Sunday I drove to Grandcamp for lunch at the Hôtel Duguesclin. I was hoping to follow in Liebling's gustatorial footsteps. He was one of those people who, like M. F. K. Fisher, constantly blur the line between travel and food writing; inseparable from his love of Normandy was his love of eating. In *Normandy Revisited* he made the exalted claim that "Lower Normandy has the best sea food, the best mutton (from the salt marshes of the Avranches region), the best beef, the best butter, the best cream, and the best cheese in Europe."

The night before I had driven to Port-en-Bessin, a town on the coast fortuitously situated between the British and Canadian beaches of Gold, Sword, and Juno and the American beaches of Omaha and Utah. It had a special place in Liebling's heart because of a "magnificent *sole normande,* bedewed with shelled mussels" he had once devoured there. In fact, from his landing craft on D-Day, he had tried to pick it out. (The town, not the restaurant, I think.)

Returning in 1955, he had eaten another memorable meal—*araignée de mer* (a local type of crab) followed by skate in black butter—at the Hôtel de la Marine. So naturally, as I drove along the harbor, I looked for the Hôtel de la Marine. And I found it, only a newer version. The young man at the front desk wasn't even sure where the old hotel had been. I ate a decent dinner—prawns followed by scallops (which in France go by the ecclesiastical name of *coquilles Saint-Jacques*), washed down by a bottle of local cider—but I knew it was not where Liebling had eaten.

Neither was Duguesclin, but it was more Liebling's kind of place. Perhaps because it was May Day, or simply a sunny Sunday in spring, or perhaps it is always this way, but the dining room at 1 P.M. was like Renoir's *Déjeuner des Canotiers* come to life.

Families, couples, children, and dogs all produced a convivial chatter; waiters bustled back and forth with imperturbable smiles. Mine brought me a nearly bottomless tureen of the freshest, plumpest mussels I had ever eaten, followed by the famous black-buttered skate. Lilies of the valley, the traditional flower of the day, sat in small bowls on some of the tables, and on the far wall hung a large painting depicting the U.S. Rangers' assault at Pointe du Hoc. (This famous cliff is just a few miles away, and the town now features a Rangers museum.)

"Did you see it in *Le Figaro* yesterday," Marie Madelaine Brard, the proprietor, asked me about the painting. "We just had it refurbished. You know the Rangers are coming here. We're having 400 people to dinner on June sixth."

I asked her about the meaning of the name Duguesclin.

"He was a chevalier who chased the English out of Normandy. But," she said, smiling, "that doesn't keep us from having good relations with them."

## The Schoolboys

Around noon the next day I stopped at the western edge of Omaha Beach. It was another unusually clear day; a British family had stuck a wicket in the sand and was playing cricket with a tennis ball; a busload of French high school students were staking out seats on a bunker for their boxed baguette lunches.

The cricket, especially, seemed a sacrilege on the very spot where so many men had given their lives. But then I reasoned that the players were simply restoring the beach to its proper use, and that it was the Germans—with their barbed wire and booby traps—who had desecrated this ground in the first place.

The students were from a high school outside Paris and happy, the boys especially, to give me sarcastic, bloated speeches on the importance of this field trip "to their historical and cultural understanding." It was only when I said I was from around Miami that we got on a natural footing.

"Me-a-ME! You like the Heat, no?"

"They're not bad," said a boy with an impressive, grease-free pompadour. "But I prefer the Bulls. Sco-TEE Pip-PIN." The accent on the upbeat made him sound like a French comic book hero; a cousin of Tintin.

We talked "le bas-KET" for a while, praising the exploits of giants in baggy shorts. They were, in these kids' eyes, the new G.I.s, men of glorious feats and enviable wealth.

## The Writer

Back in my rented Peugeot 106, I headed west on Route 514. The villages were all huddled against the wind, which had smoothed their sandstone edges. They had a stark fundamental uniformity—piles of tan stone under gray slate roofs—softened by the surrounding meadows, misty with cows.

Not far from Isigny-sur-Mer I saw a sign, pointing south, for Vouilly. It caught my eye like a lodestar—it does exist!—and I nearly made the turn. But there were still some things I wanted to see first.

On my way to Sainte-Mère-Église I stumbled upon Sainte-Marie-du-Mont. It is only a mile or so inland from Utah Beach, one of those small French towns that make you pull over and pine for a while. In the main traffic circle—devoid, for the most part, of any traffic—sits an ancient dome-steepled church surrounded by a ring of linden trees. Neat stone houses rim the circle. In one of these lives Gilles Perrault.

He graciously invited me in, though he hadn't been expecting me. A woman in the town hall across the way had told me that he'd written books on D-Day, as well as, he informed me, "a number of other subjects. But now," he chuckled, "I'm in demand again. I'm precious every ten years."

He was in his early sixties, handsome and modest. (He is well known in France; every French person I met afterward said, impressed: "You met Gilles Perrault?!?") His interest in D-Day, he explained, went back to his childhood, when both his parents had taken part in the Resistance. During his military service, he trained as a parachutist, which gave him a certain understanding of the undertaking. And then, at the age of thirty, tired of practicing law in Paris, he moved to Sainte-Marie-du-Mont to become a writer.

"I didn't know the town. I saw an ad for the house, came out to take a look, and bought it.

"Manche is not nearly as well-known as Calvados; even the French don't know it. It is very beautiful, very diverse: wild in the north, while here you have the *bocage* [hedgerowed fields]. Most of the people here make their living from dairy farming or raising horses."

I told him I had heard that Normans were generally cold, tough characters. (Liebling had often compared Normandy to New England.)

"Not cold, not hard," he said. "Reserved. They have a great reserve. They don't welcome you with open arms. They observe you for a while. But they respect the rights of others, and they expect the same, to be allowed to do as they wish.

"To give you an example: I often take positions that are very controversial. And I go on TV, so everybody knows what they are.

If this were a town in the south of France, people would be pointing at me as I went down the street. Here nobody says a word to us about it. And I think that's the test of a great civilization.

"You have to remember that this region was completely martyred during the Hundred Years' War, and then during the Protestant-Catholic conflicts. And I think there remains in the collective conscience this virtue of tolerance."

I mentioned that, up until an hour before, I had never heard of Sainte-Marie-du-Mont; that Sainte-Mère-Église was the town everyone talked about.

"Ah," he said, smiling, "that is our great tragedy. We're very jealous of Sainte-Mère-Église. And all because nobody got stuck on our church steeple. But the paratroopers landed here as well. They were scattered all over the area. When I moved here in the early sixties, children still wore pyjamas made from parachutes the Americans had left behind. People made curtains from them.

"Today there is still a rivalry between the two towns. When our soccer team plays theirs, a few people often end up in the hospital." I tried to imagine the headline: "Holy Mother mauls Saint Mary."

Before leaving, I asked him what he thought about the American veterans wanting to jump again, and the French refusing to grant them permission.

"If they want to take the risk and jump, I say let them. They took the risk in 1944. And," he added, grinning, "they didn't have government permission then."

## The Pharmacist

Sainte-Mère-Église, when I finally reached it, looked like Sainte-Marie-du-Mont gone Hollywood. It was an attractive town, but it seemed to me that the writer for *Le Figaro* had gotten it about right when she wrote: "At some point the history of the town got lost in the history of D-Day. It's as if nothing, absolutely nothing, even the famous church, whose foundations date to the eleventh century, existed before."

There was an Auberge John Steele and a hideous parking lot in the main square where Howard Manoian, a paratrooper who had retired here, regularly parked his Lincoln Continental. And, in a perfect Disneyesque touch, a dummy of a paratrooper hung from the church steeple.

Henri-Jean Renaud worked in the pharmacy facing the church. His father was mayor in 1944—a plaque to him now stands in the square—and his mother tended the graves of American soldiers with such loving care that *Life* magazine called her "The Queen of Normandy."

"Oh," Renaud said dismissively, when I mentioned this fact, "journalists always have to come up with some catchy title. I prefer this," and he pointed to a framed item hanging on the wall of his office. It was his mother's obituary on the front page of *Static Line—"Your Airborne Lifeline"*—in February of 1988. "It's the journal of the paratroopers," he said.

I asked him about the current paratrooper controversy. "In 1944 they didn't ask us if they could come. And we were very happy that they did. My only concern is that it's a little exhibitionistic. Those who jump are going to take attention away from those who don't. And I want all the veterans to be honored equally."

Across the square, in the Airborne Museum, I read the latest entries in the visitor's book:

> *Thanks to those who gave their life for France*
>
> —Pierre, 8.
>
> *We must attempt, with these relics of the slow reconquest of liberty, to perpetuate the memory of that which no one has the right to forget*
>
> —Benoît, 15.

## The Schoolgirl

"Do you recognize this?" Geneviève Cousin asked, showing me the metallic plate she was using to feed the chickens in her backyard garden. And I did, from the movie in the Airborne Museum: a G.I. mess kit that had been left behind.

"It's very sturdy," she said.

I had decided to make one more stop in Sainte-Marie-du-Mont to see another family I had been told about in the town hall. And the Cousins—Geneviève, her husband, Émile, and granddaughter Mélanie, who was visiting from Saint-Lô—had been kind enough to tell me their stories. Geneviève had shown me the scar on her forehead, received the night of June 5 when a bomb hit her house, and pictures of the American doctor, Eugene Klein, who had treated her. Émile, pouring me another glass of homemade cider, had talked about cutting grass for the Germans to use as camouflage on their bunkers. "We were just kids. We had to do it. Otherwise . . ." and he had formed a gun with his hand and put it to his head.

They said they would spend the sixth this year in town, as always. "Sainte-Mère-Église," Geneviève said sharply, "has a ball. I've never gone to that. My mother was killed on June sixth. My brother was gravely wounded. My father was away in prison. For me it's not a celebration." She was not bitter toward the Americans (war is war) but toward what she saw as a lack of due respect in Sainte-Mère-Église.

They asked if I'd been to Saint-Lô. I said no, and they suggested I take Mélanie back the following day to show me around.

"Well, I have to get to . . ."—it was the first time I had actually said, or attempted to say—"Vouilly." In desperation I wrote it down. Mélanie, laughing, helped me out, pouting her lips to expel a sound that resembled "phooey."

"You can go there afterwards," her grandmother said, smiling.

So the next morning I pulled up to the house at nine o'clock. Mélanie kissed each grandparent two times on each cheek—her head going back and forth in that touching, bobbing ritual—then hopped into my Peugeot and rode away.

Though living in Saint-Lô, Mélanie was going to high school in Cherbourg. From one bombed city to another. A child of modern France. But she had listened to her grandparents' stories with genuine interest. "I've heard so many," she told me as we headed south. "My grandfather didn't tell you the one about the boys peeing in the milk pails before they gave them to the Germans."

It was raining when we arrived in Saint-Lô. "The weather's turned miserable," I said.

"But typical," Mélanie replied smiling. It was also cold. "At least it's not cold," she said.

We wandered around town, poking into rebuilt churches, and then drove to a modern apartment building to visit her other grandparents. Before pulling into a space, I asked if it was okay to park there.

"That's funny," she said. "You said *parker.* That's not French. The word is *garer.* You've heard about our Minister of Culture, who's trying to ban the use of English words? His name is Monsieur Toubon. At school we call him Monsieur Allgood.

"It's ridiculous, what's he's trying to do. The other week a bunch of us went to a café and we asked the waiter to bring us a slice of ham between two pieces of bread. He looked at us as if we were crazy. But you see, we were trying to avoid saying 'sandwich'."

Upstairs her grandparents fed us coffee and cookies and more war stories. Then they asked if I were going to visit Mont-Saint-Michel.

"It is the marvel of Normandy," the grandmother said.

"Of France," the grandfather said.

"Of the world," Mélanie said.

I said I had to get to Vouilly.

As a consolation, the grandmother gave me a postcard of Mont-Saint-Michel. Then they sent me off with a fragrant stem of lily of the valley.

## The Cows

I drove slowly to Vouilly, to savor the moment. At Saint-André-de-l'Épine I took Route 59 north, the road the Twenty-ninth Division had taken south to the front. It was still, in places, bordered by high hedgerows that had hampered their advance. Liebling described the Twenty-ninth's progress as "slow, bloody and sometimes nearly imperceptible." As I drove, I tried to imagine "the fire going over the road, clipping leaves from trees and making you feel important." But it was all vernal quietude.

Finally, I came to Vouilly. It looked as Liebling had described it, "a crossroads, an old church, a harness-maker's shop, and a grocery café," except for the absence of the last two. In the cemetery beside the church I found the large granite tomb of the *Famille Hamel.*

A sign at the crossroads pointed to Le Château. I followed a leafy country road that led quickly to a sign I had seen all over Lower Normandy, identifying the farm as a *gîte,* or bed-and-breakfast. The journalists had been replaced by tourists.

I headed down the treelined drive, green pasture stretching on either side, and parked on the gravel in front of the large, stately, white-shuttered château. A woman in her forties, with short reddish hair and a gentle expression, came out to greet me, introducing herself as Marie-José Hamel.

She led me into what is now the guest breakfast room, though it was still labeled, I was happy to see, "Press Room." I recognized, with muted excitement, the ornate pieces of furniture made by Madame Hamel's son, and, just below the windows, the moat from which Madame, sitting in her living room, would casually fish for carp.

"It still has carp," Marie-José said. "But the water's stagnant so they're not very good."

I caught up on news like an old neighbor. Madame Hamel had died in 1968 (four years after Liebling), and her grandson—Marie-José's husband—ran the farm today. They still had fifty cows, but now they were Dutch. Traditional farming, she said, was dying in France, as was Vouilly.

"We are now the youngest people in the village," she said, laughing with a mixture of dismay and disbelief. "The baker closed shop a couple of years ago. He held out the longest. There is no school anymore. Children have to go to Isigny."

Old correspondents still dropped by. "I can always spot them, because when they get out of the car, they look first at the pasture."

Marie-José got up and brought me the guest book that the Hamels had kept over the years. I paged through it, finding Andy Rooney ("all the Americans who come point him out"), John Thompson of the *Chicago Tribune* ("he's very loyal, he comes back frequently") and, finally, the man I was looking for. The handwriting was execrable, the French flawless. It was dated 16 June 1955:

> *Happy to find you all smiles, as always in my memories*
> *—A. J. Liebling, of the New Yorker.*

When her husband, James, came in I showed him Liebling's *Normandy Revisited,* pointing out the chapter on their farm. They had never seen it.

I translated a few passages—descriptions of Madame Hamel and James's father. He stood with his muscular white forearms crossed, a smile of wonder and recognition passing over his boyish face. "That's true," he said nodding. "He was very observant."

I asked if there were any new Nitouches.

"No," he said smiling. "I give them geographical names now. There's Volga, Bogota. I have a few American names: Nevada, California, Michigan."

Monsieur Hamel's cows.

# 9

# *A Sentimental Journey*

The discount supermarket on the outskirts of Szeged still looked like the factory it had recently been. György pushed our cart across the concrete floor, picking from waist-high piles foods unfettered by marketing strategies. Two cans of stuffed cabbage, two cans of frankfurters and rice, an airtight packet of salami, a box of cookies, bottles of water and grapefruit juice. Supplies more befitting a camping trip than a week in Romania. "You don't worry so much about finding food," explained Ildiko, "but about the quality." I had forgotten the travel habits of Eastern Europeans.

György went in search of tonic water, his high forehead and thin ginger beard gliding above the heads of his fellow shoppers. We had met in Warsaw in the early 1980s, where we had both found ourselves in the novel position of teaching our native tongues. György was an English literature scholar, specializing in the Renaissance, though recently he had also become the head of the Hungarian Studies program at his university, József Attila. It was in this capacity that a few years earlier he had taken a group of American students around Transylvania, a trip he was now eager to repeat with me and his girlfriend.

Back home I sat in György's living room with a three-volume photographic book on Transylvania. One cover carried a picture of an equestrian statue rising from a square in Cluj-Napoca (which the book called by its Hungarian name of Kolozsvár);

another showed an ornamental wooden gate consisting of a large swing door for wagons and a small side door for humans. This was identified as a Székely gate, from the Székely Land.

Turning inside, I read the introduction:

> *Transylvania, do you bear in mind your sons, do you hear the beating of our hearts like a mother? We are still your sons, even if we live far. We are keen on you, follow all the news about you in anguish. We have got far from the motherland. . . . But we feel and know that the land of our ancestors expects us to return. We understand the mysterious and deep meaning of being sons of Transylvania through tears and smiles. We step out of time and are amazed at the beauty of the motherland, at the motherland that attracts us unceasingly till the end of our lives.*

On the evening before our departure, we visited György's mother and sister. In an elegant, pre-war apartment, we were served tea and snapshots of Transylvania. (The two of them had gone on a bus tour several years earlier.) There were pictures of peasant gatherings—which Ildiko examined with an ethnographer's eye—and more Székely gates, which everyone pronounced "*SAKE-ay.*" György studied a detailed map while his mother looked on with searing plaintiveness. When she kissed her son good-bye—making at each cheek a puckered litany of smooching sounds, in that Hungarian way that at first sounds cartoonish but eventually becomes touching—her eyes were damp.

Her feelings were understandable. Every book I'd read before this trip featured travelers in Hungary being warned about Romania. In Patrick Leigh Fermor's *Between the Woods and the Water,* a beautiful book describing his walk in the 1930s from the Hook of Holland to Constantinople, he is told by his Great Plain's hosts, "It's a terrible place! They are all robbers and crooks!" and then, on his departure, he is given an automatic pistol by the lady of the house. In *Stealing from Deep Places,* Brian Hall, a young American riding through on his bicycle in the 1980s, notes that "the Hungarians had warned me repeatedly about physical violence in Romania. . . . They had told me to buy a knife to protect myself." More recently, Eva Hoffman writes in *Exit into History* of the stories she'd heard of "tourists disappearing in the dark Transylvanian woods." Hungarian friends cautioned her not to go in a car with Hungarian license plates. We would have not only Hungarian plates, but a Russian car.

Out on the street, György looked preoccupied. "It makes me feel guilty," he said, "when my mother says she wishes she were coming with us."

I had not been prepared for the Hungarian attachment to Transylvania. There are islands—the Falklands, Taiwan—that incite nationalistic passions, but they are more of a political than an emotional nature. The desire, verging on a duty, to visit seemed reminiscent of American Jews and their feelings toward Israel, except that Israel was a promised, not a lost land. Poles talk wistfully of the cosmopolitanism of Lwów and Wilno—the national epic *Pan Tadeusz* begins, "Lithuania, my fatherland, you are like health!" —but they don't obsess about their erstwhile borders.

Transylvania—*Erdély* in Hungarian, with the same basis in "forest"—has long been claimed by both Romania and Hungary. The Romanians argue, not illogically, that the ancient Dacians, from whom they are descended, secured their kingdom here; the Hungarians counter that when they arrived the land was virtually uninhabited, emptied by years of vicious invasions. The embittered debate has a "chicken-or-the-egg" quality, yet there's no disputing the fact that for most of the last thousand years Transylvania was ruled, often repressively, by Hungary. Finding itself on the losing side in World War I ended its run. The words

"Treaty of Trianon" still haunt Hungarians worse than "Waterloo" ever nettled the French. For Waterloo, for the French, represented only a dream of grandeur.

After Trianon, not only was Transylvania gone, but so were its northern and southern lands to Czechoslovakia and Yugoslavia. A country that had been, in its own part of the world, of respectable size, was reduced by two-thirds. (Imagine the U.S. losing everything west of the Mississippi.) It also said farewell to about half its pre-war population, albeit much of that minorities. Still, an estimated two million ethnic Hungarians live today in Transylvania.

But the pain was not just in the sum of what had vanished but in the nature. With Transylvania, Hungary lost a part of its patrimony: the intellectual cafés of Kolozsvár, the spiritual bastion of Gyulafehérvár, the seminal folk arts of the Székely Land. (Much of what we think of as distinctly Hungarian—red-and-white patterned embroidery, for instance—is Transylvanian.) And, just as tragically, it lost its mountains: gone were the Carpathian peaks, the pellucid streams, the conifer forests. After Trianon, Hungarians had to accustom themselves to a life of prosaic flatness. It was as if the country had been not only abbreviated, but emasculated.

Late Monday afternoon, it took us several trips to load the Lada: suitcases, food boxes, cooler, camera bag, loose plastic bottles. When it looked as if we were finally ready, György insisted on filming us getting into the car. With a painful groan, he took the camera down from his face. "I can't believe it! I pushed the wrong button and erased the opening frame that I just spent an hour working on upstairs."

Once in the car, Ildiko tried to console him. "Where are the tapes?" he asked. We had left them upstairs. We were not leaving quite yet. "I'll go get them," said Ildiko. "No, I'll go," said

György, and he yanked open the door. When he returned, he said with his ironic half smile, "Don't worry, Tom, it will get only worse." A few minutes later, just after five, we crossed the Tisza River and headed for Transylvania.

We reached the Romanian border a little before sunset. (György had taken a longer route to a less crowded crossing.) A stout Hungarian in a short-sleeved white shirt stamped our passports and chatted stiffly. "Quite pleasant," said György, pulling away. "Obviously part of the new image."

Just ahead of us loomed the old. Five long lines of cars stretched haphazardly from two distant booths. The majority were Romanian Dacias, their taillights dusty, their engines turned off. A few drivers had resignedly gotten out, and now stood smoking in the waning light, while a trio of shady young men weaved suspiciously among the cars. That particular southeastern European atmosphere of tedium, disorderliness, and threat.

"Ildiko's scared," said György, smiling, trying to console her.

"I don't like Romania," she said sharply.

Forty-five minutes later we reached passport control. A taciturn man studied our documents through heavy glasses, stamped them, wordlessly handed them back. We drove a few feet to the customs booth. A svelte blonde emerged, dressed in a blue blouse, bright yellow tie, and tapered gray slacks. She looked as if she had just stepped out of a 1950s Chesterfield's ad. She walked back toward the passport booth, picked up a barrier, and placed it about ten feet behind our car. "Uh-oh," said György, stepping outside. But as soon as he opened the trunk, revealing our suitcases and food boxes, she told him to close it. We were free to go.

After the self-important border, the land turned scraggly. The flat road ran through lumpy fields veiled, in places, by laundry lines of embroidered cloth. (The combination of folk crafts and roadside commerce reminded me of Mexico.) A peasant woman sat by each collection, knitting as intently as if snuggled before a hearth. At one point a strange contraption lumbered onto the road and, as it slowly made its way across, we recognized it as an enormous sow. Four high-heeled piglets daintily followed.

Soon the road became a wide street leading through a corridor of new apartment blocks. It looked less like a city than a construction site: people waited at dusty intersections and clothes hung from partial balconies. Some buildings had obviously been abandoned in mid-construction, others simply looked that way. The unfinished and the decaying fused in a squalid harmony.

The town was Arad, site of an eighteenth-century Hapsburg citadel, though I knew it better as the place where Patrick Leigh Fermor had gone on a double date. In *Between the Woods and the Water,* the second volume of the still unfinished trilogy of his epic walk, Leigh Fermor tells of a sketch he made of the fair-haired Izabella that is still in his journal, "pressed like a petal" and titled, "Iza, Arad. May 16, 1934."

If the purpose of this journey, in György's mind, was to see a vanished homeland, a subtext for me was visiting the setting of one of my favorite travel books. *Between the Woods and the Water,* like its predecessor *A Time of Gifts,* is an ornate, intoxicating work that brilliantly captures the adolescent wonder and hard-earned joys of travel. And some of its finest moments occur in Transylvania, where the nineteen-year-old Englishman—passed from one amusing, superannuated manor house to another—drinks amber wine and dances to Gypsy songs. Toward the end of his stay, in a dream-like idyll, he joins two Hungarian friends in a touring car—"on a secret journey to the interior of Transylvania"—though, in his version, he is the one who has the girl.

Just as I was wondering whether we would see anything remotely resembling what Leigh Fermor had found, we all three hit the roof. György stomped on the brake. "Romanian roads!" he howled, then picked his way through a cratered stretch. "And this is the European highway!" I suddenly sympathized with Leigh Fermor's descriptions: "The roads were not good. The car pitched about the ruts and the potholes like a boat in a choppy sea . . ."

That was about it for nostalgia. Runaway trucks swirled out of the darkness—practically the only traffic at this hour—nearly bowling us over with their drafts. Lonely roadside cafés appeared, often strung with colored lights and hung, inevitably, with a Coca-Cola sign. In the darkness, and to a backdrop of Bach concertos, they looked rather inviting, but we didn't stop. We were in the Partium, a kind of neutral cushion between Hungary and Transylvania. Sometime around midnight we crossed into the latter. Then a sign appeared for Deva, and György and Ildiko cheered.

The streets were empty save for a troupe of street cleaners—baggy coveralls, twig brooms, horse-drawn wagon—looking like grim reapers in the dim light from the street lamps. We found a hotel—the Bulevard—and walked inside, György leading and contracting something sticky from the door handle.

The receptionist lifted her head dreamily from a pillow concealed behind the counter. She had short black hair, beautiful skin, and a large sweater divided into the national colors of blue, yellow, and red. She did not speak anything but Romanian; we spoke, among us, six languages, though Romanian was not one of them. She tore off a piece of newspaper and wrote on it "75,000."

György asked how much that was in dollars. She did not understand. A policeman entered—appearing, I assumed, for his nightly tryst. He too spoke only Romanian though, after a word with the receptionist, he picked up a pen and wrote carefully in the palm of his hand: $100 = ? "Precisely," said György. "How much?" The officer wagged his head blankly.

We assumed that the price wasn't exorbitant, and got from the receptionist the name of a hotel where we could exchange dollars. György's ability to understand was increasing by the minute; Ildiko and I were still futilely banking on help from our French. Back in the car, György said, "That scene reminded me of an old Hungarian policeman joke. Two policemen are standing on a street corner in Budapest and a man comes up and asks them something in German. They don't understand, so he tries English. Nothing. French. Nothing. Italian. Nothing. Totally frustrated, the man walks away. At which point the one policeman turns to the other and says, 'You know, it would be good to learn another language.' 'Why do you say that?' his partner asks. 'That guy spoke four and what did it get him?'"

It was a short drive to the Hotel Sarmis. Two men stood outside the entrance, smoking. "*Bună seara,*" I said, with a man-of-the-world air. I had just picked that up. I had just given them the signal to pounce. "*MO-ment!*" said György, with surprising authority, and they retreated meekly as we walked inside.

At the reception desk I changed fifty dollars, getting 150,000 *lei* in return, in 10,000 notes. As I began counting the wad, Ildiko whispered sternly, "Tom. Don't." I stuffed it into my pocket and kept my hand there, clasping it tightly, as we headed out past our new friends.

Back at the Bulevard, György moaned: "Oh, no, we're going to get that sticky stuff on our hands again." And all our anxiousness—of the border, the ruinous roads, the dimly lit city—dissolved into a late-night giddiness. We broke into laughter. "I wonder what it could be?" he said. Still smiling, I gave the receptionist 75,000 *lei,* and we carried our key up a winding flight of stairs.

The door to our room, Number 112, stood next to a door that had a sign in place of a number. It read: *Partidul Aliantei Civice.* Luckily, the members of the Civic Alliance Party were not celebrating any victories tonight. We entered our room. It had a high ceiling, a window overlooking the street, three low single beds, an armoire, a sink, a mirror, and a picture frame with nothing behind the glass. It seemed fittingly symbolic.

"No reading lamps," said György, cracking us up again.

Ildiko wanted to use the bathroom but refused to go alone. When she and György returned, there was cause for more mirth. (One must take the hour into account.)

"There are two toilets," György said, like a maitre d' presenting the night's seating arrangements. "One is marked *WC Personal* and the other is marked *WC Clienti*. The shower is an absolute horror," he added cheerfully. "Tiles are missing and the pipes are exposed." Discreetly, we got ready for bed.

"This reminds me," said György, "of that hilarious scene in Sterne's *A Sentimental Journey* when he shares a room with two young women. Do you remember it? It's a very delicate situation, of course, so he puts up a partition, but he can't sleep and changing position he stretches out his hand and there's all this confusion and just when he's about to tell us what he's grabbed the book ends."

We breakfasted in: stale bread, salami, jam, yellow peppers. Outside, casually dressed people walked to work down the middle of the street, many of them casting glances at our Lada. At the far end rose an old volcanic hill topped by a citadel. But we drove in the other direction, east, toward Hunedoara.

The town was coated in a rust-brown film, the skyline spiked with belching smokestacks and tin church steeples that shone, miraculously, through the dust. (The only thing for miles around to keep its original color.) Up a hill, hemmed in by factories, stood the famous castle of Vajdahunyad, no longer solitary and now surpassed in imposing menace by its coughing neighbors.

It seemed a sad fate for what had been the seat of János Hunyadi, "the most celebrated hero in Hungarian history," according to Leigh Fermor, "and . . . the greatest fifteenth century champion in the whole of Christendom . . . not only a great commander and statesman, but a rock of uprightness in a kingdom and an age that seethed with conspiracy." He was Romanian by birth, but at an early age he fought for King Sigismund of Hungary. As his prowess grew, he achieved stunning victories of his own, rousting the Turks out of the Balkans and eventually becoming the ruler of Transylvania.

We walked toward the narrow bridge that led to the barbican, the soiled fortification now rising grimly into the murky sky. Sándor Petöfi, the great poet who died at the age of twenty-six while fighting for Hungarian independence from Austria, wrote to these battlements: "Glorious walls, accept me." An information board, in Romanian and French, spoke glowingly of "Iancu de Hunedoara," and called this "the most precious monument of the Romanian people." Next to which someone had written, in French, "You lie."

"Probably a Hungarian," Ildiko said, with satisfaction.

The count who showed the castle to Leigh Fermor in 1934 commented similarly. "They seem to think the Treaty of Trianon awarded them Hungarian history as well as territory." To which the countess replied, "Well, I suspect the Hungarians underplayed the Rumanian side."

We headed in a northeast direction toward Alba Iulia (Gyulafehérvár). As much as I tried to sympathize with my friends, I found myself quietly favoring the Romanian when it came to names, not only for the towns, but for the things within them: *librarie vs. könyvüzlet, florarie vs. virágüzlet, bijuterie vs. ékszerész*. It was like choosing, for a dark alley meeting, between a vague acquaintance and a total stranger.

Alba Iulia had the most pleasant collection of *libraries* and *bijuteries* that we had yet seen. Even the ubiquitous new apartment houses displayed architectural flourishes—rounded corners, pitched roofs—that distinguished them from the monotonous boxes one usually sees in Eastern Europe. In a department store, though, we found sparsely stocked shelves and drab merchandise. "Like a hangover from socialism," groaned György.

At the top of a hill, under an ornate archway, sat a tranquil precinct of leafy streets and conflicting towers. Two cathedrals—one recent and Orthodox, one historic and Catholic—stood side by side, and their positioning—both facing in the same direction, each ignoring the other—seemed to epitomize the story of Transylvania. We strolled gardens shadowed by onion domes and brushed shoulders with workmen in the yard of St. Michael's. "It's so nice to hear Hungarian," György said, "and to see Hungarian inscriptions." We entered the austere side chapel—"After Esztergom, the most beautiful Renaissance chapel in Hungary," pronounced György, willfully unmindful of the twentieth-century realignment of borders. But he was correct in that this was still a Hungarian see; the bishop's residence stood next door. At the far side of the lofty nave we found the tomb of Hunyadi. A fresh holly wreath lay atop a graceful stone likeness of the White Knight in repose, its red-white-and-green ribbon trailing down his leg and carrying the name of the Hungarian Library Association.

Outside, we walked down a side street past the Museum of Unification—"Unification," scoffed György, "it should be Appropriation"—and came to a dilapidated palace. "That was the home of a Hungarian landowning family," said György bitterly. Trying to enter the library next door, we were brusquely turned away by a Romanian guard.

"I'm totally baffled," György said. "Let's move on to the Hungarian territories. This is not Hungary, this is Romania."

At Medias I took the wheel. We traveled through fertile fields rimmed by rolling hills and marred, every few miles, by the reiterated factory plopped crustily in the middle. We would be sailing along past horse-drawn wagons and lopsided hayricks and the occasional Gypsy caravan parked under a tree when all of a sudden smokestacks would appear, rising in the distance like an indecent mirage. In this arcadian tableau, they looked not only out of place, but out of time. "That's Ceauşescu's legacy," said György. "He wanted to industrialize so he could make Romania independent."

"From the Soviet Union, right?"

"From everybody."

In the last light of day, we entered Sighişoara. Sturdy houses spilled down hills, their faded façades of mustard and grape and evergreen washed now in an angelic glow. Brown-shoed children rode gearless bicycles over flowing cobblestones. It was not just the hour, or the giddy up-and-downness, that gave the place a fairy-tale quality; it was the prim Teutonic squares rimmed by wealthy burgher houses. In the heart of Transylvania, on our way from "the Romanian to the Hungarian territories," we had entered an old Saxon town.

Saxons were an additional element in Transylvania's ethnic muddle, brought here as settlers by Hungarian kings in the twelfth century. (Despite their name, most of them came from the Middle and Lower Rhine.) Because of repatriation over the last few years, the population has dwindled from about 300,000 to 40,000. György said that at one point Helmut Kohl was paying Ceauşescu 1,000 marks for every Saxon who returned to Germany. "That's how Ceauşescu was able to make Romania the only Bloc country without any debt."

Many of the abandoned Saxon houses, indeed whole towns, had been taken over by Gypsies (who, according to György, hastened their decline), though Sighişoara still looked well-kempt and much as Leigh Fermor must have found it when he spent a bittersweet night here with his soon departing Angela. "The gable windows upstairs," he wrote, "surveyed a vision of great unreality."

We walked past the stately house where Dracula was born—the plaque on the wall, bearing the name of Vlad Dracul, appeared like an unwanted cliché in my evening masterpiece—then ducked under the Clock Tower and headed down winding steps that dropped us onto a lively street of umbrellaed cafés. We chose the pizzeria—why not add one more ethnic imprint?—where our black-haired waitress tattooed our order into her small left palm.

I could have spent a couple days here, but György was eager to reach Oderheiu Secuiesc or, as he preferred, Székelyudvarhely. After about an hour of driving he made a momentous left turn and announced with a gritty half-smile, "Now the roads get really bad. The Romanians don't improve them for the Székelys."

The Székelys, according to most historians, were sent here by Hungarian kings to serve as border guards. Though of the Magyar family, they are always spoken of separately from the Hungarians of Transylvania—a shrewd, strong-willed, tight-lipped people.

"We have Székely jokes," said György. "A young man is hitching a ride and a Székely picks him up. The man asks, 'Is it far to Szováta?' 'Nope,' the Székely says, and the man hops in. They go quite a ways and don't say a word. Finally the man asks again, 'Is it far to Szováta?' And the Székely says, 'Now it is.'"

"Look!" said Ildiko. "The village names are in Hungarian!"

"Yea," said György, "the Romanians take them down, but the Székelys put them right back up."

Suddenly, György stepped on the brake. "A hedgehog!" cried Ildiko.

"A Hungarian hedgehog," clarified György. And we all burst into laughter.

In the morning, a comely young woman in a short, tight skirt changed my travelers' checks in a modern bank. "A few years ago," said György, "these girls would have been in peasant dresses." We then went to get some gas. Everyone spoke Hungarian.

We drove out to a neighboring village where there was a Calvinist church with frescoes from the fourteenth century. A gaggle of geese waddled down a dirt street decorated with Székely gates. Two women stood washing clothes at tables set in the middle of the river, the prettiest kept cool in a French-cut bathing suit. Nearby, two storks confabulated in a nest they had built on the roof of someone's house, and as we stood taking pictures a policeman walked up and demanded our passports. He peered down at them and ordered us inside. Only then did we notice the small Romanian flag; the house was the police station.

We were led before the chief of police, a short bespectacled man with a thick head of reddish gray hair. He listened patiently while the arresting officer ranted. I recognized the words "video" and "negative report about Romania." Indignation was turning his dark cheeks scarlet.

The chief quietly heard him out and then turned to György, whom he addressed in Hungarian. His speech was soft and easygoing. We had stumbled, I realized with relief, upon the Andy Taylor and Barney Fife of Transylvania. While Andy and György chatted and joked, Barney slumped in a posture of disappointment and shame. Andy said he didn't even know about the stork nest—"Ya hear that Barn? We got us some baby carriers right over our heads!"—and came out with us to take a look. Barney, manfully trying to recover, returned our passports, tipped his hat, and said "Good-day" in Hungarian. He slunk off, no doubt for lunch with Thelma Lou.

Back in the car, György said: "That's what they did during the Ceauşescu years. He put a few policemen in every village to harass the Hungarians."

On the way back to Oderheiu, we stopped by a Székely gate crowned with straw hats. I had noticed them on all the peasants—the narrow brim always turned up in the back and down in the front—and thought they might work nicely against the Florida sun. I tried a few on and settled on one for 6,000 *lei.* It seemed strange to pay in Romanian money. György, with his ironic grin, said, "Now you look like a real Székely."

Lunch was at the home of one of György's academic acquaintances, who lived on the second floor of a drab apartment block. "Look," said György, pointing at the mailboxes in the baleful hall. "All the names are Hungarian."

A man with thin hair and heavy glasses greeted us warmly; we had just caught him, he said, laboring over some runic inscriptions. We squeezed around a table in his cell-like kitchen, where, next to my shoulder, Ildiko heated our can of franks and rice. This was preceded by cold cherry soup. Small white dishes were provided for the seeds, which accumulated with the watermelon for dessert.

After eating we moved into the slightly less cramped living room, where György pulled a heavy, two-volume work down from the shelves. "This is the definitive book on the region," he said. "*Description of the Székely Land,* by Bálazs Orbán. Orbán was a Székely aristocrat—one of the few—and he spent years traveling around to every village and town, recording everything."

His grave, a few miles outside town, sat at the top of a knoll set back from the road. Leading up gradually to it was a series of Székely gates, all of them doorless, and set not in a straight row but in a seemingly random curve. The blatant disregard for the customary order and regimentation of death had a definite charm, and the airiness of the gates produced a feeling of release. They had come from all over the region, and though they were all of the same traditional pattern—even down to the pigeon holes carved in the top beam—they varied in size, hue, etched decoration, and inscription. "This gate is full of hospitality," Ildiko read from one, "but the owner will have a club for the wicked people."

A few miles north, the village of Corund appeared like a drive-through crafts mart: sheepskin rugs hung on gates, hats and woodwork covered roadside tables, the famous hand-painted pottery filled garages. There were pieces in the original color scheme of green, brown, and black, as well as some in more nouveaux shades. Sitting with the straw hats was a rounded, velvety mountaineer's cap—with cutout designs on the side of a deer and a pine tree—made from a local mushroom. A boy of about eight approached me and asked for some *forints;* I gave him fifty and he said, "God bless you." *Áldja meg az Isten.* A Gypsy girl walked by, blinding in her flowered pink apron over her flowered yellow skirt, and licked a vanilla ice cream cone.

The streets off the main road were quiet and sprinkled with bucolic peasant houses, some painted blue and set behind graceful gates. Firewood piles sat in courtyards and grape trellises dripped from porches.

We seemed to have left the world of industry. The road climbed into a forest of pine; young Gypsy men stood along the road holding out buckets of raspberries for sale. In a clearing, two high-booted peasants leaned mythically on scythes, while a saddleless white stallion, choreographed off to the side, flicked his tail.

Farther in we came to balding mountainsides, some shaved so recently that the felled trees had not yet been cleared away. "Look at that!" said György, shocked. "It's all new from three years ago." In the current economic free-for-all, people were buying up land and stripping it bare, selling the timber to, among other places, Hungary, where, György said, it was fashionable to build with wood again. I thought of the old Eastern European joke: "What is the difference between capitalism and communism? One is the exploitation of man by man, the other is the opposite." Debatable, perhaps. But we had seen conclusively in the last few days—from uncurbed pollution to unregulated deforestation—that both entail the exploitation of nature by man.

Coming down from the mountains, we dropped into a great flat bowl, its vastness given an almost Biblical cast by shafts of sunlight breaking through distant thunderclouds. Storks picked fussily in a sodden field and the raspy voice of Gábor Presser boomed from our speakers. Ahead of us rose the eastern Carpathians, hiding Moldavia.

Lazarea, or Gyergyószárhegy, sat to the left, at the foot of its own modest slope. A Franciscan monastery clung to the side as did, slightly higher and to the right, a fifteenth-century Catholic church. In the village below, we found a house with two signs in the window—the larger in Romanian, the smaller in Hungarian—indicating that it took in guests. The lady of the house came out to welcome us just as her son arrived home and, in one swift motion, kissed Ildiko's hand.

Emma quickly set the table for us, chattering away as if we were family from Esztergom who needed to be brought up to date. Then she ran out to finish kneading her dough, which she brought back shortly and slid into the oven. Next, she went to fix up the front room—she and her husband would move out to the back. In her apron and cheerful busyness, she reminded me of the Hungarian mothers of childhood friends in Alpha, New Jersey.

It was a cozy, ample farmhouse kitchen, its walls decorated with cloths in the traditional red-and-white designs, old wedding photographs, a dangling rosary. Emma sat with us for a few minutes, adding to our supper her homemade salami and four fresh eggs. Then her hay arrived and she was out again, directing the horses into the yard and dealing with an inebriated deliveryman. "He's a good fellow," she said, returning to the table. "If only he didn't get drunk so often."

She and her husband farmed a few plots. They had been part of a cooperative during Ceauşescu's time, and now some of the land was being given back to families. But neither of her sons was around to help; both, even the one we had seen earlier, had moved to Budapest.

They'd had to serve in the Romanian army, working in decrepit mines because the officers did not entrust guns to the Hungarians. It was a terrible time—she worried about them constantly—but Ceauşescu's project of bulldozing villages and putting the population into apartment blocks had not really reached here. Emma and her husband were actually able to build a house, though it had to conform to the dictated two-story style. Not having the money for a second floor, they built the façade of one. (I had seen the window coming in, and only now noticed there weren't any stairs.) When Ceauşescu was executed, on Christmas Day in 1989, the village was quiet, she said; most of the people were too afraid to show their relief. Though some young men went down to the town council building and set it on fire. Before the blaze could be extinguished, some old records were destroyed.

Emma kept in a closet the traditional dress of the region, though the last time she wore it was in 1992, when she traveled to Hungary to see the Pope. The Romanian authorities tried to prevent people from going, but she and her friends managed to make it to the border, where the Hungarians had buses waiting to take them to Pécs. On the way back, they had to take nine different buses. "It was a true pilgrimage," she said laughing.

Her grandparents' generation was the last to wear traditional dress on a daily basis. But we'd see some examples tomorrow, she said, up at the church for the Day of the Assumption.

My bed was all made in the living room, its fluffy pillow the size of a sow. Above it hung a painting of Jesus with a fiery heart enwrapped in thorns and sprouting a cross; tucked into the corners were two picture cards, one of the Pope and one of Márton Áron, the popular Bishop of Transylvania who died in 1980. It was a long way from the empty-framed room in Deva.

I woke around six and walked out on flagstones past the stable and into the outhouse. It was clean, with a pinching vinegary smell, its walls made homey by taped pages from Hungarian fashion magazines, an Ikea Christmas catalogue, a tourist map of Budapest and, just above the little window on the door, a black-and-white picture from *Playboy* of LaToya Jackson.

After breakfast, Emma, still in her apron, came out to bid us farewell. She kissed us each like cousins and insisted repeatedly that I come back, next time with my wife.

A soft rain fell as we made our way up the hill toward the church. The procession followed shortly after, each group led by dark-coated men bearing red-and-white banners. A few were dressed in high, black boots and the traditional white wool trousers with a thick black stripe running down each side (similar to those of Polish mountaineers). One handsome white-haired man wore a waist-length black jacket, collarless and with elegant black braiding around the tightly spaced buttons. Some of the women appeared in wide skirts of broad red and black stripes and red bodices over billowy white blouses. Many of them sang as they walked, in the dirge-like cadences of Eastern Europeans, and the closeness of the clouds added to the mood of rigid and long-suffering piety. The whole pageant, reenacted for us here on this hillside as it had been for centuries, seemed a testament to the triumph of faith over ideology. As we turned to leave, all voices joined in a stirring hymn.

"That's the Transylvanian anthem," György said. "It was strictly forbidden during Ceauşescu's time. You could be sent to prison for playing it."

The rain followed us into the Carpathians, but it let up long enough to allow us to lunch on the shores of Killer Lake, where vacationers—Hungarians and Romanians—rowed their boats through an obstacle course of petrified tree trunks. Back in the car, we climbed a slippery switchback, looking down occasionally at the tiny cars, our former selves, creeping far below. On the way down, we squeezed between towering sheets of massive rock. One soaring pinnacle, with a flattened top, thrust a white cross into the sky.

"There used to be the Roman numeral three up there," György said, "representing each decade of Ceauşescu's rule. A few days after he was killed, in the wind and sleet, some Székely youths climbed to the top and replaced it with that cross."

A minute later we slipped through a crevice, and out of Transylvania.

We returned the next evening, north of here on the Tihuta Pass. The road was steep but not as tortuous, rising through brooding forests swathed in mist. Not surprisingly, this was where Bram Stoker had placed Dracula's castle—though he himself had never seen the place—and the inclement weather merely improved the vision of Transylvania that everyone I'd told about this trip had imagined for me.

We drove through the night to Cluj-Napoca, the old intellectual city of Kolozsvár.

Green-gray turrets pricked the morning sky, rising from faded wedding cake façades. The city was a busy memory bank of *fin de siècle* urban detail: Tram lines cut along mounted Corinthian columns and roof cresting curlicued out from Scheherazade domes. I was entranced, though György and Ildiko said casually that they had more of this Austro-Hungarian architecture at home, and in better condition. György especially seemed uncomfortable in the city of Gheorghe Funar—"the mad mayor of Cluj"—who rose to power partly on his anti-Hungarian policies. For the first time since Alba Iulia, most of the people around us were speaking Romanian.

The Cock Church provided a relief: a Calvinist sanctuary with an interior of soothing purity. Its motif, taken from the parable of St. Peter, was repeated in hanging iron lamps and delicately painted pew decorations—every detail designed by the architect Károly Kós, a Transylvanian who, according to György, brought to Hungarian Art Nouveau a simple peasant quality that distinguished it from the more flowery style of the Great Plain. It seemed odd to find in this fusty city the most beautiful twentieth-century church I'd ever seen.

We went for cake to a café with its own decorative theme: A bright red Coca-Cola sign stood atop an enormous Coca-Cola refrigeration case, while another Coca-Cola advertisement hung above the coffeemaker. On the wall ticked a large Coca-Cola clock and above the door, outside, waved a Coca-Cola shingle. Communism's red replaced by capitalism's.

The rain was getting to us. In the main square swam the statue of Hunyadi's son, Matthias Corvinus, which I recognized from the book cover in György's living room. (A few years earlier, the mayor had had the word "Hungarian" erased from its base.) A downpour held us captive in St. Michael's church. We splashed, at my insistence, over to the Hôtel Continental on the corner, a faded lemony palace that turned out to be (as I had hoped it would) the old New York Hotel where Leigh Fermor had stopped for cocktails with his friends. Inside, a post-socialist neglect had taken over the old "Regency neo-Roman decor," so we paddled down the street again to the modernist Diesel Café. Through window dressings of engine parts, we watched the rain.

I thought: This is how it should end, a journey to a place as irretrievable as childhood.

But the next day, Sunday, broke blue and calm. On our way home we stopped at the Calvinist church in Vistea, where women in colorful dresses and flowery kerchiefs worshiped in a billow of red-and-white cloth. They were seated according to age—the youngest in the front pews, the oldest in the back—and dressed chronologically as well, the brightest primary colors becoming more muted in middle age and turning eventually to hunched widow black. But even these long dark skirts carried intricate patterns. The pastor spoke in a tempered monotone but with such clear conviction that György, a Catholic, shed a few tears. And I remembered the command of Count Imre Miko: "Live like a Transylvanian. Believe in any church you like, but love with a true heart."

Then we went to a confirmation ceremony in the nearby village of Turea. The service was already in progress when we arrived, and in the churchyard two young escapees—Katalin and Helga—shyly practiced their English on me. We were nearly on to the subjunctive when the congregation filed out in a flurry of flowery blouses and skirts. Katalin's parents introduced themselves—György and Margit, who'd been told of our coming by the director of the college where we'd stayed in Cluj—and as we were getting acquainted, gliding toward us like an apparition, came their fourteen-year-old daughter, Lilla. It was not just her attire—full peasant regalia, including a beaded headdress that resembled a confection—but her poise and bowed head and shy, enigmatic smile that dazzled. She looked like a princess emerged from a storybook.

They invited us back to Helga's parents' place—a shabby farmhouse in a courtyard of mud. Through a messy kitchen we were led into a dark chamber that, as our eyes adjusted to the natural light, filled with a treasury of folk artifacts. It was like walking into your plumber's house and finding a wing of the Smithsonian.

The room was preserved to look exactly as it had a hundred years ago, with ceiling-scraping cupboards and armoires clashing in a riot of red and white. Hefty pillows were neatly stacked in crimson piles atop the antique bed—hidden by beautifully embroidered curtains—and a row of hand-painted dishes hung along the top of patterned walls. The profusion of color and detail—even the wooden chairs crawled with tiny floral designs—made the room seem as if it were spinning.

The wardrobe was opened to reveal a kaleidoscope of dresses, and while Lilla quietly changed back into a teenager, Ildiko was ceremoniously dressed for a wedding. It took half and hour. "This is all Hungarian," Lilla's father said laughing, though making sure I understood. "Not Romanian."

We were late for the confirmation party. A muddy street led to another tumbledown farm where lively music carried out of the barn. Inside, long wooden tables stretched between bales of hay and Brueghelesque peasants sat before tall green bottles. We squeezed onto benches in the back.

The first course arrived, a combination of the unrecognizable and the inedible: duck liver in casing, nuggets of fried lard, a jellied gray wedge that turned out to be a pressed compound of pork, fat, gristle, and bone. Quickly reaching for a bottle, I washed it all down with honey schnapps.

Fiddle bows flew and the confirmation girl twirled, spun in the arms of Lilla's father. To my right, the other György was deep in conversation with a neighbor. How many American academics, I wondered (not for the first time this trip), would be so comfortable in such earthy surroundings? Part of it, of course, was the working of a cultural solidarity, but much of it was simply his winning, unpretentious nature. I could not have found a better guide, or friend.

Lilla, now merely beautiful in her schoolgirl sweater, extracted herself from her friends to come sit down next to her mother, whom she gave a sweet kiss before returning to her seat. The young man to my left stood up to address the room, and the end of his speech was greeted with laughter. "He was supposed to give the greeting and the blessing," explained György, "but he got the two of them mixed up. He's a little bit drunk."

The second course arrived, a greasy chicken soup, while the fiddlers galloped into a *csardas.* I looked around the barn—at the hands dwarfing spoons, the lips smacking in appreciation—and thought: This is what Ceauşescu wanted to destroy. And the celebration, which to everyone else was just a simple village fête, took on for me an air of sweet revenge. These people had succeeded, through many dark years, and against great odds, in perpetuating not only their ethnic heritage but also their ancient livelihoods. In a land that seemed sometimes almost a metaphor for loss, they had retained their identity. The dictator was dead, and the confirmation party was in full swing.

Amid loud protests, we got up to leave. A plate of cakes arrived from the kitchen, for the long journey. A farewell committee gathered in the courtyard. György and Margit and Katalin and Helga insisted on walking us back to our car, where the girls, still in their Sunday dresses, tightly clasped our shoulders and pulled themselves up to kiss our cheeks. Then—as if we were leaving home, not returning there—they stood and waved until we drove out of sight.

# 10

## *Calypso Carnival*

A night flight to carnival. The man in the window seat was getting a head start on the rum and cokes. The *Daily Express,* "The National Newspaper of Trinidad & Tobago," was rife with letters. "Moreover, over the past five weeks calypsonians such as Luta, Shortpants, and I have been speaking to thousands of schoolchildren all over the nation with a view to lifting the art form out of the abyss of filth and debauchery, where many of today's singers in their rush to make money have dumped it." It was signed: Hollis U. Liverpool (Chalkdust).

Peter Minshall, attacked on page five by Paster W. Cuffie—for giving his carnival band the name "Hallelujah"—was defended on the letters page by Arthur Ghany. "Mr. Minshall is merely exercising his God-given right instituted in the garden of Eden."

"You've already missed a lot of the parties," José said, pulling out of the airport parking lot. He spoke in a suave, clipped manner at odds with his unshaven, stevedore appearance.

"Now tomorrow night you've got Panorama. That's the steel band finals. Then Sunday night are the Calypso Monarch finals." (Filth and debauchery?) "I've got a couple of extra tickets, if you're interested."

We raced down the left side of a divided four-lane highway, passing warehouses and shopping centers. Kentucky Fried Chicken blazed in the distance.

"Are you playing mas?" he asked.

"I'm sorry?"

"Mas. Masquerade. You can buy a uniform and join a band. Most of the people in the mas bands are women. Carnival is really for women. It allows them to behave differently. If they are normally shy, reserved, they can be outgoing. They can live their fantasy. And what's good for women is also good for men." He flashed a lush, yellow-toothed smile.

"There's quite a bit of promiscuity. Every November there are always a lot of births. But you have to watch it. Carnival is like a drug. You can get addicted to it."

We entered Port-of-Spain, zipped past twin office buildings, and looped around the Savannah, the Queen's Royal College clock tower glowing fuzzily in the darkness. A landmark from literature, it magnified the already unreal quality of arrival in a new place. For I knew the school from V. S. Naipaul's *A House for Mr. Biswas,* a novel I had taken out of the British Institute library while living in Poland in 1978. I had been enthralled by the story—a young man's drive to escape his stultifying surroundings hung on his father's dream of owning his own house—and the rich language used to tell it. (It was where I learned the word prognathous, which, as I now see by this red line, my computer finds suspect.) My drab Warsaw apartment filled with the heat and lushness of the tropics, creating in me that curious, two-timing longing, which always surprises you in a foreign country, for the exoticism of another. The book made Trinidad a significant place for me, one that, even after Poland, I would want to visit.

We left the city and followed a winding road into the hills. After about ten minutes we passed a house surrounded by cars and reverberating with *soca.* José explained, as he stopped the car, that *soca* is a combination of soul and calypso. My hotel was next door.

"Well," José said, "you won't get much sleep tonight."

★ ★ ★

At nine the next morning—five hours after the *soca* stopped—eight middle-aged Germans sat eating fried eggs and tomatoes on the terrace.

"Winston, what time is it?" one of them asked the manager.

"Time? I don't know. It's carnival."

Then Winston went and put on some calypso.

Downtown, by Woodford Square, swarms of bumblebees fidgeted in the sun. Children's carnival. What a deal: To parade—costumed and headdressed and sprinkled with gold dust—through the streets of your capital. People loitered the length of Frederick Street, watching the pint-sized bands. T-shirts read:

*"If you don't like my attitude, quit talking to me."*
*"100% black family. Yo, it's a pride thing."*
*"I may live in another country, but I'm 200% Trini."*
*"Who framed O. J. Simpson? 100% innocent."*
*"If you don't like my attitude, dial 1-800-EAT-SHIT."*

On a side street, the Wish and Take restaurant advertised "Dagwood hamburgers, seamoss & soursop."

Later in the day, Frederick Street—from the Savannah down past Royal Victoria Institute, the prison, the Sportsman's Bar, the *roti* shops, St. Mary's College, City Hall, Barclays Bank, Greyfriars Church of Scotland, all the way to Independence Square—became a river of writhing bodies. They bunched in front of *soca*-blasting speakers stacked on the sidewalk. Young women—girls—motored their bottoms into boys' crotches and tried to stick, hips slowly, serviceably grinding. (Synonyms for this type of dancing are *wining* and *dingolaying*.)

Near the square a nine-year-old girl *dingolayed* solo with a precocious, carnal instinct, while her mother looked on, laughing with pride. Only when she stopped to gulp from her

Thermos, sweat beading on her forehead, did she look like a little girl.

That evening the steel bands rolled onto the Savannah stage. Some had as many as 500 drums. It took almost half and hour to get one off and the next one on, all for the performance of a song that lasted about five minutes. Like at the racetrack: a burst of thunder between long pauses.

Down in the pit, the chariots sat like tin and tinsel wagon trains. When the call came, they knocked back spectators and stirred up dust that hazed the lights and muffled the aroma of fried chicken, oranges, and marijuana.

By the gate, two young Indian women stood with children. They were waiting for the Renegades and had not bothered with seats. "There," the pretty one said, pointing to the south stands, "is where the society people sit. The north stands are where you go if you want to have fun."

When the Renegades finally came on, the women cupped their ears to catch the sound. It arrived as a distant, metallic cacophony.

Sunday began quietly. Along the western edge of the Savannah the Indian coconut vendors stood with machetes by their truckloads of "Cold Nuts." Men in long white pants played cricket on the grounds of Queen's Royal Collage.

The school was closed for the holiday, but in one of the outer hallways a bulletin board displayed the carnival poems of the school literary society. The winning work was titled "J'Ouvert"—contracted French for "the day opens," and the name for the official start of carnival, which occurs at 2 A.M. Monday morning.

> *The embrace of slumber pinioned by the furor*
> *Of carefree children throwing colours.*

*Soon, the rebirth of light*
*But the mas continues;*
*The children have only just begun to play.*
—Phillip Lou-Hing

Downtown, I stopped in a bookstore. It was a spare shop with low shelves along the walls and down the middle. But it carried a selection of Penguin paperbacks, including *A House for Mr. Biswas.* Picking it up, I searched for the scene, near the end, when Anand walks out of his "exhibition examination," disheveled and spent, and finds his father. I still remembered the pen stain on his shirt pocket—"as though his heart had bled ink"—and the triumphant reunion. But reading that passage now, I found a different scenario. On spotting his father, the boy feels irritation and embarrassment; he scolds him for still wearing his bicycle clips. I stood in the bookstore aisle shocked, both by the heartlessness of the scene and by my capacity, over the years, to coat it with a filial warmth. No less daunting was the author's unflinching honesty.

At dusk, people headed along the Savannah toward the stadium. Inside, in a clear, sonorous voice, the emcee declared: "Tonight we will choose the best calypsonian in the world."

Sparrow—the Mighty Sparrow—led off, followed by M'ba, Luta, Sugar Aloes, and others. The songs spoke of drug dealers, family life, philandering, cricket, Peter Minshall, Haiti, the fate of calypso, and the late-night wanderings of the prime minister. M'ba sang: "Put me in jail/And leave the bandits free." A man with dreadlocks and the improbable name of Black Stalin sang the even more improbable "A Message of Hope."

Intermission featured the junior calypso champion, the only female singer of the night. Her song was about her father not wanting her to bring her boyfriends home—for a variety of reasons.

*If they're talking Yankee*
*And they never went to Miami.*

Then brilliant gargantuas took the stage—inspired visions of feudal dragons (houselights dimmed to reveal burning eyes) and futuristic Lepidoptera. Looking closely you could pick out the small human, camouflaged at the bottom, who shouldered the construction. Each represented a band, and was vying tonight for King, or Queen, of the carnival.

The Queen, it turned out, in flowing white wings with pastel swirls, was from Peter Minshall's *Hallelujah* band. Black Stalin was voted Calypso Monarch.

The crowd filed out at midnight, J'Ouvert now only two hours away. People flowed down Frederick Street, where speakers blared, and filled up Independence Square, there to await the march out of costume called "Dirty Mas."

The wide avenue had taken on two identities. On the landscaped median, spectators—including some families—milled about in quiet expectation. Behind the viewing stands, out of the cutthroat bars, a drunken lewdness spilled, with dreadlocked wobblers and toothless whores. I drifted from one side to the other, like a spirit traveling between heaven and hell.

In the middle, KFC was setting a record for chicken sold after 1 A.M. Girls lined up outside the Ladies Room; others waited patiently in the Men's Room for the single stall, while boys calmly went about their business at the urinals. A respectful modesty after the animalism of the street. Heading to the washbasin, I noticed the girls giving me—the white man—shy, curious looks. Intruder to intruder.

A melodic tinkling sounded in the distance, gradually inching closer. A steel-band chariot, surrounded by bodies, floated toward us as if carried atop shoulders. This was it, the beginning of carnival in the middle of the night. Another band followed, its shirtless minions caked with chalk-like mud, giving the wearers—the whole, fantastic scene—an otherworldly quality. Troglodytes on parade. I had a sudden vision of something mysterious and tribal playing out before our eyes.

A few of the men carried plastic pails of muck and grease that they—with eerie, exaggerated gestures—slapped on spectators. Others, darker-hued, passed by smelling of chocolate. Half the city, it seemed, had been turned into ogres, and those of us as yet untouched watched with a mixture of repulsion and awe.

Around five, the patch of sky above the cathedral leaked blue. The long, primordial night was over. Half an hour later I vaulted a bench to avoid being trampled by the contagious fury of a crowd in panic. "A fight," someone gasped. "The man has a knife," another said. A few minutes later a muddied man was led down the street by another, streams of blood flowing down his left leg.

*The children have only just begun to play.*

There were no taxis at 8 A.M. I was given a lift to my hotel by a marriage counselor.

"I think, with the economy the way it is, the government needs carnival," he said. "The people are under so much stress. If they could not let off steam at carnival once a year, this country would really be in trouble."

Tuesday morning, the *Trinidad Guardian* reported that J'Ouvert celebrations were "responsible for several persons being stabbed or chopped." One of them, a Savannah coconut vendor, had lost his hand in a morning attack.

But the carnival, rather than degenerating, took an almost genteel turn. On the final day, families laid picnic blankets in Memorial Park and children held foot races during the long intervals between bands. (They were later joined by the elegiac, white-robed figures from *Hallelujah*.) Three girls sat on the iron fence of the park as if posing for a photographic book of sisters. Graying "Bob Skate" appeared on roller skates, as he has every year since the age of fourteen. The young women in Marie's Grill Castle refused to let orders interfere with their dancing. "Are you enjoying carnival?" strangers inquired earnestly.

The bands continued to march through the city after their performances on the Savannah. Each one had at its heart a hollowed out tractor trailer piled with speakers and surrounded by jumping flesh strategically spangled. The vibrations, if you came close to the source, rattled your heart. I wondered if it was carnival that gave Naipaul his loathing for both music and noise.

The band Ecstasy blasted its way—"I cannot take your ragamuffin behavior"—down Tragarete Street, bringing entire families out of their houses. By the entrance to the Princess Elizabeth Centre for Physically Handicapped Children, winsome-eyed boys *wined* in their wheelchairs. "I cannot take your ragamuffin behavior."

On Ariapita Street, the steel band Exodus took the lead. The soothing, unamplified music of pans. Men and women in the garb of sailors, many of them older, soft-shoed it up front. They set feet to tapping in lawn chairs strung along the sidewalk, and straw hats bobbing on wooden porches. They passed, with a certain defiance, Lapeyrouse Cemetery. The setting sun elongated their shadows as the strains of "Heavy Roller"—by the great Lord Kitchner—tickled the air.

That night other steel bands roamed the streets of Port-of-Spain, their fatigued supporters shuffling behind. The sound of pans splintered off in a dozen directions, like the light carried by candles from a Greek Easter Eve mass.

"I thought you were a Jehovah's Witness," Mr. Lee said. "They often stand on that corner."

It was the next morning, Ash Wednesday, and I was hitching a ride into Port-of-Spain. Mr. Lee taught at one of the country's better preparatory schools.

"The school has a population of 500," he said. "Today, forty students showed up." His voice carried a tone of minor annoyance. "In Japan, the day after a holiday, I think 90 percent of the people would go to work. It's a question of discipline, perhaps, but it's difficult to say. It's a complicated subject."

He asked where I was headed. I said downtown, to get a taxi to St. James. I explained that I was going to try to find the boyhood home of V. S. Naipaul.

"The house of Mr. Biswas," he said. "I started that book once. Never finished it."

I had mentioned to Winston, back at my hotel, that I had heard Naipaul wasn't very popular in Trinidad.

"He makes some stupid remarks now and then," Winston had said after a long, pensive silence. "But it's nothing like Salman Rushdie."

Mr. Lee said he could take me to St. James. We drove down neat, treeless, residential streets with names like Agra and Kandahar. At the corner of Calcutta and Delhi he said, "Let me ask this chap," and I thought how an Englishman would gloat, hearing that word used by an Asian to refer to an African at the cusp of South America. When he dropped me off, he refused any payment.

The house was easy to find because Naipaul's younger brother, Shiva, had provided the address—No. 26 Nepaul Street—in his book *Beyond the Dragon's Mouth*. Shiva, who died in 1985, was a wonderful writer in his own right.

It looked exactly as Shiva had described it, "a small, box-shaped, two-storeyed house . . . situated not far from the corner where Nepaul Street met the Western Main Road." I stood in front of the high white wall in silent homage, like an Elvis fan at the gates of Graceland. Then I noticed a neighbor across the street.

"Do you remember the boys?" I asked the woman.

"Yes," she said. "They were quiet, very quiet. All the Naipaul children were quiet."

Later that day, walking along the Savannah, I came upon the "blue-and-red Italianate of Queen's Royal College." I entered the side gate and told the guard I just wanted to have a look around. Inside, two students directed me to the Assembly Hall.

Slabs of late afternoon sunlight filtered through tall jalousied windows; three plain chandeliers swayed high above a sea of wooden desks. Printed atop a side wall was the long list—going back to the turn of the century—of scholarship winners. Next to the year "1948" appeared the name "V. S. Naipaul." It glowered like an admonishment to work and learn and escape your small, ragamuffin world.

# 11

# *Town of Letters*

I picked up my rental car on an unlikely overcast morning. (Texas, like that other vast spread, Australia, always appears in the mind under brilliant blue skies.) Trucks barreled philosophically, as far from one coast as the other, and streamlined totem poles lifted heavenward the names of Shell and Sizzler.

"There are times when one just feels like driving," Larry McMurtry wrote in his essay collection *In a Narrow Grave.* And one of them is after getting off an airplane. It's like a release from prison, leaving a regime of enforced confinement for a realm in which, still moving, you are now alone and in control. The world, lately glimpsed from afar, unattainable, is all around you. Your head spins with possibility and the novelties of freedom—new car, new roads, new landscapes. It's amazing there are not more accidents around airports.

I skirted Fort Worth, and pointed west before heading north on 281. In Mineral Wells I stopped for lunch in a main street café and read the morning's *Fort Worth Star-Telegram.* At the bottom of the Life & Arts cover was a quote from Flannery O'Connor. "Everywhere I'm asked if the universities stifle writers. In my opinion, they don't stifle enough of them."

Then I paid and drove north to Archer City.

On the literary map, Archer City—situated about twenty-five miles south of Wichita Falls—holds a unique position, for it is both setting and repository. It is the town that Larry McMurtry has mercilessly depicted in a trilogy of novels, beginning with *The Last Picture Show,* and the home he has returned to with a quarter of a million of the books he has amassed in his second career as an antiquarian bookseller. People who come looking for Duane and Jacy are rewarded instead with one of the finest secondhand bookstores in the country. It's like going to Yasnaya Polyana and finding Hay-on-Wye.

It was that Welsh town, brimming with bookstores, that McMurtry had in mind when he returned to Archer City in the early 1990s. Then he had mainly geography working against him—situated as he was on a road to nowhere in the middle of the country; today, with the advances in e-commerce, he has technology. A development that, while far from desirable from his standpoint, nevertheless strengthens his bond to his ancestors and many of his literary characters. In his essay/memoir, *Walter Benjamin at the Dairy Queen,* he draws a parallel between his own passion, book collecting, and ranching. "Unfit for ranch work because of my indifference to cattle—if sent to fetch a particular animal I usually came back with the wrong one—I went instead into the antiquarian book trade, becoming, in effect, a book rancher, herding books into larger and larger ranches (I now have filled a whole town with them, my equivalent of the King Ranch). I couldn't find the right cow, but I *could* find the right book, extricating them from the once dense thickets of America's antiquarian bookshops." Later he writes: "Because of when and where I grew up, on the Great Plains just as the herding tradition was beginning to lose its vitality, I have been interested all my life in vanishing breeds." He stops short of acknowledging that, as an independent bookseller, he has become one himself. (Though the book's last chapter is poignantly titled: "The End of the Cowboy—The End of Fiction.")

The road sped through fields of fresh spring grass. I had never seen a two-lane highway with a speed limit of 70. The land was not as runway flat as I had imagined it, and the scattered trees had a surprising fluffiness. There was the feeling, just on the outskirts of town, of entering a hallowed place, one that had been scorched and validated by words.

These were not the impressions of a devoted fan. In preparation for the trip, I had read *The Last Picture Show* (wishing for more description) and then in *Texasville* got as far as page seventeen when the predominance of dialogue became too much. I much preferred the essays—*In a Narrow Grave,* published in 1968, and the more recent *Walter Benjamin at the Dairy Queen*—because they spoke directly about the place, and the man. I imagined myself one of the few pilgrims to Archer City who had read more of McMurtry's nonfiction than his fiction. I had also written him a letter, stating my intentions to come out and do a story. And he had replied, in a handwritten note, saying I was welcome to stop by, he was usually around, "though sometimes Hollywood beckons."

Gradually the pastures between houses shrank to yards, which in turn gave way to a block of storefronts—forlorn, one-story affairs of brick and glass. A stately stone courthouse rose from the square opposite, and at the intersection—of Main and Center—a blinking red light hung like a worn literary device.

Down on the right, just past the abandoned service station, sat the Spur Hotel. I parked diagonally in front and walked inside. A cowhide spotted the wall behind the reception desk. A medley of antlers sprouted from a pillar, and a bobcat ran in frozen stride above the entrance to the sitting room. On my way upstairs I was careful not to knock the stuffed rooster off the banister.

I dropped my bags and headed out into the storied town. A cannon stood on the courthouse lawn, along with two signs: One painted like a basketball that read: "Champions State Class AA, 1988, Wildcats," and the other, in the shape of a football: "State Class A Champions, Wildcats, 1964." "A few years ago," McMurtry wrote in a meditation on football as a form of sexual compensation ("Eros in Archer County," *In a Narrow Grave*), "our local eleven won the state One-A Championship, and the enraptured citizenry bought a commemorative cannon and set it on the courthouse lawn, a proud reminder, and probably the nearest thing to a penis ever to be exhibited in those parts."

Across Center Street, joining the line-up of usual suspects—café, florist, general store—was Booked Up Inc. No. 3. Building No. 1 occupied a low, tan-brick structure in the next block. I opened the door, walked past tables handsomely set with hardbacks (a readable feast), and asked at the counter if Larry McMurtry were in.

"He's not here," the young woman said. "He left for L.A. this morning."

I stood speechless. It was only later that I thought: "I'm glad I didn't stick with *Texasville.*" I told her that I'd come all the way from Florida, where I'd written to him of my visit.

"He's not the most organized person," she said.

I asked when he'd be back.

"Next week." I'd be in San Antonio.

"Well, I'm going to look around."

"You'll need a book," she said solicitously. "It'll be a long night."

An old campaign poster ran along the top of the back wall: "In your heart you know he's right—Vote for Barry Goldwater." Under it a T-shirt read: "A woman's love is like the morning dew. It's just as apt to fall on a horse turd as it is on a rose—*Leaving Cheyenne.*" In *Texasville,* Duane's wife Karla wears T-shirts printed with life lessons from hillbilly songs, and I wondered if this slight variation on a fictionalized behavior—using as fodder one of his own bons mots—was as intentionally self-mocking as it appeared. (Self-mockery is not a trait that comes through in the essays.) More souvenirs congregated in a corner—mugs, caps, CDs (of songwriter son James)—and made understandable Susan Sontag's remark, uttered during a visit, that McMurtry was living inside his own theme park.

The other walls were padded with books. There was the refined, soothing orderliness that row upon row of leathery volumes produce, but also a keen, stately defiance here on the main street of a dusty town on the Texas plains. Starting at a middle shelf, I found Edmund Wilson's *A Piece of My Mind* ("crotchety, old-fartish assembly of gripes and complaints about the deteriorating quality of American life . . . intensely readable," *Walter Benjamin at the Dairy Queen*) next to Yukio Mishima's *The Temple of the Golden Pavilion.* "In my view," McMurtry writes elsewhere in his memoir, "half the fun of a bookshop is serendipity. I try to compose, first off, walls of books that please and hold the eye—indeed, that hold it so tightly that the eye will desire closer inspection. Sometimes this doesn't work—people will stare at the wall in befuddlement, unable to discern any pattern. And indeed, the only pattern may be that all the books on the wall are pleasing books."

The prices were high—rare books and first editions here in the front—but back in the adjoining annex they dropped encouragingly. When my head tired of the tilt of reading every spine (my eye still pleased, and tightly held), I took the second volume of Kate Simon's memoirs, *A Wider World,* up to the counter.

"That'll be ten dollars," said the woman.

As she made change, I asked about the store.

"It used to be a Ford dealership." Books do furnish a showroom. "And then, as you probably saw, we have three other stores around the square."

"Has he gotten any other booksellers to move here?"

"He doesn't talk about that anymore."

"Well, nowadays people can buy on the Internet."

"Yea, he's waiting to see how that goes. He doesn't own a computer. I just introduced him to the Internet the other day—I showed him some frogs jumping and he was totally disgusted. He got up and walked out."

Yet, animated cuteness aside, what is there in the lightening efficiency of a computer for a man who refuses to alphabetize? And what is sound marketing sense for a merchant who fills a cow town with books? Everything about McMurtry's business goes against the grain: Peddling great works in a far backwater, in an increasingly aliterate and impatient age, through a system that demands minute, painstaking scrutiny. The paradox is that in his journey from book writer to bookseller (a short and logical if infrequently made trip) he has gone from someone perfectly in tune with the tastes of the reading public to someone magnificently out of touch with the times. The beloved, best-selling author is a difficult, buyer-be-damned dealer. It is almost as if his bookstore were a conscious reaction against his literary popularity; as if he were saying: You may be able to breeze through my novels, but here in my store you're going to have to work—taking time over words, stumbling across unfamiliar names—to reap your rewards. And, as such, in an oblique way, it seems an act of revenge on the sort of people who failed to see the demythicizing he was committing in *Lonesome Dove* and made it instead "a kind of American Arthuriad."

I chatted a little longer with the woman behind the counter (I had time on my hands). She was from the East, and didn't like talking to reporters.

"They're always looking for some juicy stuff. Somebody from Houston wrote about us and made it sound as if I hated Archer City. I thought I'd be lynched."

"Nobody could say anything worse about the place than what McMurtry has said."

"But he's from here. He's the favorite son."

On my way back to the Spur I stopped in the general store, which was more of a crafts mart. I asked the woman snug behind the counter about business.

"We get a lot of people from Texas. They come out on the weekends."

"Were you surprised when McMurtry came back?"

"No. He never really left. He got the family ranch."

She continued, no more pressed for time than I. "His father was one of the great old cowboys around here. As soon as he couldn't work anymore he died. First his horse died. He called my husband—my husband has bulldozers—and asked if he could come out and dig a hole, a pit. It had to be done that night—it couldn't wait till the morning. When it was dug, he led his horse down into it and shot him. He was crying all the time. The horse was thirty years old. It had been his life."

I mentioned how sorry I was to have missed the son.

"He was here yesterday. I saw him walking all over. He's reclusive. He walks looking down at his feet—and dresses like nothing special: slacks and a sweater. He drives his father's old Cadillac. That's his heritage.

"It's because of him," she continued, "that we have no industry. He doesn't want any. Him and the landowners—they'd rather pay higher taxes than have to put up with all that. We've had a drought for the last four years, so we don't really have the water for any industry. An aluminum company wanted to come in. A recycling plant was a possibility.

"We lost our hospital. And our pharmacy. The man who ran it retired, and nobody wanted to run a pharmacy in a town without a hospital. Oil is about up—the small operations have been put out of business by the big companies. And it's hard to get help. A lot of young people are messed up with drugs.

"You have drugs out here?"

"Ye-e-s, drugs. But not gangs. Wichita Falls has gangs. You see graffiti up there for the Cripps and the Bloods.

"So we're looking to tourism. But we need a restaurant that stays open for dinner. Unless you drive into Wichita Falls, about the only thing here is the Dairy Queen." The celebrated Dairy Queen.

She helped a customer with a purchase, and then said: "A while ago some people came out from New York—they bought about twenty-five hundred dollars worth of books. The man said: 'I'm not leaving here until I see Larry McMurtry and get him to sign these books.'

"I saw him walking down the street and I said, 'Larry, these people would like to meet you.' And he yelled, 'All these people coming in here and buying out my first editions.' The New Yorkers were surprised. He said, 'I wasn't talking about you. I was talking to her.' But he meant it—he was upset with me. Later he said, 'Etta Mae, I like you, but someday I'm going to get back at you.' And then he said, 'I get tired.'"

Before leaving, I asked her the name of the tree on the courthouse lawn.

"That's a mesquite," she said. The bane of McMurtry's father's existence.

"I didn't know they grew that big."

"Well," she said, "that one has been there since time."

Outside the sky hung low and the wind pushed briskly down the wide open streets (Though it wasn't a cold norther). I thought of the opening paragraph of *The Last Picture Show* when Sonny, in this same emptiness, "felt like he was the only human creature in the town." But there was no pool hall now, that I could see, or even a tavern. Just the works of thousands of rounded-up writers.

I had another whole day for them—with great hopes, I had booked two nights at the Spur—so I got in the car. At the blinking red light I took a right onto Main, passing modest houses set back in unfenced yards. At the edge of one stood a sign announcing the

Lonesome Dove Inn. I headed up the walkway to the red-brick house and knocked at the front door under the portico.

A woman with a weathered face and a gentle expression and an easy, self-assured manner invited me in. Her name was Mary Webb.

"This is Texasville," she said, standing in the living room. "Each room is named after a novel. And I put a copy of the novel in each." We walked on through.

"This is Bolivar's kitchen. He was a cook in *Lonesome Dove.* The dining room is Buffalo Girls and the video room is The Last Picture Show."

We climbed the stairs. "This house used to be the old Archer City Hospital," Mary said. "Till about the '60s. Janet here is in surgery."

A young woman smiled up at us from her laptop; on the nightstand sat novels by Grace Paley and Virginia Woolf.

"I've got a group from SMU staying here right now. It's a continuing education class in creative writing. Their teacher brings them out for four or five days. They spend the days writing and in the evening they have a critique session."

The windows looked out onto the backyard, where four pecan trees were starting to sprout leaves. "I want to put in a balcony," Mary said. "In the summer you can't see the oil equipment."

She had grown up with McMurtry—he dedicated one of his novels to her mother—and, like him, left Archer City only to come back, in her case to care for an ailing parent. She seemed extremely respectful of his privacy—which is to say she didn't offer any information and made you, by her principled demeanor, reluctant to ask. Though when I expressed concern that he might have fled to L.A. to avoid another interview, she said, "No, something really did come up that he had to attend to."

The creative writing teacher—a small, spry woman in her sixties—told me downstairs: "He's a bit eccentric. Well," she admitted, "I came here and stepped on his toes. I asked him to come speak to the students. He came once. He just sat there—didn't say anything to the students, whatever he had to say he said to me. Then all of a sudden he said: 'I have to go'—and he got up and left."

I asked her if I could come back and sit in on the evening critique. She said she'd have to check with the students.

The road out of town ran flat and straight. I had never approached a Dairy Queen with a feeling of reverence before, but this was the most glorified, most literarily significant Dairy Queen in the world. It was London's Café Royal, Paris's Closerie des Lilas, transported to Texas, with a table for one.

It was here that McMurtry got the idea for the book that would eventually feature the famous red-roofed restaurant on its cover and in its title. It was a hot summer morning in 1980; he was sipping a lime Dr. Pepper ("a delicacy strictly local, unheard of even in the next Dairy Queen down the road—Olney's, eighteen miles south—but easily obtainable by anyone willing to buy a lime and a Dr. Pepper") and reading Walter Benjamin (a German literary critic unheard of surely in the next Dairy Queen down the road but nowadays easily obtainable by anyone willing to make the trek to Archer City). The book was *Illuminations,* and the essay that caught his interest was "The Storyteller," for it addressed, in McMurtry's words, "the growing obsolescence of what might be called practical memory and the consequent diminution of the power of oral narrative in our twentieth-century lives"—two of the recurring themes of his memoir.

And despite his obvious delight in the mix of high and low (European intellectualism set down on grease-filmed Formica; his personal pilgrim's progress), McMurtry makes a good case for his choice of fast-food reading. He writes that when they arrived in north Texas in the late 1960s, Dairy Queens filled a void that was more social than culinary, for they gave people, for the first time, a place to gather and share news, exchange gossip, tell stories. "The oilmen would be there at six in the morning; the courthouse crowd would show up about ten; cowboys would stop for lunch or a mid-afternoon respite . . . and the women of the village might appear at any time. . . . And always, there were diners who were just passing through . . ."

When I arrived, around six-thirty, two women of the village were licking soft ice cream cones. They were plumpish, with the kind of hair that looks like it will crack if you touch it. I immediately ordered a lime Dr. Pepper and was taken aback when the teen in his blue "Team DQ" cap had to hunt around for limes.

"You do make them, don't you?"

"Oh yea," said a young woman, coming to his rescue. "We also make cherry limeade. That's good too." There seemed no point in explaining its literary inferiority.

I then ordered a cheeseburger, though the chicken fried steak sandwich tempted me. "Only a rank degenerate would drive 1,500 miles across Texas without eating a chicken fried steak," McMurtry wrote in *In a Narrow Grave.* But I hadn't driven 500 miles yet and I imagined that trying the delicacy swathed in a soft bun would be akin to eating escargots buried in a baguette. (Which may explain why there is no "McMurtry Special" of lime Dr. Pepper and chicken fried steak sandwich.)

The walls, befitting the establishment's cultural importance, were decorated with framed covers of McMurtry novels and stories from the local paper about the filming of *Texasville.* (A scene was shot here at the Dairy Queen, giving it early cinematic fame before its more esoteric connection with Walter Benjamin.)

As I took my seat, a man entered wearing a tan cowboy hat with a sheriff's badge attached. He placed his order and sat down at a table next to the women.

"What ya'll doin'? Come to get your ice cream cone for the evenin'? You're lookin' good."

"You want my glasses?" one of them asked him, chuckling.

"Ya know, I go home in the evenin' and I say to my wife, 'I can't wait till tomorrow.' She says 'Why?' And I say, 'Because I get better lookin' every day.'"

The diminution of storytelling, and the recrudescence of wisecracking.

I knocked again at the front door of the Lonesome Dove Inn, and Mary let me in. The students had not objected to my presence. The five of them were already seated in the living room in a loose circle around the coffee table. They looked to be in their thirties.

The teacher, sitting on the sofa, picked one of the women to go first (there was only one man) and she then passed out copies so everyone could follow along. This, I was told, was the latest chapter of a novel-in-progress.

Then one of the other students read it aloud. It was a mystery story, about a female detective whose good friend, a woman, is brutally murdered. Tonight was the murder scene. It went on for quite awhile. When it ended, the other students voiced their opinions, questioned usages, suggested changes. It was all done in a kind, constructive, well-meaning fashion. When everyone was done, the teacher asked me if I had any comments. I had been afraid of this. I explained that I was a travel writer, and didn't write fiction, so was probably not the best judge; then mumbled some faint praise about a rare descriptive passage.

The next story, the man's, was from a novel about the West. There were settlers, and Indians, and arrows piercing breasts. It was followed by a psychological thriller. As my mind wandered it fell on two thoughts. The first was that this Monday night salon in Archer City could not have been further from the tenor of the novels about the place, yet they, and others by the same author, had served as the inspiration for it. The second was that here, in the living room of a small north Texas B&B, the seemingly lost practice of storytelling was being resurrected, in an extremely literal if perverse fashion. People were gathering for the precise purpose of telling their stories and hearing those of others. It was as close, in structure if not surroundings, to a starry-night campfire as one could get. Yet the stories being told were not about what McMurtry in *Walter Benjamin* calls "local lore or incident" (in this case Dallas lore and incident); they weren't even highly embroidered variations on events and scenes from personal experience; they were romantic inventions, borrowed fantasies with little or no basis in the writers' own lives. These greenhorn novelists were telling stories for the sake of telling stories, not to probe their consciousness and then convey important information about the species, or to illuminate hidden truths, or even to capture a genuine feeling or celebrate the commonplace. It was a storytelling that seemed to derive less from a desire to share experience than from a dream of making sales. McMurtry of course, as the name of the inn demonstrates, can serve as a potent inspiration for the latter, but his triumph is that he achieved it through the tireless execution of the former.

The red light blinked pointlessly as I turned on to Center Street. No cars slept sideways in front of the Spur. I took out the key—which the receptionist had told me I'd need, for she went home at five—and opened the door. With visions of fictional mayhem still fresh in my head, I walked quickly past the stilled fauna and up the creaking stairs.

After a restful sleep I came down the next morning and met the owner. Etta Mae had told me that I should talk with Abby Abernathy, the man who had fixed up the Spur, and now was in the process of rebuilding the Royal Theater (the last picture show), which burned down in 1965.

We moved to the sitting room adjacent to the lobby and plopped down into two fake cowhide chairs. "They're from my grandfather's house," Abby said. In the corner a bobcat stood on its hind legs, in an eternal tango with a stump, a belittling red kerchief tied around its neck. "I killed him. Not too many who get that big. He's trophy size."

Abby wore a black baseball cap atop a boyish face, a long-sleeved white shirt, blue jeans, and boots. He had grown up with cattle—"I'm a fifth-generation rancher," he said with a distinct note of pride—but had left Archer City, first to go to SMU, and then to pursue an acting career in New York and Los Angeles.

"*The Last Picture Show* was shot here in 1969. I was the mascot for the Volunteer Fire Department, which was right behind the American Legion Hall. I'd go over in the evening and sit and watch them filming in the parking lot. I didn't really know what I was watching, but it was glamorous." (Already his story was more interesting than anything I'd heard last night at the inn.)

His father was the high school principal, and a Baptist minister—a leader in the protest against the film. "McMurtry offered to have a public debate with him, but it never came about. He didn't try to stop them from filming, but he didn't want them using any high school students in a film that was going to be R-rated. He was afraid of the light that had been put on the town—the book had made it sound like it didn't have any morals. I was forbidden to see the film when it came out. I didn't see it till I was twenty-five."

Because the Royal Theater had burned down—they rebuilt the façade for exterior scenes—the film premiered in Wichita Falls. To this day, it has never been shown in Archer City.

That may change. The new Royal Theater, which had its grand opening four months after my visit (thirty-five years to the day after it burned down), is going to be used initially for theatrical performances, music shows, weddings, and banquets. But movies will eventually be shown via a video projector.

"We did an entertainment feasibility study," Abby said, "and found that there are three legitimate theatergoers in Archer City. That means three people who would choose theater over any other type of entertainment, including sports."

"You have sporting events here?" I asked.

"Sure. High school football, Little League."

I had been thinking "professional." I remembered, from *In a Narrow Grave,* McMurtry's exasperation at the local obsession with football.

"That was written at an angry time," Abby said of the book. "I don't think he's bitter about it now. You get older, more mature."You move on to Walter Benjamin.

"He's an interesting phenomenon, a great guy. When I moved back here at the end of '96 we formed a relationship. He'd let me use bookstore No. 4 for productions, and he'd speak at events to get donations for the theater."

I told my sad story.

"Well, I don't think you would have gotten more than twenty minutes with him. He's not much for sitting down for interviews. Now with students, he'll sit for hours. At Midwestern State University in Wichita Falls there's the McMurtry Center for the Arts and Humanities. It's one of the only places where he'll do public speaking anymore. And he'll let the students run around the house, the bookstore."

"What about his being against industry coming into town?"

"It's not like he's on a campaign to keep industry out. Nobody's unemployed here anyway. Some people still ranch, some are in oil, then there are the courthouse employees. But it's primarily a bedroom community for Wichita Falls.

"Look what's happening in the town. The high school just completed a two-million-dollar expansion. The First Baptist Church a quarter-of-a-million-dollar expansion. The Assembly of God is doing major renovations. The Methodist Church is doing major renovations. The Archer City Museum is undergoing renovations. The city park is near completion of renovations. There are building renovations going on across the street here. The Texas Department of Highways has a new million-dollar facility on the north side. You have the Royal Theater project. The theater is a national icon—it's still visited on a daily basis by people from around the country.

"With industry you need to increase the police force, city maintenance. The industry that needs to come here is tourism. I think it's happening, but people don't see an immediate result. They don't see an extra five dollars on the dinner table.

"The main tourism is for hunting. I run and operate my own hunting business, and that pretty much keeps the hotel going. McMurtryism traffic is starting. On any given weekend here you have 200 people from out of town."

He was perfectly sanguine. And ready to leave.

"I've missed Manhattan a lot. First year was very difficult, very frustrating. Middle year I dealt with it, spent a lot of time in Dallas and Austin. Last year was one of the most difficult because I could see the light at the end of the tunnel, but it wasn't getting any closer.

"I miss acting more than anything. I don't know that I could go back and start the process over again. It's hard to say where I'd go. But 'one more winter won't find me here,' to quote from James McMurtry. That's a line from one of his songs. It's about living in these cultural deserts. I tell people it's my autobiography."

Clouds hung coolly over the town. It took some effort to imagine the numbing winter gusts, the scorching sun of summer. A moment of moderation in a land of extremes.

At the intersection the red light blinked with the steady regularity of a healthy heart. I turned left, walked down a few yards to watch the work on the theater, and then came back up to bookstore No. 4. I was the first customer of the day—alone in a large room full of books. Unlike in the main store, there were no display tables, no attempt to show that this was anything other than a gutted shop whose bright confines had rudely been shadowed with shelves. Though half of the front was still open space, giving the feeling of a work-in-progress and a clear view onto the courthouse opposite.

In travel writing there is always a thin line between work and pleasure—sleeping in hotels, eating in restaurants, meeting interesting and attractive people—but as I scanned the shelves the line seemed to dissolve (and then disappear altogether when I got to the Travel section). In looking to add to my library I was, inevitably, researching my story; the selfish act of acquisition merged, indistinguishably, with the slightly more reputable one of reporting.

What impressed, after you had accustomed yourself to the arranging anarchy, was not just the scope—which you had been prepared for—but the quality. As a customer, there was no taking shortcuts—no starting at the ABCDs before skipping down to the Ms and Ns (with perhaps a brief look-see at the Fs and Gs) and then crouching before the STUs and Ws. But you were rewarded for your diligence by spine after engaging spine. The number of books you wanted far exceeded the number you could carry, or perhaps even house. And even the ones that didn't interest you personally had a clear intrinsic value, an air of import, a reason to be here. There was almost nothing in that category that Charles Lamb called "biblia abiblia" ("books which are no books"). The closest I saw, perhaps, was a copy of Jerry Seinfeld's *Seinlanguage,* though it could still transcend its sit-com origins and become a lasting work of humor.

Unlike a librarian, a bookstore owner—especially one as idiosyncratic as McMurtry—need not bow to fashion, nor represent, at the mercy of outside interests, the duly under-represented. He need not compromise his artistic and intellectual integrity.

Instead, he freely creates his own universe, after his own whims and desires (in his own image, if you will); he builds a personal utopia between covers. It is said that two of the most common fantasies of middle-aged Americans are sailing off on a freighter and owning a used bookstore. Which is perfectly logical, since together they are physical manifestations of two popular and opposing human desires: to see the world and to retreat from it. For, despite the inescapable realities of the marketplace, a second-hand bookstore constitutes a refuge, an adult's treehouse made out of pages, and the more irrelevant that books become in people's everyday lives the more vital and enticing a refuge it becomes.

The layered beauty of McMurtry's store is that it is a world of books created by a prolific writer of books (the nearest equivalent being an author's—seldom seen—private library) who happens to be one of the greatest readers of books. This is a man who takes Walter Benjamin to the Dairy Queen. In the subsequent book, an entire chapter is titled "Reading," and begins with the story of the cousin who gave him nineteen "common boys' books of the twenties and thirties" when he was six. That started him on a habit that was not stilled until 1991, when he underwent heart surgery and woke up to find that he no longer had any interest in reading. A few pages later he writes: "I am only now [1998] regaining my velocity—the ability to read several books more or less at the same time, at a fast clip." By the end, he confesses: "In my seventh decade I feel a new haste, not to write, but to read." Sad news for his readers; inspiration for his customers.

After an hour I headed out looking like a freshman with a long night of homework ahead. On Center Street there was an occasional clash as stetsoned rancher passed bespectacled bibliophile. Boots versus loafers, dirt versus dust. The locals seemed to pay little heed to the treasure in their midst, rather like the residents of an old Adriatic town who blithely run their errands around useless ruins. Except that here the treasure was not something that, however ignored, was deeply integrated into the culture; it was a fluke, an aberration that had recently landed in town as if from another planet. And it had brought with it this strange cult of asocial, middle-aged men on a mission. (You find few giggly girls among the stacks of secondhand bookstores.) Though we had, it seemed to me, something in common with the weekend hunters, who also come here with hopes of taking home trophies and spend long hours of what to any outsider look like unrelieved boredom but are in fact blissful periods of exhilarating pursuit.

After some time in Nos. 2 and 3 I wandered with A. J. Liebling, M. F. K. Fisher, Bernard DeVoto, James Thurber, George Mikes, and Malcolm Muggeridge down to No. 1. (Signs in all the buildings direct customers to the main store, the only one with a cash register.) The young assistant from the day before had been replaced by an older woman with a rugged face and a sharp but pleasant manner. Mary had told me that McMurtry's sister worked in the store, and I asked if she were Sue McMurtry.

She confirmed that she was, and after some pleasantries said, "Two of us liked horses and two of us didn't. He and my sister didn't. She's got the Abstract Company on the square."

I asked about him. "He writes in the morning, and then comes in around eleven. He goes home for lunch and then comes back and stays till five. He unpacks about twenty books a day. That's what he loves doing." I had visions of him, erudite yeoman, sitting in a drafty old warehouse up to his elbows in hardcovers.

Sue said she'd mail the books, making sure to wait a week so I'd be back from my trip by the time they arrived. I told her to tell her brother I was sorry I missed him.

Outside, the bells of the neighboring Methodist Church pealed a hymn which seemed to come out of nowhere:

*All glory, laud, and honor to thee Redeemer King!*
*To whom the lips of children made sweet hosannas ring.*

Abby had told me where McMurtry lived, and on my way there I stopped at the high school. It was a classic brick fortress fronted by a flagpole. The students wore the requisite indigent outfits and surly expressions, then ruined it all with polite "Hi's."

The superintendent's office occupied the neighboring annex. He didn't think any of McMurtry's novels were on the syllabus, but added that individual teachers might use them. "We're proud to have him in the community," Randel Beaver said. "He supports the reading initiative program. If you pass a test you can win a T-shirt. It's quadrupled interest in reading among elementary school students.

"He's an interesting character, a regular Joe. He wears jeans, and has his hair down to his shoulders."

"He got a haircut," one of the women in the office said with approval. "I saw him the other day."

Thomas Wolfe, and most of the people he wrote about, had to die before Asheville embraced him. Today in Archer City, Larry McMurtry is not only accepted, he is treated as if he were still in high school. Obsolescence of practical memory, or the tolerance of more liberal times? Or perhaps the diminishing power of the written word?

The house sat at the end of the street, a rambling mass of tan brick rising three stories to a green tile roof. It had been, I knew from the memoir, the house of a rich oilman who had lost his only child in an oil field accident and taken solace in books. McMurtry writes of how, as a boy, he would look across the hay field late at night and see the light burning in the man's second floor study. It is a scene of potentially Gatsbyesque power, but McMurtry explains it simply. "Mr. Taylor and I were the only two people in Archer City who liked to read all night."

I took in the windows of the neighboring houses, and wondered if there was anyone watching the survivor.

# PART FOUR

## *Rio, Meet Waterloo; Where Is My America?*

I didn't make it to Woodstock, but I saw the movie. It was obligatory. Thereafter I became a member of the generation. It was beyond my control.

Quite an illustrious career that sylvan word has had—evolving from the name of an unremarkable hamlet in New York State to the defining label of a nation's youth. Small town name makes good.

It wasn't the first. Our globe and language are littered with names that have expanded in meaning to transcend place. We have the Amazon for size, Gibraltar for strength, Timbuktu for distance, the Sahara for emptiness, Siberia for bitter, unbounded misery.

The Bible probably started it all, recounting tales of Canaan and Sodom. Ancient history added quite a few new names, so that even today you will hear of someone crossing the Rubicon even though she is nowhere near north central Italy.

Byzantium (now better known as Istanbul) gave us the political analyst's favorite adjective, Byzantine. The name Babylon is so rich in dreamy associations that most people, if asked where it is, would be hard pressed to place it in Iraq. While Transylvania—taking into account its country's twentieth-century political life—seems right at home in Romania.

War has been a vicious aggrandizer of place names. Carthage, Gallipoli, Auschwitz, Hiroshima. Waterloo, won on the playing fields of Eton, has become something even an accounts executive can meet. In this country, the Civil War brought us towns whose names are forever bathed in blood and glory. Antietam, Gettysburg, Appomattox. Like Woodstock, Gettysburg has gone—to give another example of name expansion—Hollywood. Hollywood, of course, being that Mecca for aspiring actors and filmmakers.

Korea and Vietnam are still, for many Americans, more wars than countries.

Even the Cold War created new catchwords. In Eastern Europe, the Crimean city of Yalta, often dropped into conversations with a bitter shaking of the head, was universally taken as shorthand for Western betrayal and postwar malaise. And the Finns, like the Balkans before them, watched helplessly as their country's name was suffixed into a geopolitical process—Finlandization.

In a similar vein, Shanghai remains perhaps the only city to have ever been verbalized. Though how long will it be before tourists, returning walletless from Brazil, complain of being "Rioed"?

Chernobyl is no longer just a city in Ukraine, nor is Chappaquiddick simply an island on Martha's Vineyard. Likewise, Watergate has long ceased to be an apartment building in Washington, D.C., and Stonewall is much more than a gay bar in Greenwich Village.

Certain cities have become synonymous with misery and decay. Sarajevo replaced Detroit as the next Beirut, which was once the Paris of the Levant.

London and New York—as befits the two great English-speaking metropolises—have introduced an impressive number of geographical neologisms, many of them drawn from thoroughfares: Bond Street, Fleet Street, Grub Street (leave it to the English to champion a coinage for literary failure), Wall Street, Broadway, Madison Avenue (the American contributions are, instructively, all money and show). Greenwich Village is not just a neighborhood in New York, it is the American answer, in art and metaphor, to England's Bloomsbury.

As big a country as the United States is, the name by which it is known around the world looms even larger: America. It signifies—depending on where you are—dream, bully, savior, promised land, murder capital, Great Satan, heartbreaker. "I am waiting for Madeleine," Jacques Brel used to sing of the woman who never showed for their dates. "She's my own America."

# 12

# *On the Trail*

*A man didn't make history, staying close to home.*
—A. B. Guthrie, Jr. from *The Way West.*

The story of America is the story of movement. The Europeans sailed in and gave birth to pioneers. First boats, then wagons.

Other countries have been peopled by emigrants, but only the United States saw an emigration of emigrants, a second, internal migration almost as significant as the first. The homesteaders from Massachusetts and Virginia who journeyed west on the Oregon Trail did so for the same foggy, often unarticulated reason that their forefathers had sailed from Germany and Ireland: the perception of a better life. In the mid-1800s, the West became for Easterners what America had already become for Europeans: a freewheeling, savage promised land.

The two migrations shared other characteristics. Costs were high, both for passage in steerage across the Atlantic and the oxen and wagons that traversed the plains. Both journeys were arduous, though the one on land exacted a heavier toll. Today there are people in the Willamette Valley who talk of themselves proudly as sixth-generation Oregonians in the same way that certain families in New England consider themselves twelfth-generation Americans.

But the most remarkable quality linking these two great migrations is their staying power. Americans are still attracted to the West—more than a century and a half after the first emigrants set out on the Oregon Trail—just as much of the world is still drawn to the United States, which has come, in the minds of many, to symbolize the West. Haitians sneak ashore in Palm Beach County while a fast-food chain boasts on a billboard in Portland: "91,059 people have moved here this year. Because of Burgerville?"

Restlessness is in our genes. It shows itself in everything from our national literature—*Moby Dick, Huckleberry Finn, On the Road*—to the short life of the average address book. "At Thanksgiving," the British writer Jonathan Raban has observed, "the airport is a bee-swarm of people coming and going home. They cross each other in the skies—millions of bits of families trying to reunite for the holiday." It seems no coincidence that our largest export company is Boeing. From a historical perspective, no other country could have beat us to the moon. If, as is said, England is a people and France a civilization, the United States is an experiment in perpetual motion.

"You can have a four-door sedan or a station wagon."

It was a soft Friday evening in August and I was standing at a rental car counter in the Boise airport. I had flown in to drive the last leg of the Oregon Trail in its sesquicentennial year, and the wagon, I thought, would have provided an excellent touch. But I needed a trunk. I pulled out my plastic and took the sedan

Most emigrants began their journeys in Independence, Missouri. They bought their wagons—not the Conestoga variety popularized by Hollywood (they were used on the Santa Fe Trail), but small, narrow, top-heavy farm wagons with canvas coverings. These had an easier time going over the steep hills and through the thick forests of Oregon. The emigrants' first major decision was whether to hitch mules or oxen to their wagons. The first were faster, more intelligent and had tougher hooves. But oxen ate anything, pulled heavier loads, had more pleasing dispositions, and were less attractive to thieves. They also cost less.

Saturday morning I got in my sedan and steered it onto Interstate 84, the modern-day trail to Oregon. The flat land west of Boise was fenced into fields and cramped with houses. About the only thing I shared with the emigrants was the weather, which was hot and dry. For they, too, arrived here in August, having left Independence in late April or early May. Their start had to be timed to fall after the prairie had hardened from the snows but before the sun scorched the grasses. And they had to make it over Oregon's Blue and Cascade mountains before the new snows. The 2,000-mile journey from Independence to Oregon City—crossing Kansas, Nebraska, Wyoming, Idaho, and Oregon—usually took five or six months.

Oregon Trail road markers directed me off the Interstate and into Parma, near the Oregon border. In later years, emigrants also got guidance, not from markers, but from ruts carved into the ground by earlier wagons. (Some of these are still visible today, most impressively in Wyoming.) The peak years of travel were the early 1850s, though in 1849 someone at Fort Kearny in Nebraska counted 500 wagons rolling by in a single day. In the eighteen years of the Trail—1843 to 1860—a quarter of a million people kicked up its dust.

Parma was a typical small western town, a blot beside some railroad tracks. When I finished my lunch at the Fort Boise Café—grilled ham and cheese with a mountain of fries—the waitress asked concernedly "Didja git enough to eat?"

Fort Boise, situated on the banks of the Snake River just outside of town, was established as a fur-trading post in 1834. It was the trappers, or "mountain men," who forged the route that would become the Oregon Trail, finding a way through the Rockies at Wyoming's South Pass. And it was, in large part, the rugged missionaries who later accompanied them who spread the word about Oregon—the abundant fish, the fertile land, the temperate climate—when they returned back East.

I visited a replica of the fort—the original got washed away in a flood—at the edge of town. The bright red Hudson's Bay Company flag flew overhead. Although a British outpost, at a time when the United States and England were contesting the Oregon Territory, the fort had been famous for its hospitality to emigrants. Inside I learned that Edgar Rice Burroughs had come to Parma during the Idaho gold rush—before he'd penned the Tarzan books—and served on the city council.

Then I drove down to the banks of the Snake to see the site of the original fort. It was marked simply by a chest-high stone topped by a comical looking lion's head. Nearby, two young men sat by fishing poles.

"There's good fishin' here if you like that," one man said. "Catfish, bass, perch. And there are places where you can walk to the other side. I guess that's how they got their wagons across."

A few miles up the road I crossed the Snake easily enough—by bridge—into Oregon. At this point, the emigrants had covered more than fifteen hundred miles and had fewer than five hundred—about a month's worth of travel—to go. But these last miles loomed with more parched plains and the steepest mountains of the whole endeavor. Histories of the trail invariably comment on the fact that the most grueling part of the journey came when the emigrants were at their weakest and most fatigued. In fact, it has been suggested that had the trip been made in reverse, it would not have been considered such a remarkable feat.

The sign welcoming me to Nyssa told me it was "The Thunderegg Capital of the World," but I didn't see anybody who could tell me what a thunderegg was. It was a still, hot, deserted afternoon. The road to Vale was bordered by fields of wheat, corn, beets, and alfalfa. I know this because each field posted a sign that said, "Malheur County presents—Wheat (or Corn or Beets or Alfalfa)—the Oregon Lottery."

Malheur (for a land so ruggedly western, it has an awful lot of French: Boise, La Grande, The Dalles) means "misfortune" and there are few more appropriately named places. For it was here that Stephen Meek, the pilot of an 1845 emigrant party, persuaded two hundred families to follow him on a shortcut across the desert to the upper Willamette Valley. When they found no water to the west, the group turned north toward the Columbia River. But twenty-four of its members died.

The proper route was grim enough. Sarah Sutton, writing in 1854, called the area between the Snake and Malheur rivers "the most dusty, dry and hot bare desert that any person ever travers'd." Just outside Vale I found the tombstone of John D. Henderson, the date "Aug 9, 1852" engraved above the words "Died of Thirst." Historians contend that the cause of death was actually invented by a local schoolboy; nevertheless, I stopped at the Dairy Queen and ordered a large lemonade.

Back on I-84, heading north to Farewell Bend, I listened to *A Prairie Home Companion* on National Public Radio. What a lift, I thought, it would have given the emigrants if they could have listened to Garrison Keillor. Not on radio, of course, but around the campfire—his quintessentially American voice, resonant and wry, telling stories and humming concertos. A big Midwesterner, too, he could have given them a good day's work.

Farewell Bend was where the emigrants said goodbye to the Snake River, which had been their companion, off and on, for the previous three hundred miles. (Here it flowed north, while they continued northwest.) The parting was bittersweet, for the river had given them fish, while occasionally taking some wagons, and lives, in the crossings. Today it is a state park with Winnebagos grouped like wagons in the parking lot. Driving the Oregon Trail you begin to see how any long car trip now borrows—with its breakdowns, its rest stops, its mounds of provisions—from this first epic overland journey.

A family picnic was in progress, while off to the side a man sprawled in a chaise longue. He looked out over the silvery expanse of water, more like a lake than a river, and the bald, mustard-colored mountains muscling up the other side. The landscape had something of the parched majesty of the Dead Sea. A long, graceful Union Pacific train floated into the picture, winding its way south along the eastern banks. It looked small in the distance, like a model in a roadside attraction, and as much an aberration in this fabled setting as the happy reunion and the man of leisure.

The drive to Baker City was up and over miles of steep, spherical, desolate hills that gave no sign of life. It was not the last time I wondered how wagons had made it.

Yet the Oregon Trail Motel, at the entrance to town, had the "NO" in its vacancy sign well illuminated, and the only empty bed, it seemed, was at Sagebrush Sadie's Bed & Breakfast.

Baker City was experiencing a boom from Oregon Trail nostalgia that harked back to the gold rush days. The Interpretive Center, a few miles outside town, was the only one of four in the state to be completed in time for the sesquicentennial, and it was profiting handsomely from its exclusivity. Lorinda Jones, proprietor of Sagebrush Sadie's, still bore scars from the horse that trampled her during the center's grand opening.

Main Street was a pantheon of wagon worship. A painting on the window of the Blue & White Café depicted a cook in an apron feeding an emigrant. Wooden covered wagon toys decorated the windows of not only the Heirloom and Creative Gallery, but also Bruce A. Nichols, CPA. At Tumblewood Toys and Tales you could buy Wagon Wheels to Oregon: A Game of Historic Adventure. A poster for the Oregon Trail Theater advertised "the finest in evening entertainment." The bookstore offered *The Oregon Trail Cookbook,* which sounded about as appetizing as *Recipes from the Mariel Boatlift.* Children's drawings, taped to one window, marked the twenty-fifth anniversary of the filming in town of—what else?—*Paint Your Wagon.* A wagon stood on the lawn outside the offices of Oregon Trail Properties.

"That's a real one," Andy Arstein told me that evening. "Before I bought it, it was sitting in a garage in Missouri."

Arstein and I were sitting at the bar of the Main Event on Main Street. "It's incredible what they did," Arstein said, looking into his beer. "We went out last year when they opened the center, with a few wagons and horses. We covered about seven or eight miles and it was grueling. There were some spills.

"I grew up on a sheep ranch in Idaho. No, I'm not Basque, but my dad had two hands who were Basque. So I know this stuff. Even still, it was tough.

"You've heard of the wagon train they've got going this year? It started at the Wyoming-Idaho border, should be on its way to The Dalles right now. They've had their problems. One of the wagons overturned and the wagon master got badly hurt. He's rejoined the train, but the last I heard he was just walking alongside.

"They try to follow the old trail but they can't. It's another world out there now—highways, ranches. A lot of it's fenced in and you can't just go through somebody's land."

"By the way," I asked, "do you know what a thunderegg is?"

"Never heard of it," he said.

As impressive as the contents of the Baker City Interpretive Center, with its dioramas and theatricals, is its dramatic setting atop Flagstaff Hill. As I ascended the sagebrush-dotted mound, overlooking the alkali flat below the hazy Blue Mountains, Henryk Górecki's *Symphony of Sorrowful Songs* played on the radio. And these searching, mournful notes, written by a living Pole, seemed somehow to speak to the emigrants' struggle.

One out of every twenty people who started on the trail died on the trail. Emigrant diaries constantly refer to makeshift graves passed along the way. Very few of the deaths—an estimated four percent—came at the hands of Indians, who, especially in the early years, often aided the emigrants. Mundane accidents and diseases like cholera thinned the ranks; novels of the trail inevitably include a misfired gun or a child crushed under a wagon's wheels.

Ruts are still visible on Flagstaff Hill and you can trace the trail as it descends toward the flat. On an August afternoon the land is bare, bright, unforgiving, open to the harshness of sun and wind. You can almost see them coming over the hill, legions of the ragged, the thirsty, the footsore, and the spent, urging their oxen through whirlpools of dust.

Inside the center, sneakered families wander with the same dutiful sense of patriotic edification that they bring to the monuments in Washington. Yet the most striking thing about them is their softness. Their baggy, pastel shorts and T-shirts conceal a flab that seems to mock the hungry, tested faces in the photographs. It is like observing the process of natural selection in reverse.

In the late afternoon I left for La Grande, where I planned to spend the night. It was forty miles away, not a great distance, but four times as far as the emigrants usually traveled in a day.

The Grande Ronde Valley, in which the town sits, was named by French trappers for its vast circular shape. Emigrants often found large numbers of Indians gathered—Cayuse, Nez Perce, Walla Walla, Umatilla. Their diaries remark on the attractiveness of the spotted ponies and the tall conifers on the bordering mountains. "An enchanted valley," one emigrant called it, "after a thousand miles of naked rocks." It was the first sign that the Oregon they sought was getting nearer. Some settlers, in fact, returned here after failing to make it in the Willamette Valley.

As I came into La Grande, I, too, found a gathering, not of Nez Perce, but of teenagers and families and old-timers in lawn chairs. The progeny of pioneers. They stretched along the main street as if waiting for a parade.

"What's going on?" I asked an elderly gentleman in a painter's cap.

"We're waiting for our girls' Little League team," he said. "They're coming back today from their first World Series."

"Did they win?" I asked.

"No. But we're still proud of 'em."

And the pioneers gave birth to ballplayers.

I was getting the hang of small western towns. Each one was composed of the same set of seemingly interchangeable parts—a movie theater, a café, an heirloom shop, a bookstore, a Chinese restaurant, a rationing of trees, a park with a covered wagon by the jungle gym—strung along the two parallel constants of train tracks and Main Street. A rodeo arena often sat on the outskirts, like the baseball diamonds of the East and Midwest. The ingredients were so predictable that, after I'd seen a few towns, they all tended to blur as one.

La Grande stood out, though, for the Oregon Trail went right through it. In the morning I drove to Birnie Park, where the coverless wagon next to the jungle gym actually looked reasonable. For it was here, on this green where an Eastern Oregon State College student now studied in the grass, that the emigrants camped before climbing the first hill over the Blue Mountains.

Just behind the park ran B Avenue, which was used by wagons before it was given a name. Now it was lined with modest houses, their living rooms all overlooking a street of history.

At the foot of the hill, in the corner of a split-level's yard, stood a stone marker. I gunned the car up the steep grade, thrust back in my seat like an airplane passenger during takeoff, and was actually relieved to see that the gravel, after only a few yards, ended in a private driveway. Coming back down I saw the mailman driving his truck—as he does every day—across the Oregon Trail.

Interstate 84 now zooms over the Blue Mountains. An emigrant had called this stretch "the worst road yet, worse than the Rockies." The crossing took at least three days, longer if they stopped in the meadows to feed their livestock. At a pull-off near the top, you can walk along the rut-marked path they cut through the conifers.

Taking a back road, I wound my way down the other side of the Blues. The sky was low and cottony gray, but two fat sunbeams split the clouds and illuminated the vast amber bowl of the Umatilla Valley. "The sight from this mountaintop is one to be remembered," wrote emigrant John Minto in 1844. "It affects me as did my first sight of the ocean." At an overhanging curve, I pulled to the side near a parked pickup.

"You're not broken down or anything?" asked the driver as I came near his window. When I told him that I'd gotten out to take a look, he said, "I'm just checking on my cattle. Hundred and fifty head." They appeared as small, dark dots on the undulating fields below. "Not much, but it keeps me out of trouble. We own some of the land," he said, "but most of it we rent from the Indians. This is Umatilla Reservation, you know." And I recalled that the emigrants traded here with Indians—not only Umatilla, but Cayuse and Walla Walla—to replenish their dwindling food supplies.

After reaching the valley and being immersed in wheat, I finally came into Pendleton. It was a larger version of earlier towns, with its famous woolen mills and round-up grounds (housing the Cowboy Hall of Fame).

The place still possessed a definite western feel—Red's Clothing Co. offered goods "For Every Cowboy"—but it had lost its distinction as the "Town That Couldn't Be Tamed." The famous Pendleton Underground, once the province of Chinese laundries and gun-happy speakeasies, was now a guided tour for the entire family that ended at the obligatory gift shop. A barber on Main Street offered "back-to-school haircuts." A mother at Armchair Books interrupted her reading of the *New York Times Book Review* to tell her daughter, "You better get a sack for that honey, or it will be all over the pickup."

Still, some touches remained. In Crabby's Underground Saloon and Dance Hall, the only subterranean establishment still in operation here, a sign was posted claiming "Whiners will be shot." In a town that once boasted eighteen bawdyhouses, I got a room at the Working Girls Hotel.

"It used to be a boarding house," Pam McKay, the owner, told me. "And the girls would come in through a doorway in that wall—it's been bricked up now—to service the lodgers."

McKay had the air of a smart young businesswoman. When she learned I was following the trail, she asked if I'd heard what had happened to the Sesquicentennial Wagon Train.

"You know about the Interpretive Centers?" she asked. "I assume you stopped at the one in Baker City. Well, there were supposed to be four, one of them on the Umatilla Reservation. But Washington never gave the Indians any money for it, so when the wagon train came through they held it hostage.

"The chiefs arrived on horseback in full regalia. It was very tastefully done. And of course all the TV stations came out—it was a perfect PR ploy to get their message across. One of the chiefs said 'We will lead you through the mountains, just as our ancestors did.' And then the Indians invited them to a salmon feed."

The next day's route was hot and dry between rolling brown hills. A road sign warned "Blowing Dust Area—next 40 Miles." Like the emigrants, I'm sure, I'd hoped I'd seen the last of dust.

Echo, unlike Pendleton, was a smaller version of earlier towns. Here the trail splits off, for the first time in Oregon, from I-84. (The Interstate heads for the river, while the wagons stayed on the plains.) The trail now goes through the Ramos family farm; a billboard in town told of the Portuguese emigrants, often from the Azores, who settled here as sheep ranchers; not far from the sign stood St. Peter's Catholic Church. On the back of the sign, someone had scrawled: "Echo sucks."

The Columbia depressed me with its barren grandeur. Never had I seen such a large body of water in such an arid space. I had always associated water with life, but here, sun-burnt hills on either side were relieved only by rock and sage. They darkened the bluffs the same way the wind-churned whitecaps lightened the river. When, at the town of Arlington, I detoured south, and came upon endless fields of wheat, it struck me that the Columbia was the exact opposite of the Nile, whose banks support the only greenery in the surrounding desert.

I could tell, as I drove into The Dalles, that the Sesquicentennial Wagon Train had recently arrived from the freshly squashed horse chips along the road. I found the wagons outside the rodeo grounds, parked in a neat circle and decorated with people in period dress. The two semis that carried their kitchens and showers sat in the nearby parking lot.

"My ancestors came out in 1952, '53," Jim Conner said. He was from Fruitland, Idaho, a retired deliveryman who'd built his own wagon expressly for the train. "We've got ten wagons, four from Idaho. One is the Idaho State wagon, and it'll be on permanent display in Boise. As far as I'm concerned, if anybody's got $17,000, they can have mine.

"We've also got eight outriders—men on horseback who can help you if you have a problem with a runaway. We had one rough moment when four of the horses got scared and ran. The wagon master fell off, broke his pelvis in three places and bruised a kidney. It was a pretty exciting four or five seconds. They took him to the hospital. That was on Sunday. By Friday he was back in his motor home. Last week he was driving his team again."

The train historian, Mike McKinley, stood with his rifle answering questions while Pat Slovik gathered her things from the Nike wagon.

"Nike's one of the sponsors," she explained. "I'm a receptionist and they had a lottery for employees who wanted to ride for a day. But it wasn't like I thought it would be."

"How so?" I asked.

"Well, we went on I-84 and stopped for lunch at Les Schwab Tire."

But that evening, as if to make it up to her, the town gathered in force for a cookout—chili, cornbread, and apple cobbler—and square-danced by the light of the moon.

The Dalles (French for "rapids") is a conservative town—"there are two paychecks here," someone told me, "aluminum and farming"—with a population that hasn't changed much in the last hundred years. But I could still sense, in a strange way, that I was edging back into a more familiar world. A bed-and-breakfast on West Fourth Street accepted only windsurfers, and Baldwin's downtown was a "non-smoking saloon." Go far enough West and soon you're back East.

The emigrants, too, were getting closer to more familiar, or at least more soothing, landscapes. But at The Dalles they faced their toughest decision: Whether to put all their possessions on a raft and go down the Columbia, or follow the Barlow Road south of Mount Hood and over the Cascades. In his novel about the trail, *The Way West,* A. B. Guthrie, Jr. ends his story here, as if the float through the rapids was like an afternoon on the Intracoastal.

It wasn't. Emigrant rafts frequently wrecked. You can imagine, even today, looking out over the river now plugged with dams and trivialized by windsurfers, the emigrants' dilemma. For those fed up with walking, the swiftness of the current must have been a powerful lure—just push out from the banks and off you go!

But on land, at least, you didn't risk sinking everything you'd carried for the last 1,900 miles, including yourself. Many of the emigrants didn't know how to swim.

The Barlow Road was forged by Samuel K. Barlow and Joel Palmer in 1845. Pictures of Barlow show him looking, with his upstanding coiffure, like an ascetic Lyle Lovett. Palmer climbed the 11,235-foot Mount Hood, the first white man to do so, and, looking down, found the pass that would carry them across the Cascades. The following year Barlow opened the road to traffic and, in a gesture that would later warm the hearts of highway commissioners everywhere, charged five dollars a wagon.

"You can follow us. We've got a cellular phone."

I had been reading the warning about low-level vehicles on the Barlow Road when the White sisters pulled up. They had a four-wheel drive Jeep with two children in the back. "We're doing it," they said. "We promised the kids we'd show 'em some ruts. Come on, it'll be fun."

We turned onto a dirt road through a forest of pine. I had to hang back to let the dust clear. After a mile or so, the road turned to rock. The car barely made it between the trees. For the first time in days, I thought of the man who'd rented it to me. I swerved nervously to avoid deep holes, and then inched my way over protruding boulders, bouncing wildly and listening all the while for the scrapping of the chassis. It was like driving through a stream that had been emptied of water. Eventually, we came to a clearing.

"I'm going to turn back," I said, hoping to sound jaunty. "I don't think the car's going to make it."

"Oh, come on," the White sisters said. "We haven't reached the road yet."

When we got to the Barlow Road, they wanted to go east. "Our ancestors came this way," the White sisters said. "I'm pretty sure Whites didn't take the wheels off any wagons and float them down the river. We're still not all that great on water."

"Do you know what year?" I asked, trying to retain my reportorial composure.

"No, but Grandma White does."

They were clearly the children of emigrants—adventuresome and fearless. Cursed with more sedentary roots—my family never left New Jersey—I fretted over my rental car. Now I had to decide: stick with the Whites for the security of the phone, or push on alone, hoping to find the next dirt road back to the paved one. I bid them farewell.

Shortly after I got in the car, it overheated. Speeding up to give it some air was out of the question. I entertained visions of a gasket break, even though I'm not quite sure what or where a gasket is. The path, obviously not meant for cars, continued to throw sharp rocks in my way. Between frantic looks at the thermometer, I thought of how close I'd come—for the first time in the journey—to approximating the feeling of emigrant anxiety.

The next day, my last on the trail, I ran into A. D. Anderson at Laurel Hill. (The car was dusty but unharmed.) It was here where the emigrants made their perilous descent, often tying their wagons to the trunks of trees and letting them down inch by inch. Anderson had just pulled up on his bicycle, bundled against the cool mountain air, having ridden from Independence, Missouri.

"Actually, I started from home in Asheville, North Carolina," he said. "I've always wanted to do a western trip. I didn't even know it was a big anniversary until I got to Missouri."

He had started from there on June 15, "not hurrying," he said. We walked up the hill—"the real hill they came down is across the highway," a local in a cowboy hat told us. He added that the last tree with rope marks on its trunk had been cut down by treasure hunters several years earlier.

And then, after a slow afternoon drive, I arrived in Oregon City. Almost a suburb of Portland today, it seemed to have neither the amenities of a city nor the charm of a small town. It sat dull and confused, with its two separate levels, above the Willamette Falls.

Down at Abernathy Green, where the emigrants officially ended their journey, I found Anderson cradling a pay phone to his ear. The roar of nearby highway traffic drowned out his voice, but I imagined him saying, in his southern drawl, "Honey, I made it! Hurrah for Oregon!" Then I headed the car toward Portland, my next assignment, remembering the journal entries of James Nesmith, the man who went on to become Oregon's first senator:

> *Friday, Oct. 27: Arrived at Oregon City at the falls of the Willamette.*
>
> *Saturday, Oct. 28: Went to work.*

# 13

## *Mother of Mystics*

William Buck Taylor, Jr. stood backstage at the Mobile Civic Center in white tie and black eye patch. It was Saturday, Coronation Night, and Taylor was sidelined from his traditional role as usher by injuries resulting from a recent fall (unconnected to any carnival revelry).

"The King and Queen are not chosen democratically," he said in a voice that fell somewhere between a shout and a growl. "You understand that, don't you, Tom?!?

"Tonight we are observing three momentous anniversaries. Before the King and Queen arrive, you're going to see the seventy-fifth anniversary Queen! Now how old would she be?!? THINK ABOUT IT, TOM!!! That's right! Somewhere in her nineties!!

"My daughter is also going to be introduced. She's the twenty-fifth anniversary Queen. My great uncle Hannis Taylor was Emperor in 1887! HE RODE INTO TOWN ON AN ELEPHANT!!! He was a bit flamboyant!"

Suddenly he took my arm, led me out into the arena and, still clutching at my sleeve, walked me in front of the stage and the eyes of Mobile. "I'm taking you to your seat! You're being ushered by a man who ushered you uniquely!!"

After the lengthy introductions—of past Queens and the current court—a costumed man unfurled a scroll of parchment and read a proclamation from the King: "In observance of ancient custom and in celebration of honored ritual, I, Felix, Emperor of

Mirth and Lord of Misrule, do herewith proclaim my glad return . . . to fair Mobile, most beautiful of cities in the most noble Southland, the Mother of carnival in the New World . . .

"It is our imperial edict that during this royal visitation no stripe of industry, labor, or toil will be permitted except in furtherance of the frippery and frivolity which this season demands: Be not misguided by Yankee notions of application or enterprise; rather, let wit and joy and the pursuit of happiness be the order of our days, until our call to penitence and Lent."

He added that any "miscreants found in violation" would be sent to Birmingham or, if truly wayward, Montgomery.

It was in 1704 that a Frenchman, Nicholas Langlois, established the Société de Saint Louis at Mobile's first settlement, inaugurating a tradition of secret societies and Mardi Gras celebrations that predates New Orleans's. The Spanish, when they arrived, added their own touches, and pre-Lenten bacchanals flourished on the bay until the start of what is still sometimes spoken of here as "Mr. Lincoln's War." Then carnival, like so much else in the South, came to an end.

But like the South, in fact well before it, it rose again. On Fat Tuesday in 1866 a city clerk and local wag by the name of Joe Cain dressed up as an Indian, christened himself Chief Slacabamorinico, and, with six of his friends, paraded through the streets in a coal wagon drawn by mules.

"He said he was a Chickasaw Indian chief who had emerged from Wragg's Classic Vale," said Wayne Dean, who was sitting on a bench by Claiborne Street early Sunday afternoon. "There was a Wragg Swamp back then, out where the Springdale Mall now is."

The warm February sun had emerged, causing Dean's synthetic black braids to glisten. He was dressed as Joe Cain dressed as Slacabamorinico: wig, mustache, goatee, Confederate army shirt with Indian trim, deer-tail bonnet of turkey feathers.

"He wanted to revive the city's spirits, but he was also taunting the Union troops—parading around in a Union-occupied city in Confederate garb and as a member of a tribe that had never been defeated. Everything he did had a double or sometimes triple meaning. He was out to have a good time but he also wanted to make a statement.

"The following year he got sixteen men—they called themselves 'The Lost Cause Minstrels.' They started portraying themes. It lasted for about thirteen years."

A trolley passed—long, black-gloved arms waving lugubriously from out its windows. "There go Joe Cain's widows," Dean said. "Every Sunday before Mardi Gras they go to Church Street cemetery and moan and groan and dance around his grave. We used to have a party in the cemetery after the parade—people would picnic on family graves. We moved it out because it got too big. Not—as you might have heard—because of desecration of the graves. The vandalism was mostly done at night."

In 1967, Dean came home from college to participate in the first resurrection of the Joe Cain Procession; for more than a decade he has been its head. He is the author of the book *Mardi Gras: Mobile's Illogical Whoop-De-Doo,* which tells of the days when invitations to balls were sent by special messenger and often wives didn't know what secret societies claimed their husbands. "Now it's a kind of pretend secrecy," he said. "But most societies will fine members if they reveal their association. And obituaries in the *Mobile Register* still state simply: 'He was a member of a mystic society.' They don't say which one."

As we talked, families wandered up and asked if they were looking at Joe Cain. "Chief Slacabamorinico," Dean would gently correct them, the sliding board name tripping effortlessly off his tongue. Then they would place their children on his lap for a picture. Dean was unfailingly serious and obliging.

"Where y'all from?"

"Atlanta."

"Up north."

Though most were charmed Mobilians.

"Carnival is a 25 to 30 million dollar business in Mobile," Dean said, carefully putting a child back on the pavement. "Costumes, floats, food, gowns. Probably one million alone is spent on ball gowns."

The Living Section of the *Register* that morning had proved a fascinating study. Gracing the cover were the two royal couples. (There are, apparently by mutual preference, two separate carnivals: the white one and the African-American one.) Profiles of the four monarchs ran inside.

"It's tradition that she adores," the white Queen's mother said of her daughter, "and she is a true, traditional Southern girl." But, "anything but stuffy or parlour-bound," the reporter quickly added. "She loves," her mother explained, "a satin dress as much as she loves camouflage."

There were also pictures and brief write-ups of all the attending knights and ladies. Each began with the names of the parents, and each lady's ended with a description of her robes. "Lady Rhen's gown of ivory silk had a sweetheart neckline that extended into a deep oval in the back and flared into a peplum at the waist. The bodice was edged with gold metallic passementarie and accented with Austrian crystals, gold seed beads, and hand-stitched gold treillage and scroll designs."

"The King and Queen are almost like royalty," Dean said, "in that they come from moneyed families that have long been involved in Mardi Gras. They have to be well off because they end up spending about $100,000 each. The Queen has to buy a gown and train and presents for her court. And then there are the parties. I heard that one family spent $5,000 this year just on food and drink for people stopping by the house to see the royal robes.

"The first balls start in November—the big Strikers Ball is on New Year's Eve—and they last until Mardi Gras evening. Then they start up again Easter Week.

"Kids in Mobile learn to dance. I remember as a child, before that, playing 'Mardi Gras' along with 'Cops and Robbers.' One kid would stand up on a box and throw beads to the others. And then on my twenty-first birthday my grandmother gave me tails. You wear them at fraternity balls, even sometimes at high school dances. Mobile uses more formal attire than any other city in the U.S. except Los Angeles."

A little before two-thirty Chief Slacabamorinico said goodbye, walked over to the start of the parade, and took his seat not in the wagon but on one of the mules. The procession led down Church Street, turned north on Royal, then west on St. Francis, where it brushed the live oaks of gracious Bienville ("Be-n-vul") Square. People lined the route, though usually no more than three or four deep; downtown parking lots bulged with pickup trucks and simmered with the suburban aromas of grilled sausage and hamburger. Well-dressed folks leaned from the few wrought-iron balconies that survived, like mournful veils, amidst the faceless façades of the 1950s and 1960s. What a lovely city this must have been at the turn of the century.

I followed the parade down Conception Street. "This is the gay and lesbian district," a young woman said, standing in front of a lawn chair and cooler. "Just thought you'd like to know. Now, what can I get you to drink?"

Kim and her companion had been here—at the corner of Conception and Conti—since six in the morning; they were both from Mobile. "You know this is the oldest Mardi Gras in the United States? When we were kids, the floats were pulled by mules. Now it's GMC trucks. And at night, blacks would walk alongside them with torches."

Taking my Bloody Mary, I asked how their Mardi Gras differed from the one in New Orleans.

"It has all the decadence," Kim said smiling, "with none of the violence."

Back in my room at the Admiral Semmes, I had one message, from the man I had met the night before. "Tom, this is your old friend Buck Taylor!"

I tried to take a nap but was kept awake by children playing in the hall. Mardi Gras? The elevator had been packed with happy fair-haired families, all from Mobile and renting rooms downtown until Ash Wednesday. Earlier someone had asked me, on hearing of my hotel, if I was getting any sleep. I had assumed it to be an allusion to the coming wild parties, not children's romps.

Unable to sleep, I dipped into the book I'd bought about Mobile. Among its native sons, I read, were not only Hank Aaron but also Willie McCovey and Billy Williams—a powerful triumvirate that surely makes Mobile, self-proclaimed as the Mother of Mystics, also America's Mother of Home Runs.

Soon it was time to get ready for Le Krewe de Bienville Ball. Even though it's something of a bogus affair, held for out-of-town visitors, it still requires white tie and tails. I had never worn white tie and tails. I pulled the rented outfit from its bag, certain that an essential element—the bow tie, for instance—had fallen out on the train ride up and was now being worn dashingly by one of the conductors as he rolled through New Mexico.

But everything was here. Studs and cuff links pushed their way through the starched-tight openings like icebreakers in the Arctic. I had to shorten the loop on the tie, which apparently had last been worn by Zach Thomas. And I hesitated briefly before positioning it under the flaps of the stand-up collar. What a target,

I thought, for the mudmen in Trinidad. Then, as I reached for the vest, my heart began to race. I was seconds away from looking the best I possibly could.

Sartorially speaking, that was the highlight of the evening—standing in the bathroom and looking in the mirror. The thing about formal events, when you're a man, is that you think you look exceptional—you *do* look exceptional—until you arrive at the affair and see that every other man is dressed exactly like you. In about the time it took you to get dressed, you move, crushingly, from unprecedented elegance to unrelieved uniformity.

The other thing about formal affairs, especially balls, is that they're best enjoyed with someone else. (I can only assume.) After the opening ceremony, I wandered around a lot. At one point I ran into a young man with strawberry blond hair and a pinkish complexion. (You know what he was wearing.) I asked him if this was anything like the secret society balls. I was still intrigued and feeling deprived.

"To be brutally honest," he said, more or less answering my question, "this is the first time I've ever been to this ball."

"Well," I explained my presence plaintively, "I'm from out of town and this was the only one I could get into."

"Here," he said, handing me his card. "Give me a call tomorrow and I'll see what I can do."

Monday morning, I telephoned Paul. (In observance of the mystic societies' rule of secrecy, I have changed his name.)

"How long do you have the kit?" he asked.

"The what?"

"The white tie and tails."

"Oh, until I go back to Florida."

"Good. I'll put you on the list for Tuesday night. In the meantime, if you just show up tonight in white tie and tails, chances are nobody's going to ask any questions."

The rain that had teased all day fell in earnest just after dark, soaking the Infant Mystics parade. There had been so few people along the route that the floats, when they reached the Admiral Semmes, still contained vast reserves of trinkets, which the Mystics now unloaded with artless abandon. For twenty sparkling minutes it literally rained Moon Pies and beads on Government Street. A few of the members, too drenched to bother with individual tosses, heaved entire cartons of pies, belying the whole purpose of the marshmallow-and-biscuit sandwich, which had been introduced into the parades as a replacement for Cracker Jacks after the carnival association banned the throwing of boxes. But not all traveled in flocks. I followed the brief life of one lunar disk as it sailed through the ribboned sky, skidded on the glistening pavement, and was retrieved and removed from its rain-dropped wrapper by a portly policeman in a globular helmet who, with one hearty chomp, reduced it to a waning crescent.

Then I went up to my room and dressed—transformed myself—for the Infant Mystics ball. It was a wonderful feeling. Even if I hadn't had a ball to sneak into, I think I would have wandered around town all night in white tie and tails.

I almost ended up doing just that. Over at the convention center, they weren't asking questions but they were taking invitations. I had none. I strode confidently up to the desk and slipped in quickly behind a broad-shouldered man as he offered his.

The ball opened with a procession of the members, still in costume, and their ladies, in floor-length gowns. This was followed by a playlet about pirate Jean Lafitte. Invited guests watched from the balcony seats. Then, after the introduction of the King and Queen, they came downstairs and joined the others.

It was then that I realized that the only thing worse than being solo at a ball is being a gatecrasher. Not only did I not have a date, I didn't know anyone in a room where everybody knew everybody. My work was cut out for me. Thank God I was dressed for it.

The feel, even with the penguin factor, was more that of a college mixer than of an antebellum cotillion. The drafty hall, the cans of Lite, the little sausages on toothpicks, the pervasive cloud, especially in the lobby, of cigarette smoke. Several bands played at various locations; an all-black R & B group tucked in one of the corridors attracted the largest and most sensuously clinging crowd.

"I'm a debutante lawyer," a pleasant young woman introduced herself. She had thick short hair and thin dress straps over straight white shoulders. "No, I was never a Queen, but I was a lady in the court. It was the worst year of my life. Nobody else will tell you that. But you couldn't do any work. At Thanksgiving and Christmas there'd be three parties a day.

"People here still ask 'Who are your people?' Really! It's worse than Charleston, because we think we're like Charleston and we're not." I had no idea what had set her off, but I had no intention of asking her to stop.

"You know what they say about Mobile? That it sucks—but it sucks you back. And it's true. I live in Birmingham now. It's comfortable. I can go out by myself in the evening and have a salad and a glass of wine. You can't do that in Mobile. If you're over thirty-five, you're married and have children. Go out by yourself and you're obviously trying to get picked up. And yet I always return. There's something here that pulls me back."

On Fat Tuesday, the last day, parades flowed through the city one after the other. Fraternity brothers set up sofas in a corner of Bienville Street, and revelers turned Dauphin into a PG version of Bourbon Street.

Elephants marched in the final, Order of Myths, procession—a nod to Hannis Taylor?—and appeared at the ball. The crowd here was older and more subdued than the one the night before. Near the dance floor, two men in costume discussed the editor's column from Sunday's *Register.* (He had offered suggestions on how to make Mardi Gras more civically responsible.)

"That putrefying sack of excrement. He's from Louisiana. Shr-e-e-veport," added contemptuously for my benefit, to indicate his provenance from a part of the state, the world, that doesn't understand carnival. "We don't need some scalawag coming in here and telling us what to do."

"We're a Gulf city," the satin harlequin now addressed himself to me. "We have more in common with New Orleans and Biloxi and even Tampa than we do with Birmingham and Montgomery. People up there think we're all Catholics, not good Protestants like one ought to be. And Mardi Gras they see as just another example of our decadence.

"Sometimes they come down for it. And they see a ball like this and they ask what charity is it for? And we say it's not for any charity—it's to have fun. That's all it is. And they can't understand that. That its sole justification is having a good time. Are you having a good time? Here, you look much too respectable."

And he lifted several of his numerous necklaces over his head and placed them roguishly around my neck.

# 14

## *The Last Summer*

Fans arrived early for the games—or rather, the gatherers of keepsakes did. Season ticket holders came and found their way cluttered with tourists posing for pictures under the familiar green letters of C-O-M-I-S-K-E-Y P-A-R-K spanning the curve of whitewashed brick. The new stadium, going up next door, attracted more looks than photographs.

People who for years had not set foot in Chicago's South Side headed down the Dan Ryan Expressway that summer to pay their last respects. Americans made detours on cross-country trips. A man from Wyoming, driving home from New York, made a special stop in Chicago to show Comiskey to his son. His son was eleven months old.

For Jim Georges, it was too early for nostalgia—it was only the end of July and the second-place Sox were desperately trying to catch the Oakland Athletics. If they had been in any division other than the American League West, they'd have been in first place. But for the Sox, there was no other division. And for Comiskey Park, there was no next year.

Today's game—moved up from a 7:30 P.M. to a 12:30 P.M. start because CBS decided to televise it—was against the Milwaukee Brewers. When the White Sox played their first game at Comiskey, on July 1, 1910, there was no television, no team in Milwaukee, no team in either league that called itself the Brewers. There was, however, a team called the Browns. Visiting from St. Louis, they defeated the White Sox 2–0 on opening day of the stadium christened "the baseball palace of the world."

Comiskey was not only old but, people suggested, cursed—despite the fact that its cornerstone was a green brick laid on St. Patrick's Day. (The man who built the stadium, Charles A. Comiskey, was Irish, as was the neighborhood surrounding it.) A workman fell to his death twenty-four hours before opening day. And after only three days in their new home, four Sox players were on the disabled list.

In its eighty years, Comiskey Park was host to everything from auto polo to a record pyre—billed, in 1979, as Disco Demolition Night. It boasted an exploding scoreboard (inspired by the pinball machine in William Saroyan's *The Time of Your Life*) and a barber's chair in the center-field bleachers.

As the oldest of the major league stadiums still standing in 1990, it had probably seen more Hall of Famers than any other; Babe Ruth was rumored to have ducked across the street between innings to have a beer at McCuddy's Tavern, recently demolished. But throughout its long history it had been home to only one world champion—the 1917 White Sox—a team whose notoriety was eclipsed two years later by the infamous "Black Sox," the team that threw the World Series to the Cincinnati Reds. All of which would have made a championship in this, Comiskey's final year, ring forth like a redemption.

"If I had my wish," Georges said, "we'd go play Boston in the playoffs. [Carlton] Fisk [the then 42-year-old catcher acquired from the Red Sox in 1981] kills Boston every time he goes back. Then, in the World Series, we meet Cincinnati. In 1919," he explained for those unschooled in history, "we gave it to them. If I got to write the script, we beat Cincinnati here in five games."

Today's game got off to an excellent start: Leadoff batter Sammy Sosa sent the Brewer's first pitch into the left-field stands for a 1–0 lead. Georges was sitting in his usual seat in the upper deck between third and home. He was wearing a blue White Sox cap, a black T-shirt with an action picture of shortstop Ozzie Guillen printed across the front, and denim cut-offs. His round bald knees showed the light red patina of a fan more accustomed to games at night.

From his homey perch, Georges got an unobstructed view of the action—something that was never a given with Comiskey's numerous support posts. (Holders of season tickets were known to come out to the park to check the location before they paid.) He could admire the distant sweep of dark green seats—barely showing their age from his perspective—the ribboned pattern of fresh-cut grass, and the gregarious scoreboard. The smokestack of the Illinois Institute of Technology rose above the right-field stands; a few rows back sat the house organist.

Except for the unfinished roof of the new stadium, looming over the top of the old, it was all as familiar to Georges as his living room furniture. He last missed a game here in 1988.

"June fourth," he said sourly, turning to the young man seated behind him. "For his wedding." Then he added, still in disbelief: "And he was here!"

Georges had been a season-ticket holder since 1976; he had been a fan from birth. "I was born on the North Side, but my father said, 'You're a White Sox fan.' That's the way it happens in Chicago. And he knew best.

"We hate the Cubs," he said casually of the city's North Side, National League team. "And Cubs fans can't be bothered. Cubs fans don't get it. They don't have the capacity to know that they should hate us. And that makes us hate them even more."

The South Side traditionally has been a blue-collar neighborhood, while the North Side has attracted more young professionals. Comedian Bill Murray, tellingly, is a Cubs fan; White Sox fans tend to be more anonymous. (Although Mayor Daley's family has long held a box behind the home team dugout.) And, they insist, they are more knowledgeable about the game.

"Cubs fans cheer even if their team is losing." Georges said critically, before addressing an even greater offense. "They throw home run balls back. So what if those are home runs against them? A home run ball is sacred. You don't throw it back. You take it home and put it in a shrine."

A walk around Comiskey Park uncovered a wealth of baseball stalwarts. In the picnic area under the left-field stands—created in 1960 by the colorful owner Bill Veeck, so that fans could see the game from a player's perspective—three young men were discussing politics.

"But should they keep him out of the Hall of Fame?" one of them put the question to his friends.

"No," another answered unequivocally. "Ty Cobb is in the Hall of Fame. You know some of the things he did. Babe Ruth is in the Hall of Fame. So why not Rose?"

Up in the press box, top of the fourth. A long fly ball was caught by Sosa to end the inning.

"A year ago that would have been out of here," one of the sportswriters declared. "Why," a newcomer asked, "were the fences pulled in last year?"

"No," he replied, "the Sox are lucky this year."

Down in the dim, beer-soaked caverns under the stands, two young men were contributing to the spill.

"You want to know what the Comiskey experience is?" one of them asked loudly. "Here's the ultimate Comiskey story. My brother comes home from Vietnam. First thing he wants to do is come out here. 'Let's go to Sox field,' he says." (With the flat Chicago vowels it came out like "Sax.") "No pizza, no nothing. Just go to see the Sax."

"In all my years in this city," his friend added proudly, "I've never been to Wrigley Field."

★ ★ ★

"Is this for attribution?" Georges inquired when asked if he had ever visited the hated team's park. "I took friends there twice. It was out of charity. I wore my Padres hat—the Padres beat them in the playoffs the year before. And," he added critically, "nobody got it.

"Wrigley's a quaint little park," he admitted, "with the worst organist, the worst food, and the worst announcers. And they have vines and things on the walls. So it's not baseball. They have stuff growing out there. I guess they can't get rid of it."

The histories of Chicago's two baseball teams have often intermingled. Comiskey Park and Wrigley Field were designed by the same man—Zachary Taylor Davis. Wrigley's devotees will tell you that Comiskey was his rough draft. And the idea of ivy on Wrigley's walls was dreamed up by none other than Bill Veeck—the same man who installed the barber's chair and the outdoor shower in Comiskey's center-field bleachers. At the beginning of the twentieth century, the Cubs and White Sox played a city series, or "serious," as it was called by Jack in Ring Lardner's classic *You Know Me Al*. The two teams also share an unshakable reputation for never finishing on top.

It was the bottom of the eighth, and the Brewers' pitching coach was headed out to the mound. Georges stood and yelled to the organist: "Nancy, play the theme from *Green Acres*."

The organist acknowledged the tip, and played a few bars. Georges explained "Their pitching coach is named Haney, and there was a Mr. Haney on *Green Acres*."

Nancy Faust, who could easily play the role of Peter Pan, was in her twenty-first year as the White Sox organist. She had begun today's game by playing, among her medley, 'On Wisconsin.'

"Kinda big of us," she acknowledged, laughing. Later, a Brewer walked to the tune of "The Long and Winding Road."

She had mixed feelings about the end of Comiskey Park. On the one hand, she was looking forward to the new sound system;

on the other hand, she was worried about losing some of her friends in the upper deck.

"We've all gotten to know each other over the years," Georges said. "We get together for dinners in the off-season. The beer vendor here, Bobby Chicione, gives a couple of beers away each game on trivia questions. Things like: 'Who pitched the most shutouts in the majors last year?' So he's part of the show, too.

"And I like to help Nancy out. LET IT ROLL FOUL!" he shouted to the pitcher eyeing a bunt down the first-base line, not losing track of the game for a minute. "When Luis Polonia of the Angels came to bat—you know, the guy who got caught in bed with a fifteen-year-old—I told her to play 'You're Sixteen, You're Beautiful, and You're Mine.' She said, 'You want me to lose my job?'"

We had reached the bottom of the ninth and the Sox were trailing 4-3. Leadoff batter Ron Karkovice smacked a double off the left-field wall.

"Y-Y-Y-YES!" Georges said sharply.

The next man up, second baseman Scott Fletcher, laid down a picture-perfect bunt.

"Y-Y-Y-YES!"

Men at first and third and nobody out. Fisk—"Commando" to Georges, since he didn't like his more familiar nickname, "Pudge"—walked to load the bases.

Guillen, the shortstop painted on Georges T-shirt, stepped up to the plate. He got behind in the count on two weak swings. With the third, he ripped a single up the middle to drive in the winning run from second.

Pandemonium in the upper deck.

"DID YOU HAVE FUN!!??" Georges yelled at the people beside and behind him. "DID YOU HAVE FUN??!!" he shouted at strangers filing past. "DID YOU HAVE FUN??!" the happiest man in Chicago screamed as he reluctantly made his way out of Comiskey.

# 15

## *Fields of Corn*

Iowa is almost as rich in harvestable Americana as it is in corn.

There is, to begin with, the National Hobo Convention in Britt, just a few miles away from the Surf Ballroom in Clear Lake, where Buddy Holly sang his last ode to Peggy Sue. (The spot where his plane went down, also killing Ritchie Valens and the Big Bopper, is now marked with a plaque.)

Kids hit grounders on the "Field of Dreams" in Dyersville, nostalgically preserved by the farmer who got a new front porch and an air conditioner out of the movie. And there is gambling—our real national pastime—on Mississippi riverboats out of Davenport and Dubuque.

The spirit of Herbert Hoover, born and buried in West Branch, lives on in the town's annual Hoover-ball tournament. And the world of Grant Wood, creator of probably the most recognizable—certainly the most parodied—American painting, still resides in the rolling fields of perfectly ordered rows of corn and distant silos. The natives, for their part, look far more personable than the *American Gothic* couple, the models for which were not farmers anyway but Wood's sister and dentist.

For sightseeing there are, in addition to the famous Amana colonies, the smallest cathedral and the largest strawberry in the world. ("That's largest STATUE of a strawberry," an assistant at Prairie Lights Books corrected. "I know a little girl who went up there and was disappointed that she couldn't take a bite.") To get from one to the other you cross the Volga River.

Speaking of things foreign, there are the Norwegians in Decorah, Swedes in Stanton, Danes in Elk Horn, Luxembourgers in St. Donatus, Czechs in Cedar Rapids, and Dutch in Pella, where even the McDonald's bears the façade of an Amsterdam canal house. The practice of transcendental meditation is an admission requirement at Maharishi International University in Fairfield. In Spillville, not far from Decorah, Antonín Dvořák wrote his New World Symphony.

Mark Twain began his journalism career in Muscatine. Flannery O'Connor was one of the first in a long line of literati to flow from the Iowa Writers' Workshop in Iowa City. Jack Kerouac, passing through, declared that "the prettiest girls in America are in Des Moines," while Bill Bryson, the son of a Des Moines sports writer, made his name with the story, "Fat Girls in Des Moines," followed shortly after by "More Fat Girls in Des Moines." A less self-conscious Henry Luce said he always wished he had grown up in a town like Oskaloosa.

I asked the man at the car rental counter which of the two routes north from Des Moines would be the more scenic. It caught him off guard. I thought of all the people who said "Iowa?" when I told them I was going there.

"Either way, all you're gonna see is corn," he said. "Lots of corn. Maybe," he added encouragingly, "some beans."

Outside Ames, the road turned straight, the landscape flat, the houses two-storied and spaced far apart. About six in the evening I parked in front of the Surf Ballroom. The smell of manure saturated the town; the descending sun skimmed the lake. I walked into the lobby, past the period furniture, the 1950s billboard announcing the Buddy Holly Winter Dance Party, and heard Edith Piaf singing "*Les Amants d'un Jour.*"

"She's one of my favorites," said Bruce Christensen. "Discovered her when I was with the Army overseas."

Christensen had been manager of the Surf Ballroom for a year and a half, ever since leaving his banking job in Punta Gorda, Florida. He had been coming every February since 1979—the twentieth anniversary of Holly's death, when the town inaugurated its annual tribute—and perhaps figured that living here would save him the trip. He had been on the executive board of the Buddy Holly Society until it went out of business. Now he devoted himself to saving the Surf.

"This was one of the great ballrooms of the Midwest," he said. "All the big bands played here—Artie Shaw, Benny Goodman. Then, in the fifties and sixties, the Midwest became the real hub of rock 'n' roll.

"We had Garrison Keillor here. Maria Holly comes up every two years." Automatically, two lines went singing through my head: "I can't remember if I cried/When I read about his widowed bride."

We walked to the edge of the lobby and gazed out over the great darkened hall. Tomorrow it would be alive with a sock hop, but tonight—with its empty stage, its vacant wooden booths, its silent dance floor—it did look like the place where the music died.

Lord Open Road's funeral was rained out on Friday.

"We were gonna bury one of our own this morning," said Steam Train Maury. "Ten years ago he was murdered in Texas by a dope-head jackroller and robbed for three dollars." He added, sensing the need for further explanation: "He was cremated. He's in an urn now."

An urn seemed awfully domestic for a hobo, a decoration on somebody's fireplace. Whereas a coffin is like a little boxcar planted in the ground.

Steam Train Maury, for his part, looked less like a hobo than the star of a made-for-TV movie about hobos. His outfit was out of the wardrobe department: heavy work boots, striped ("that's 'stripe-ED,' with two syllables") overalls, the traditional red kerchief tied around his neck, a smoothed walking stick resting across his knee. His blue Scottish eyes twinkled above a snowy-white beard. He had suffered a stroke recently and was now in the habit of giving interviews from his trailer.

"Imagine," he said dispiritedly, "a hobo with a motor home."

Outside, the rain stopped and hobos of various stripes readied for their National Convention. You think we've truly become a corporate society when you see hobos holding conventions, but men (and women) of the road have been coming to Britt since 1900. The town, in fact, courted conventioning hobos, luring them away from Chicago. (From the hog butcher of the world to the hog breeder.)

They gave them a place—"jungle" in hobo lingo—by the tracks and created a fair and parade in their honor. Now, every August, hundreds of non-hobos turn out for mulligan stew and the election of the King and Queen of the Hobos.

"I, King of the Hobos, solemnly pledge that I will uphold the constitution of the weary Willies of the Road . . . I, furthermore, promise not to throw bricks through windows, nor will I at any time commit an act that will bring shame and disgrace to my fellowmen and the Britt Chamber of Commerce."

The people of Britt opened a Hobo Museum, built a shelter in the jungle, and consecrated a corner of their cemetery for those who, like Lord Open Road, have "caught the westbound."

"Have you met Inkman yet? He's covered in tattoos. What about Gas Can Paddy? Frisco Jack, good to see ya. There's a guy you should talk to—Frisco Jack. Some of these guys, if ya see their lips movin', they're lyin'."

Alabama Hobo was giving me the lowdown.

"Virginia Slim is here. He does the singin'. I see he brought his family this year. There's Iowa Blackie—ever hear of him? Last year he had to go to court for writing his name somewhere. He writes it all the time.

"Then there's Ohio Ned—I haven't seen him yet. He was the King last year but they took the title away because of some of his behavior."

"Well," said Bus Stop Bill, "the bums he hangs around with."

Hobos are as attuned as any minority to the potency of labels. They think of themselves as travelers who are not afraid to work. "A hobo will always carry some Windex and paper towels for cleanin' windows," explained Road Hog, a fit, hardy man who rode trains—"grainers mostly"—from California to Britt this year with his dog Lobo. "Or some tools for doing yard work."

A predisposition to labor distinguishes hobos from tramps, who will travel but won't work, and bums, who are too lazy to do either.

Men in blue jeans and red neckerchiefs and dark floppy hats crisscrossed the jungle. "Most of these guys aren't real hobos," said Bus Stop Bill. Alabama Hobo claimed he hadn't ridden in years, though he did estimate he covered about 30,000 miles before getting married and settling down.

The tracks were quiet, but an old boxcar, scribbled with chalk, stood on transplanted rails off to the side. Iowa Blackie, a sensitive, shaggy-haired young man, sat in the open doorway, hawking his poetry pamphlets. A group of young men in *Hobo Times* T-shirts chatted by a tree. Lobo scampered about, a red hobo kerchief tied around his neck. The musician Rag Man wandered by the campfire, peddling his hobo tapes—"The best forty-five minutes of music you'll never hear on the radio." The titles of his songs—"On the Road to Hobo Oblivion," "It's a Good Ol' Train Hoppin' Day"—bore a striking similarity to the titles of Blackie's poems. Two grain elevators—the cathedrals of the Midwest—rose in the background.

"We're like yuppie hobos," said Carroll Wheeler, a personable young man with a blue-and-white striped railroad man's cap on his head and a red kerchief around his neck and a pregnant wife by his side. "We have an address. To run for Hobo King, you have to have been without an address for three years."

Wheeler pulled out a business card that read: "The Piano Doctor—Piano Tuning, Regulating and Repair." The address was Musselwhite Ave., Orlando.

"I started riding trains," he said, "when I was in high school in Tennessee. My granddad had worked for Great Northern. My first ride was from Chattanooga to Birmingham when I was seventeen. It became cheap entertainment in college."

Even then, riding to Knoxville and Atlanta and Birmingham, he rarely came across hobos. "One time I met a guy going home for Christmas. And I ran across Texas Slim in Knoxville once." His last long ride, from Chicago to California, was in 1989, when he and his wife were on their way to Guam to teach for a year (he math and computers; she biology and chemistry).

"There's one guy here who's still out riding," he said. "His name's Cardboard. That's him walking over there." He pointed to a tall man dressed conservatively in a dark cap and dress slacks and carrying a briefcase.

"I have a lot of respect for him. Twenty years ago he gave up smoking and drinking. He's seventy-one now and getting forgetful—sometimes he hops on the wrong train. It took him thirty-one days to get here from L.A. It should have taken him only seven. But he knows how to live on the road. He's a Dumpster diver."

"A what?"

"He dives into Dumpsters and comes up with things."

The history of hobos goes back to the days following the Civil War. In fact, the etymology of the word "hobo" is sometimes traced to surviving soldiers who would tell strangers they passed that they were "homeward bound." This eventually became shortened to "ho-bo."

Another theory involves migratory workers who, because of the hoes they carried, were called "hoe boys." In *The American Language,* H. L. Mencken offered the improbable case of the word deriving from the Japanese word for "side"—*ho*—"and meaning, in the plural, all sides or everywhere."

Mencken accumulated an impressive collection of hobo argot and devoted several pages to it in his monumental work. "To steal washing off the line is to *gooseberry* it. The discourse heard in the mission-halls is *angel-food,* and the bum who listens to it is *mission-stiff.* A Catholic priest is a *buck* or *Galway,* and the Salvation Army is *Sally Ann.*"

In *A History of the Hobos, Tramps and Other Vagabonds* (a slim paperback book easily slipped into a hobo pocket), Steam Train Maury writes that World War I added large numbers of hobos to the ranks, and estimates that 90 percent of hobos are veterans. He believes that while the Depression put a lot of transients on the rails, only a small percentage of them ever became hobos. "It takes over four years steady on the road to become a journeyman hobo," he writes. "He must be a naturalist, knowing all the greens, herbs, mushrooms, barks, berries, grains, roots and people."

Cardboard sat at a picnic table signing his autograph for a ten-year-old girl. He hunched in concentration, printing unsteady letters in a laborious scrawl.

"You're from New York?" he asked a man when finished. It was a barked question, lacking in curiosity. "I was in Port Jervis once. I hit on a priest for money and he said, 'Here's two dollars. Go down there and get your bottle.' He knew. They're real people, priests. Most of 'em."

Up close, Cardboard's somewhat dapper appearance revealed its flaws. The briefcase, which contained his kitchen, was scuffed and battered. "Got this out of a Dumpster," he muttered. A button was missing on his dark plaid shirt, opening up a disconcertingly pale square of soft downy belly. His tanned, surprisingly smooth face was specked with white stubble. When somebody sat down next to him with an ear of corn, he said, offended, as if he had been offered it: "I can't eat that stuff. Ain't got no teeth."

A young man asked how many trips he'd been on. "I don't know," he growled. "I just go. I don't call 'em trips. I just get up and leave some goddamn place.

"There used to be some good places. Not anymore. They been destroyed. Drugs. Long hairs. Crap-makers. This'll probably be the last time I come here. It's gotten so's you don't know if you're talkin' to a goddamn hobo or not."

Oklahoma Slim was reminiscing in the stands set up for the evening concert.

"I had forty, forty-five years of road time. Very few people here can brag of that." His voice was soft, almost childlike, and had a soothing cadence.

"I haven't been inside the boxcar. I'm afraid if I get back in one I'm gonna like it so much I'll wanna go back. But I'm gonna ride one more time. Wyoming to Seattle—that's my best bet. On the Union Pacific.

"I put out a little newsletter. *The Hobo.* And I tell it like it is. This *Hobo Times* is too smooth—they never tell you about the dangers. As a hobo, you always have to protect yourself. The homeless—they don't know what to do, how to act.

"But the hobos, we've always taken care of each other. You might fight with a guy today, but if he's sick, you take care of him, and if he dies, you bury him.

"There's a different attitude among hobos about dying," he continued. "Road Hog says he just wants to crawl off into the bushes and have nobody know. I already got my tombstone back in Seattle. It says: 'Oklahoma Slim—Play the hand that's dealt you.' There was some problem with that. The cemetery committee wanted something like 'Jesus Saves.' Now, I have nothing against Jesus. If he saves, that's fine. But I wanted my saying on my tomb. And I won. 'Cause I paid.

"It's sixty feet from the tracks where the Burlington Northern runs. It used to be the big G [Great Northern]. And when it passes I want the boys to stick their heads out the windows and say"—he raised his soft voice to a boyish cry—"'Hi, Slim!'"

Half a mile away, in Evergreen Cemetery, a biker stood in front of the National Hobo Memorial, his head bowed and his hat in his hand. The tall cross, made from railway ties, was draped in burlap.

"That's a symbol of humility," he explained. "The wreath of twigs"—which hung from the center, like a crown of thorns—"is a symbol of hardship."

Small stone plaques poked through the grass, each engraved with a name: Slow-Motion Shorty, Connecticut Slim, Pennsylvania Kid, and, already waiting, Lord Open Road. At the base of the cross stood a rusted milk can planted with flowers. And flanking them both were two small flags: the Stars and Stripes and the red hobo kerchief.

Thirty-six hours with hobos and I had the urge to move. I got in my car and headed east, not stopping till I reached Decorah.

A Nordic Lounge crowned a hill on the outskirts of town; wine-red *Velkommen* banners hung from Water Street lampposts. But in the town bakery, something was amiss.

"What do you have that's Norwegian?" I asked.

"Not much," said the young woman behind the counter. "We only make Norwegian specialties for the Nordic fest. They don't sell that well the rest of the year. We do have *lefse,*" she added. "It's a flat bread made with potato. But we buy that from somewhere else."

Down the block sat the handsome red-brick Norwegian-American museum next door to the elegant Dayton House café.

The Gnome Book Store carried this title: *The Last Word on Lefse.* The Decorah Hatchery advertised "Quality Chicks."

About fifteen miles south I turned onto a dirt road to see the World's Smallest Cathedral. Set in a shady hollow beside a farm, it was not gimmicky, as I had expected, but pastoral and infinitely meek. A cardboard sign read: "The church is always open; please close the door." Inside, two small pews sat on either side of an abbreviated aisle. The silence—an ecclesiastical hush on top of the rural stillness—was as moving as a Bach chorale.

Route 150, which I rejoined refreshed, dipped and curved its way south past Eldorado and deep green fields of ripening corn. I passed the strawberry statue in Strawberry Point (raised in front of the public library) and arrived in Dyersville at dusk.

Following the sign to the "Field of Dreams," I was immersed in stalks. They seemed to close in on me along the dusty road, like converging armies of the night. I made a turn down a crunching lane, driving slowly. It was not only the gravel that reduced my speed, but the uneasy feeling that I was intruding onto private property.

I pulled into a dirt lot, my headlights flattened against thick corn rows. In the dying light, the house sat dark, as familiar, in its way, as Norman Bates's house in Hitchcock's *Psycho.* It too crowned a hill above a commonplace theater of weird goings-on. (And didn't its occupant also hear voices? And have a preoccupation with a long deceased parent?)

As I walked closer, the theater—the field—came into view. A father was pitching underhand to his children, while others ran the bases after imaginary hits. Thoughts of Hitchcock faded with the light.

It was a scene almost Rockwellian in its simplistic perfection: the neat cluster of red and white farm buildings, the flowing green fields of ripening corn, and there, carved out of a once-fertile corner, the cozy symmetry of a Little League diamond.

The Big Themes fairly shouted in the darkness: The national pastime in the American heartland. Our agrarian and sporting lives, work and play, melded into an easy green harmony, one field effortlessly becoming another. The rugged individualism of the farmer (hitter) working for the good of the community (team) as he pulls down the shutters and closes his souvenir stand for the night.

Dan Lansing's farm has to be one of the most curious of all the world's tourist attractions. It's a Hollywood fantasy built on top of an Iowa reality. Not only is the field a fabrication, but so are the white picket fence and the wrap-around porch. And the air-conditioning. "I wouldn't have put it in myself," Lansing said. It's a place for all those people who have gone to Atlanta looking for Tara.

Like *Gone With the Wind, Field of Dreams* began as a book (*Shoeless Joe*) written by W. P. Kinsella when he was enrolled in the Writers' Workshop at the University of Iowa. It did for corn what Don Quixote did for windmills. But it took the movies to make a souvenir vendor out of an Iowa farmer.

Offered at the stand, just down from the barn, were *Field of Dream* T-shirts, baseballs, caps, and cups. There were movie videos and old White Sox jerseys. In a rural mailbox plopped next to the field, small capsules of dirt sat ready for the taking, put there by the family that owns left field. "Donations," read the notice, "are appreciated."

A man from Missouri stood in the field gazing in the darkness. "For being a commercial venture," he said, "it has a mystique."

And a continuity. Like the characters in the movie, who wanted to relive the past, the tourists in Dyersville want to believe the fiction. On Sundays in summer, local men come out of the corn, dressed in vintage White Sox uniforms, and play catch with the tourists.

"Hey, is this a movie?" you can imagine one of the startled visitors asking.

No, it's America.

★ ★ ★

Dubuque had no rooms on Saturday night. Dubuque. The receptionist at the Julien Inn downtown sent me out to Michael Brennan's house.

"Thought it was flat, didn't you?" he asked as I came in the door. Actually, I was more surprised to find it booked.

"People come here for the gambling—the riverboats and the dog races," Brennan explained. A truck driver, he had moved from Chicago to get away from the crime.

"The church bells will wake you in the morning," he said, leaving me in my turn-of-the-century room. "This is a Catholic town. If there's a good view in Dubuque, it's owned by the Catholics."

The next morning I boarded the *Casino Belle.* "Business had been good," said the college sophomore summering as a riverboat waitress, "until the other boat started across the river. They have dollar drinks and no limit for betting. Here the limit's $200. But," she added sweetly, "we're friendlier."

We eased away from the dock and down the great river. Two young Polish women, spending a month in Chicago, sunbathed on the top deck. They didn't gamble; they had never read *Huckleberry Finn;* the Mississippi was nothing but a lazy brown interlude in a foreign summer.

A retired couple from Indiana sat in the shade.

"So I guess you don't gamble," I said.

"We already shot our wad," said the impish woman, "with the dogs last night and the slot machines here."

By mid-afternoon I was on the road, heading away from the Mississippi and back to the land. It was a relief to be surrounded by corn again. The river towns had a shady, profligate feel—endemic to all ports—that dissipated the deeper into the country you went. Here life was reduced to its simplest arithmetic: a farmhouse (dwarfed by shade trees), a barn, a silo or two, a pen for livestock and, spreading out from all sides, vast, undulating fields of corn.

That's all there was, for miles, until the silver dome of another silo, glinting in the sun, signaled the reworking of the same equation.

The repetitiveness was comforting, not boring, and the symmetry of planting reminded me of the inscription beneath a Grant Wood lithograph in the Dubuque Museum of Art: "His hard work," it said of the farmer depicted in the drawing, "has mastered the land yet has maintained its beauty."

Wood, who is buried in Anamosa, established a short-lived artists' colony in neighboring Stone City. The town, a dusty tan collection of limestone buildings, looked much as it must have in the 1940s, when student artists slept in ice wagons and scandalized locals by skinny-dipping in the river. The Stone City General Store, the only business in town, was really a subterranean bar, with live entertainment, a red-bandannaed Lab named Jake, and delicious tacos. It was filled with longhaired beer drinkers in T-shirts and jeans

"I'm running on two cylinders these days," a man at the bar complained to his friend. And the friend replied: "Welcome to the corn patch."

The following morning, at the Herbert Hoover Presidential Library-Museum, I found an interesting retelling of the familiar rags-to-riches story, as well as lesser-known facts about the thirty-first president. I learned, for instance, that he had once recommended that the batter in baseball be given four strikes instead of three.

A sign in front of a luncheonette in Durant read:

CH RITE & ORNGS—$2.75.

The waitress inside gave only partial clarification. "The special today is cheese rite with onion rings."

"What's a cheese rite?" I asked.

"Do you know what a maid rite is?"

"No."

"Do you know what a sloppy joe is?" She was slowly losing hope.

"Yes!"

"Well, it's like a sloppy joe but without the sloppy part."

Driving down a dirt road, I passed a farm with all the classic attributes—visual and olfactory—and a sign nailed to a tree advertising, as if we needed the adjectives, "Farm fresh eggs."

Toward evening, in the parking lot of Eldon Congregational Church, I conferred with some parishioners about the town's most famous house.

"Just go up this street and take a left," Roger Archer said. "That's where the *American Gothic* house is."

Then I asked about the town's most famous son. "Was Tom Arnold known when he lived around here?"

"Just as a goofball," Archer said. "For drawing attention to himself. He once walked from Ottumwa to Eldon in his underwear to raise money for college."

Oskaloosa, which I entered the next morning, was a Time-Life vision of an American small town. A leafy square with a pretty bandstand and Herman Davison—once "the orneriest guy in Oskaloosa"—sitting on a green bench under a balmy blue sky.

"When I moved here with my parents," said the elderly man in overalls, "there were hitching posts all around this square. It used to be a pretty good place. You could sleep here in the square all night if you wanted. But now you have to be out by eleven. 'Cause of drugs."

The same thing Cardboard had complained about. So Oskaloosa was not all that different from the rest of the country. And yet . . .

Over at the post office, an Asian woman was perplexed by postage. The man waiting behind her leaned back smiling: "We're not in any hurry, are we?" The woman behind him said, "You can just saunter through a day like this." And then they started comparing notes on their gardens.

# 16

# *The Cultural Desert*

The absurdist skyline first appears in the window of your plane as it taxis toward the terminal. A pyramid, a castle, a pastiche of Manhattan, interspersed by towers more conventionally shaped but with the same fey air. The structures stand not in a cluster, as in a normal city, but in a straight row, a line-up. ("Officer, it was the one on the left that took my money. I'd recognize that drawbridge anywhere.") The whole place—not just the Candyland turrets of Excalibur, but also the glass box of MGM—has a temporal, cardboard quality, heightened by the surrounding desert and, off in the distance, the undefiled mountains.

Las Vegas is the first city in the world built to the specifications of a board game. To walk along the Strip is to become a child again, rolling the dice, and moving your piece from one surprise to another. Stroll across a replica of the Brooklyn Bridge. Hop on a boardwalk roller coaster. Watch pirate ships fire salvos across the water. Visit the cuddly white tigers.

The city of course wasn't always so puerile. How could it be in the West? The Anasazi constituted the first civilized presence around A.D. 1000. It is interesting that of all the motifs adopted by the city's hotels—Egyptian, Brazilian, Japanese, Burmese, Roman, Venetian, Parisian, New Orleansian, New Yorker, Western, Arthurian, Debbie Reynoldsian—Native American is the one conspicuously absent, a rare Las Vegas concession to political correctness.

By 1845 the valley had become a popular camp for travelers on the Old Spanish Trail. Ten years later the Mormons arrived, followed by the miners (first lead, then silver), and then the railroad. It wasn't until the early 1930s, when Nevada legalized casino gambling, that Las Vegas took on its current role.

But it was hardly a theme park. Downtown, at the northern stretches of the Strip, you can still get a hint of the old gambling town, despite the ceiling of lights constructed over Fremont Street for the "Fremont Street Experience." (Light bulbs are Las Vegas's kudzu.) At the corner of Main and Fremont stands the Golden Gate—the city's oldest hotel (erected in 1906), the birthplace of the Giant Shrimp Cocktail (introduced in 1959), and now perhaps America's only bed-and-breakfast casino. In the dark wood bar a picture shows a succession of mayors gathered with two "Saucy Shrimp Mermaids" to celebrate the sale of the twenty-five millionth cocktail (on September 19, 1991), while old men on stools stare into sundae glasses pinkened by tiny crustaceans.

Gambling eventually took Vegas out of the Wild West and made it debonair. In the early 1960s the Rat Pack—Frank, Dean, Sammy, Peter, and Joey—turned it into their own personal pleasure ground. At Bonanza Gifts you can buy that picture of the five of them standing in front of the Sands marquee in their white shirts and thin ties and tightly tailored jackets.

"It was a small town when I was growing up here," said James Stanford. He was standing in the Smallworks Gallery in the art district which occupies, as all art districts must, a collection of old buildings in a rundown section of town. "I remember going to my allergy doctor and seeing Phil Silvers, Danny Thomas, Frank Sinatra. It was kind of a charming community."

The Sands was destroyed a few years ago. "It's a huge celebration when something comes down," Stanford explained. "They usually do it at night, because it's more spectacular." He pointed to a series of snapshots on the wall that captured the moment.

"André Breton loved Las Vegas," Stanford said of the author of *Manifestoes of Surrealism*. "It was the opposite of everything he hated—the old stodgy buildings of Europe that didn't let anything new go up. Las Vegas is a pop city. Nothing reflects our culture better than Las Vegas."

Beside him, leaned against the gallery wall, was a six-foot-tall swizzle stick, painted banana yellow.

The antonym for Las Vegas is sentimentality. The city is a blackboard on which the last lesson is erased, in one cool stroke, to make way for the next. All cities move with the times, but only Las Vegas destroys the evidence of a previous existence. After the Sands—Sinatra, martinis, tuxedos, dames—came Circus, Circus.

Opened in 1968, with acrobats and clowns, it signaled the beginning of a new era, one that would turn Las Vegas—of all places—from a playground for adults into one for children. While their parents played the slots, the kids laughed at Bozo. Gaming's answer to Montessori.

Disneyization eventually kicked in; the new casino hotels borrowed legendary themes and mimicked famous landmarks: the Eiffel Tower, the Campanile di San Marco, the Statue of Liberty. The synonym for Las Vegas—even more than glitz—is dissonance.

> *I'm about so many different things, but ever since I got my transplants you run into men who want the icing before the cake. Everything today seems even more superficial and, while there are some great people in the business, there are plenty more who are greedy and devious.*
>
> —An actress in the XXX-rated Fantasy Review, quoted in the *Las Vegas Review-Journal*

The city is changing—not just in terms of fractured syntax and metaphors—and it isn't. The same day this thespian was quoted,

Andre Agassi played in a doubles match at UNLV where, later that evening, theater critic Robert Brustein spoke on the "Decline of Serious Culture." Another story in that day's paper reported that Sunset Station casino had inaugurated the world's first slot machine with an exercise bike pedal.

Bellagio heralded the city's next phase: imposing classicism. It was no less counterfeit, but it was a fakery that was soothing.

It was named after a town in the Italian Lake District, and built at a cost of 1.6 billion dollars (making it the most expensive hotel ever constructed). It rises thirty-six stories on a manmade hill overlooking a "lake" rimmed by faux-Italian villas. Not even the sidewalk escapes its clutches: Pedestrians walk along a curved stone balustrade under old-fashioned lampposts fixed with speakers from which romantic songs fall night and day.

Inside, there is the traditional flow of lobby into casino, but the former is distinguished by a ceiling stuck with over two thousand large, colorful, hand-blown glass flowers. The floor's marble, "Colonial Dream," was cut in Italy though it comes from Sri Lanka. Behind the lobby, in the old-fashioned atrium, a grandiose floral display reflects the season. (It takes 150 workers 70 hours—they tell you on the tour—to change the 14,000 flowers quarterly.) The space provides an agreeable setting for those waiting in line to enter the museum of modern and Impressionist paintings from the Mirage Resorts' chairman Steve Wynn's collection. Inside, however, the most impressive thing is the silence; not only are you away from the eternal casino clatter, you are in a room where people are too busy listening to audio wands to utter a word. It is the quietest place in all of Las Vegas.

The hotel overflows with people. Every visitor to Las Vegas comes to the Bellagio to have a look around, check the place out, see—according to some observers—the future. Michael Jordan and Bruce Willis, they tell you on the tour that drops names as easily as numbers, have even spent the night.

Most don't. They wander through the casino, step into the designer shops (housed, richly, in the "villas") and gawk at the backlit jellyfish that float behind the sushi bar of Shintaro like mobile works of art. Some buy tickets for *O*, the Cirque du Soleil production that, in Bellagio's endless quest for originality, is built around water (*eau*). The wealthier ones dine in Picasso under original Picassos—the artistic equivalent of having your cake and eating it too. The lumpen proletariat head for the buffet—the Bellagio is not so proud as to dispense with this old gem—where dissonance (fettuccine Alfredo, spring rolls, tacos) arrives on a dinner plate.

This is the new Las Vegas: Sinatra's old high life with a soupçon of high culture.

The more time you spend in Las Vegas, the more clearly you see its similarity to a cruise.

Both cruising and Vegas are billion-dollar industries created for the consumption of leisure time. This shared fundamental irony—of a great business built around the concept of vacation—envelops a second: While both operations are run with Wharton School pragmatism, they are each founded on a fantasy—romance for cruising, riches for Las Vegas. Between them, they traffic in two of humankind's oldest dreams.

For the perceived fulfillment of these dreams, they create self-contained environments in the middle of a vast emptiness (the ocean and the desert). And this nothingness—of water and sand—serves as a buffer to keep the world out, allowing them to erect their own alternative reality whose illusive character is trumpeted by the names of the ships and casinos: Mirage, *Celebrity,* Tropicana, *Majesty,* Riviera, *Paradise.* (The liberal use of sentimental imagery makes them almost indistinguishable from one another, though, in an interesting twist, only the casinos have kept alive the old Cunard tradition of names ending in "a.")

And both environments depend for their greatest effects on a blurring of time: Just as the clockless, windowless casino leaves you ignorant as to the hour of the day, the work-and-TV-free routine of a cruise keeps you uncertain as to the days of the week. You exist in a kind of limbo, a landscape-less other world, with its own particular rules or lack thereof.

Both cruising and Vegas come out of upper-class European traditions— on some ships you can still feel something of the old *Normandie,* just as in a few Vegas casinos you can still catch a faint echo of Monte Carlo—that were successfully democratized for Middle America. Not only their successes, but the paths they took to them, have been remarkably similar. At the beginning, they each enjoyed a small and specific clientele (retirees and gamblers). They then broadened their bases, attracting couples, singles, newlyweds (both serving as popular wedding venues) until, more recently, they both began aggressively courting families. They entered a juvenilia phase (water slides and roller coasters) and then inched toward a kind of sophistication. Artworks decorate Celebrity ships, just as they do the Bellagio. Celebrity chefs now turn out gourmet meals in the hallowed precincts of the all-you-can-eat buffet.

And in the last few years the two of them have expanded beyond all expectations—with Las Vegas becoming the fastest growing city in the United States and cruising the fasting growing segment of the travel industry. The only structures on earth that can compare with the mammoth new cruise ships—in over-the-top one-upmanship—are Las Vegas's casino-hotels.

The experience of visiting Las Vegas is also similar to that of taking a cruise, the only difference being that the former makes for a better movie premise. The various casinos, like the different cruise lines, each cater to a particular type of clientele—with the Desert Inn being the rough equivalent of Holland America; Caesar's Palace, Royal Caribbean; and Circus Circus, Carnival.

Nevertheless, you encounter in Las Vegas the same overall uniformity that you find on a spectrum of cruises. There is a good amount of jewelry, on men as well as on women, and dramatic décolletage. Tattoos are more and more common. Physical fitness is generally not a high priority. Faces present a familiarly perplexed and flaccid look. Casinos have the same built-in confusion in their layouts as ships do, and they bestow an identical freedom from exertion. Everything is right there for you: hotel, restaurants, shops, bars, clubs, shows. It's not simply that you don't have to think, you hardly need to move. (Which explains why there are not a lot of intellectuals or triathletes wandering around.) The two conscious human activities that most approximate death are lying in a deck chair and staring at a slot machine, and a Las Vegas vacation consists of long periods of gambling interspersed by short stints of sunbathing, while a cruise is the opposite.

Eating and drinking also take up large amounts of time—both places being famous for binges. The amount of alcohol consumed in a week in Las Vegas is probably comparable to that downed in the same period on cruises. Drinking is the one thing you can do while supine by the pool, or planted at a blackjack table, and it is the perfect means for forgetting you're nowhere.

And the people gathered to serve America's footsore—in Las Vegas as on cruise ships—make up an impressive mosaic. Take a dozen cabs in Vegas and you hear a dozen stories in a dozen accents. The Afghan approves of the climate—"My boy always sick in Salt Lake City—here, never"—but not the gambling. The Asian American boasts of how he bought a house, with cash, after years of renting in San Diego. "They have sunsets here too," he informs you. The Hungarian hates all the casinos—"I lost too much money in them"—and is not terribly fond of Dennis Miller. "I don't like his attitude. I tell you something else: I don't think he's very funny. He had a few good moments, on *Saturday Night Live,* but now he's nothing. In fact, I don't think he's funny at all. I think he's basically unhappy. In fact, I think he's a very unhappy person."

Riding in these cabs away from the Strip, you think you are in Phoenix or Houston or any other faceless Sun Belt city: the same generation-less one-story houses, the recent yards, the small trees, the spotless shopping centers, the Starbucks and Barnes & Noble. Then you see a jogger coming down the sidewalk in boxing gloves.

# 17

# *Minnesota Twins*

Minnesota excels at producing unlikely pairs. In the field of literature, there is the dissimilar duo of F. Scott Fitzgerald and Sinclair Lewis (Riviera and prairie); in politics, Eugene McCarthy and Harold Stassen; in popular music, Bob Dylan and the singer occasionally known as Prince. The illustrators LeRoy Neiman and Charles Schulz are both Minnesotan, as are the sports heroes Greg LeMond and Bronko Nagurski. Even the Twin Cities—Minneapolis and St. Paul—have unique personalities, as distinct from each other as the two American icons to emerge from Minnesota in the twentieth century: Charles Lindbergh and Judy Garland. Currently the two celebrities most associated with the state—grandly continuing the tradition of dual personalities—are Garrison Keillor and Jesse Ventura.

As odd couples go, this one seems classic. Keillor is a writer with a nationally syndicated radio show, the latest in a long line of Midwestern humorists that stretches from George Ade and James Thurber to Ambrose Bierce and Mark Twain. He is a complex man who has brought religion into the fiercely secular world of popular culture while wryly trumpeting the cause of the chronically shy. Ventura, a Navy SEAL turned professional wrestler, was elected governor in 1998.

Yet there are more things linking them than a shared home state. Both are physically imposing men, standing well over six feet tall, and both speak in sonorous, signature voices. Both took noms de plume (or guerre) for careers in entertainment—

Garrison having been born Gary, and Jesse Ventura, Jim Janos. Similarly, both created a folksy persona—the homespun raconteur, the bombastic brawler—that played well in theaters and arenas and over time attracted a loyal following. Each adopted in the process a sartorial trademark, the red socks peeking out from under Keillor's pants cuffs being the shy person's equivalent of a feather boa.

And neither is particularly fond of journalists.

For most of Ventura's term as governor, the two men were locked in a war of words. It began soon after the election, when Keillor wrote a mocking essay for *Time* magazine. Ventura followed, shortly after, by suggesting an end to state financing for public radio. The new governor quickly became a weekly object of ridicule on *A Prairie Home Companion*—a heretofore harmless collection of music and skits—and the subject of a Keillor book. The feud attracted the attention of *Doonesbury* and ruffled, at least for non-Minnesotans, the placid surface of a state known for its numerous lakes.

Minneapolis and St. Paul are not the twins many think they are, connected at the hip by a bridge (like Philadelphia and Camden). Cross the Mississippi in downtown Minneapolis and you arrive not in St. Paul but in Old Minneapolis. Our Lady of Lourdes church rises on its hill behind Nye's Bar & Polonaise Room, which huddles just down the street from Kramarczuk Sausage Company & Deli. For St. Paul you should get on the freeway and, as if you were going from Burbank to Pasadena, head southeast for half a dozen unexceptional miles.

The Capitol sits alone on a hill overlooking downtown, skirted by rolling green lawns and animated by a golden chariot at the base of its dome. It could be the seat of government for a medium-sized country. Inside, the echoing corridors are hung with oil paintings of governors past: Floyd Bjerstjerne Olson, Edward Thye, Luther W. Youngdahl, Harold Stassen. It's difficult to make the proper chronological progression from these stern and provident faces to the silkenly shaven head of Ventura.

I made my way to his office one Wednesday morning. The governor was running late, a staff member told me, and first needed to address a group of representatives from various governmental departments. I was more than welcome to watch.

I stood in the back of the ornate reception room, already feeling guilty for taking precious time out of his hectic schedule. (He had just returned home the previous night from a trip to California.) He appeared through a side door, dressed in a brown double-breasted suit, dark-blue shirt, and tie. I had not realized how tall he really is. He moved a little stiffly, looking vaguely like a cross between Lurch and Uncle Fester. In his brief remarks, he explained that his managerial style was one of delegating. He spoke with his usual mild bluster, but seemed ill-at-ease, as if he realized, underneath it all, how agonizingly far out of his realm he was. I imagined him going home in the evening, taking off his tie and plopping down on the sofa with enormous relief at the luxury of being himself again.

He answered questions for a few minutes, deferring occasionally to aides, and when there was a lull, and the session seemed over, he asked: "Nobody wants to know about the Hollywood trip?" And everyone laughed, with the stunned relief that follows a joke at a funeral.

"I spent five or ten minutes talking with Nicolas Cage," he said in that deep boreal drawl that sounds as if it should be emanating from an animated character. "Real nice guy. I went to Elton John's party. His party was in support of AIDS, so I thought that was a good party to go to. I talked with Nick Nolte. How many of you saw *Down and Out in Beverly Hills?* Remember the scene with the dog food? The dog food was real." I was beginning to feel less guilty.

"I was a presenter at the Spirit Awards, for independent films. I got to give out the Truer than Fiction award. I thought 'how real.' Because many people thought my election was Truer than Fiction. Though Garrison will do it after the fact."

He was much less jovial ten minutes later when he stared at me across an empty desk in his corner office. (He had been quoted in *Newsweek* magazine a few months earlier saying he'd installed a special bumper on his SUV for running over reporters.) Something about the bald head, the dark shirt, the double-breasted suit—his impatient rocking back and forth in his chair—kindled unpleasant images from St. Paul's gangster past. I asked him (since I was ostensibly there to write a travel story) where he would take me in Minnesota if he had the time. I was hoping for an armchair tour of personal favorites, but all I got was a standard listing of Chamber of Commerce highlights: Stillwater, on the St. Croix River; the lakes; the Boundary Waters; Duluth ("the San Francisco of the Midwest" he said); the Mall of America ("It's like the Eighth Wonder of the World").

"But I don't want to say one place is better than any other," he interjected at one point. Two of his handlers were in the room with us.

"Like on Letterman," I said, remembering his statement that of the Twin Cities he preferred Minneapolis because, for one thing, he was always getting lost in St. Paul, the streets having been laid out by drunken Irishmen.

"That doesn't worry me!" he snapped. It was the conversational equivalent of a body slam.

After leaving, I drove up past the Italian-Renaissance hulk of the Cathedral, as noble on its mound as the Capitol, two lone sentinels—in an elevated equilibrium of church and state—watching protectively over the city. Coming around the corner, I found myself on Summit Avenue, St. Paul's pride, said to be the nation's longest stretch of inhabited Victorian houses. (Although F. Scott Fitzgerald once described it as "a museum of architectural failures.") His house, a handsome, turreted, three-story brownstone was at 599. While I was taking pictures, a neighbor came out onto his stoop.

"An elderly woman used to live there," he said. "And she'd let people come in and look around. Fitzgerald had his room up on the third floor, I think. She had a guest book that had some interesting names in it like William Saroyan. But she died, and I don't know what happened to the book."

He himself was not a big fan. "I read *The Great Gatsby* once. Not my kind of story—a man who gives up everything for love."

I mentioned I'd just come from seeing his governor; the remark on Letterman came up. "I'm Irish myself," he said, then, turning on a heavy brogue, "and I've touched nary a drop since I was twelve."

It was in this house that Fitzgerald, returning from military service, revised his first novel, *This Side of Paradise.* Years later, in *The Crack-Up,* he would write: "The test of a first-rate intelligence is the ability to hold two opposed ideas in the mind at the same time, and still retain the ability to function."

I cruised the neighborhood. A block north ran Portland Avenue, where Keillor lives, and a block south stretched Grand, with its pretty shops, steamy coffeehouses, and aromatic bakeries offering free samples of focaccia and potato bread. Inside the Tavern on Grand hung a picture of Mikhail Gorbachev, one of the more illustrious of the restaurant's numerous walleye customers.

The cozy streets supported the claims that St. Paul was more provincial, less dynamic than Minneapolis. There is something to be said for a lack of dynamism. North on Snelling things turned grittier—secondhand clothing shops and ethnic restaurants—and then, heading west on Larpenteur, I found myself in the middle of farmland. The School of Agriculture, a sign informed me, of the University of Minnesota.

In the evening, back in Minneapolis, I walked to dinner without venturing outside. Descending in the hotel elevator, I cut through the parking garage and found the famous Skywalk, which I followed imperviously over the traffic on Seventh Street, through a mini mall (most of the shops closed, though it was barely past six o'clock), back out across Marquette Avenue before arriving, Alice-in-Wonderland-like, in the Crystal Court of the IDS Center. I took the down escalator—was that Mary Richards on her way up?—and found the restaurant Aquavit, its doors opened not to the street but to the climate-controlled atrium. I was adrift in a city turned in on itself.

A branch of the New York restaurant, the place had a clean design and elegant lighting. My smorgasbord appetizer arrived in bite-sized morsels of Asian artistry. The only thing that kept it from being fully trendy was the discordant note of server friendliness.

Anoka—"Halloween Capital of the World"—lies about twenty miles north of Minneapolis, a small town turned suburb at the convergence of the Rum and Mississippi Rivers.

Keillor's family lived across the Mississippi in Brooklyn Park (the city, coincidentally, where Jesse Ventura served as mayor). But when he writes of his hometown he means Anoka: Downing Jewelry, the Anoka Dairy, the Pumpkin Bowl at Goodrich Field, in which every Halloween the Anoka Tornadoes would play their final football game.

"I remember Anoka High School," he wrote in *Preview* magazine in 1974, "as a long hallway, lined with brown lockers and brown ceramic tile, the hard fluorescent lights: the purgatory that prepares us for middle-class life. That was in the fifties.

"Back then the standards were exact and covered everything, down to the inflection in your voice and how you carried your books. Everything about me was wrong: I had the wrong shoes, the wrong clothes (my cousin Roger's), the wrong parents, and it all came down to money. We didn't have enough money.

". . . Our family was Plymouth Brethren, and Lord, how I wanted to be Episcopalian. Even Congregational."

Looked at in the context of high school, Ventura is the jock who never cracked a book and got elected class president anyway. Keillor, turning the tables another 180 degrees, is the gawky nerd who's decided to pick on the bully.

The school still stands—a flat-roofed, yellow-brick building—but it is now the Fred Moore Middle School. (An eminently replaceable name.) The graceful Carnegie library, where Keillor discovered *The New Yorker* magazine, has been superseded by a boxy Norwest Bank. Swedetown still exists, though the locals' current gathering spot is Hardee's. The white-pillared mansion whose basement served as a gym for the junior high now houses the Anoka County Historical Society. "The first place I took a shower with other people," Keillor wrote to the Society in 1988 on *New Yorker* stationery, "a disturbing event in a boy's life."

The Society was a godsend. In the Chamber of Commerce on Main Street there had been nothing of the town's most famous son, though a signed and framed jersey from Warren Moon hung on the wall. Across the street at the Avant Garden coffeehouse, the young waitress had never heard of Garrison Keillor. She had a tattoo on her left forearm and an innocent voice. She was from northern Minnesota, a fan of the governor.

"I like what he's trying to change."

"Such as?"

She thought for about ten seconds. "Well, he doesn't want us to have to pay for those tabs you put on your license plate."

At the Kozy Corner Eatery—home of the Killebrew Float—the owner's father said he didn't care much for Keillor. "He's a bit of an eccentric. I've got too much in my head to deal with eccentricities. He's a little weird. He looks a little weird too. But he fits the bill well. It's all part of his vernacular."

I'd stopped in Hans Bakery, just down from the old high school, and admired the almond tea rings and wild rice breads. I'd taken a picture of the water tower above Goodrich Field. For lunch at August Hope I'd been served a delicious soup by a young Vietnamese woman, who caused me to ponder the curious passage from Indochina to Anoka. (Two opposed ideas.) And then I knocked on the door of the Historical Society.

The attractive woman who answered was Jean Legg Smith, who had been a classmate of Keillor's at Anoka High. In fact, it was her father's bus that he rode to school. "He was very tall, of course. We all knew he was smart. He sat behind me in Mr. Faust's history class. I always," she said smiling, "wanted to call him Dr. Faust."

She went and brought me a box of writings by and about Keillor. There were magazine cover stories detailing his personal history: born August 7, 1942, father a mail clerk who moonlighted as a carpenter, the third of six children, brought up in a strict religious household—no dancing, no movies, church twice on Sunday. There were gossip columns buzzing about the romantic life, including the twenty-fifth Anoka High School reunion at which he again met the Danish exchange student, Ulla Skaerved, whom he soon married and followed to Denmark. There were articles covering his radio career: his rise from host of a drive-time music program in 1968 to creator of *A Prairie Home Companion*—which was first broadcast from Macalester College in 1974, moved to the World Theater in 1978, went to national syndication in 1980 and now—at the refurbished Fitzgerald Theater in downtown St. Paul—is carried by about 500 stations nationwide. Interspersed among these were forgotten essays, clipped Op-Ed pieces, old *New Yorker* stories, and issues of the *Literary Leaf*—assistant editor, Gary Keillor:

> The neon lights of the Musicland Ballroom flashed out their invitation in violent crimsons, oranges and violets into an all-too-passive world that cared all-too-little about dancing to the sweet sounds of the Billy Barker quintet.

At the Avant Garden, while I was talking to the waitress, a man at the bar had grumbled that he gone to school with Keillor. But he had nothing to say about him. It was as if any recollection of that time would be too painful a proposition. I recited a line of Keillor's about high school reunions, something about how the people at them resemble survivors of a shipwreck, shaken but relieved to have made it through OK. And the two of them—the faux-punk waitress who had never heard of Keillor, and the middle-aged man who couldn't be bothered by him—laughed in unison. And I thought, here was the mark of an artist: Someone who lives apart from the world and, distilling experience through a skewed personal perspective, is somehow able to make it universal. The aloof eccentric had created humor that cut across lines of gender and generation and produced pure, unaffiliated laughter.

That evening, friends took me to dinner at Murray's, home of the famous "silver butter knife steak." It was the exact opposite of Aquavit: heavy pink curtains, fusty chandeliers, cozy booths. We occupied Sid Hartman's (so the small plaque on the wall said). "He's a sports writer for the *Star-Tribune,*" Katia informed me.

Katia had grown up in east Minneapolis, attended Edison High School and St. Katherine's Ukrainian Orthodox Church, and now, married with a four-year-old daughter, lived out in one of the affluent towns scattered around Lake Minnetonka. When the waitress arrived, Guy ordered a bottle of burgundy and Alexandra asked if there were any playthings.

"Hmm," said the waitress. "Let me check."

She returned a few minutes later, balancing with impressive aplomb a tray of wine glasses on her left hand while clutching in her right a musty stuffed lion. I had never seen a waitress so perfectly poised between innocence and experience.

"We dug this up," she said, passing the animal over. "I think it was the owner's son's."

Guy and I shared the twenty-eight-ounce New York strip sirloin, medium-rare—the waitress slicing it at our table like a loaf of bread—Katia had the Caesar salad with chicken, while Alexandra got the house steak ("medium ware"), which she shared with the lion, whom we named, naturally, Murray.

On the way out, I stopped to read an article framed on the wall. It was an essay about Murray's that Garrison Keillor had written for *Time* magazine, a warm homage to its durability in the face of changing fashions, its nostalgic appeal, its unadulterated, unabashed American cuisine. And it occurred to me that this was the one place I'd been in the Twin Cities where I could imagine seeing both Keillor and Ventura, the two big carnivores tucking into a twenty-eight-ouncer.

Downtown St. Paul on a Saturday afternoon is a patient still staggering from a powerful dose of urban renewal. What life there is tends to cluster around the escapees: the Union Depot, refurbished with restaurants and an exhibit hall; the elegant old St. Paul Hotel, overlooking Rice Park and its statue of Fitzgerald; and, up at the corner of Exchange and Wabasha, the tidy, blue-awninged Fitzgerald Theater. It sits just down the hill from the Capitol, and would be looking up at it if not for the Children's Museum across the street.

Inside the theater, at approximately two-thirty on a Saturday afternoon in March, Garrison Keillor walked on stage in white shirt and black dress trousers and took his place at the center microphone. There was about him—in the clothes, the physical presence, the stern, vaguely disapproving look on his face—the unmistakable air of a Sunday preacher.

Sit in on a rehearsal, and then the show, and it does all begin to seem like church (with one or two of the elements reversed). There is the communal meal—coffee and fellowship—though this takes place before the service, at 4:15, when guests and cast (with the exception of Keillor, who eats alone in his dressing room) line up for home-cooked victuals from an angelic caterer. Members cordially introduce themselves to strangers. The congregation, when it files in, has the warm, benevolent, well-kempt look of the urban faithful. Some sing along with the music, which often has a spiritual theme (a frequent guest choir is The Hopeful Gospel Quartet). And no one stirs during the sermon, aka "The News from Lake Wobegon." When it's over, cast members' families come backstage, and children tumble in and out of the star's dressing room as if just released from Sunday school. In the midst of the commotion towers Keillor, holding his daughter from a new wife and looking for all the world like the leader of a prosperous and close-knit parish.

The only jarring notes in the whole affair were the puerile attacks on the governor. It was like hearing the priest tell his favorite dumb blonde joke before the benediction.

After that show in March—Irish music from the Boys of the Lough, the vocal chamber ensemble Kantorei, the governor accused of having the IQ of a salad bar—Keillor handed his daughter to his wife and led me downstairs to a room where we sat on folding chairs. He appeared to be under that conflicted spell—joyous relief and anticlimactic *tristesse*—that performers experience when the curtain falls. He untied his shoes, and then took them off, revealing a pair of fire engine red socks. They held me, not by their brightness but their improbable nearness—like suddenly finding yourself inches from Woody's horn-rimmed glasses. And then the voice—familiar, mellifluous—directed at no one but myself.

He began by talking about Florida, having recently spent some time (the "penitential Lenten retreat," as he described it on the show) near Sarasota. He told of a story he was working on, one that would show the state in a kinder light than he had done in the past. (Perhaps having come to the first part of the realization that Florida is as obvious a target as Ventura.) He said he had thought of telling it tonight, but he hadn't worked it out to his satisfaction. And then he proceeded to work it out on me. (It made the "News" the following Saturday.)

I asked at what point in the week he writes the story. He said he doesn't write it; he sits down Saturday morning and jots down some notes, sketches it out. It is a way of memorizing without really memorizing, having material but not being tied to a script. I had noticed during the "News" that he didn't read from notes; he sat on a stool, occasionally getting up and pacing the stage, all the while weaving his tale. It was an impressive feat: spinning a fluid, well-rounded story out of an almost spontaneous imagination. On live radio no less. And it was also a lovely anachronism: a tale that went from brain to lips to ears without ever hitting the page, or screen—a narrative unbound by letters and indented paragraphs, whose only punctuation was in the physical acts of speech and laughter.

He took off his black wire-rim glasses and rubbed large, liquidy, slightly protuberant eyes. He hadn't looked at me while speaking, but at the wall behind me. Only when I voiced an opinion would his gaze turn to me, with a kind of cold surmise, and then he would take the opposing view. I mentioned I'd been to Murray's. He told of driving by with his parents on the way to church; how the children had to memorize a verse of scripture, and how the verse got longer the older you got. "If you didn't have it down by the time we passed Murray's, you were in trouble." He said he hadn't been back since he wrote the essay; he didn't want the staff fawning all over him.

We talked of writing. He said he wasn't sure he'd be writing "casuals" for the *New Yorker* again, because they had gotten harder to do, not many older writers pulled them off. I mentioned that Perelman had; he agreed, but quickly assured me they weren't up to his usual standards. I asked how his memoirs were coming. It was the first time he laughed, or even cracked a smile, and it was short-lived. In an interview he'd been quoted as saying that he had taken up the Ventura book because this larger-than-life character had come along just when he was mired in a reminiscence of his student days at the University of Minnesota. He said he was having trouble with the chronological aspect. "It was in the fall of . . .," he said with mock portentousness, and then I laughed.

Without my even mentioning him, the governor came up. You could sense he was an affront to everything that Keillor held dear—the explanation, no doubt, for the endless abuse. He complained about his demands for more security. I mentioned that nobody had checked to see what I was carrying when I went to see him, and he said, "Why should they?" I couldn't tell if this was the Minnesotan in him speaking, the innocent protected from the harsh realities of the world, or the artist.

We walked upstairs together, back to his dressing room, then down the dark corridor lined with pipers waiting to go on stage for the evening show. He stopped to examine the regalia on one of the men. Outside, at the corner of Wabasha and Exchange, he asked if I needed a ride anywhere. It was the first question he'd asked me, a product of politeness rather than curiosity. He stood there, tall in his tan trench coat, facing into the wind coming up from the Mississippi, and said that St. Paul was on the verge of something, it was either going to become a bright, lively city or a daytime parking lot. He wasn't sure. Then he shook my hand. I thanked him for his time and said I'd send him my story. And that caused him to laugh—a kind of pained chuckle—a second time.

The lobby of the St. Paul Hotel swished with the gowns of a fading wedding party. I asked a young woman from Chicago what had brought her to St. Paul.

"I was poured into treatment," she said.

"What?"

"Alcohol addiction. You know how they say this is the land of 10,000 lakes? It's also the land of 10,000 treatment centers. This place is a mecca for recovery."

Sarah hadn't had a drink since 1994, but was in no hurry to leave. "They recommend that you stay in the area. And I like St. Paul. There are no Jaguars or Chanel makeup here. It's about people."

Before going back to my hotel, I stopped at Nye's Bar & Polonaise Room in Old Minneapolis. A blonde trouper tapped out old chestnuts at the piano bar, under a bad painting of Chopin, and in the side room people jostled to the plodding rhythms of Ruth Adams and the World's Most Dangerous Polka Band. A pretty dark-haired girl took to the dance floor with a stooped Ukrainian in a baseball hat. Suddenly the Twin Cities seemed almost identical.

On the third floor of the Mall of America, a caricature of the governor stared out at shoppers. It burst from a blow-up of the cover of the book—*Me,* by Jimmy (Big Boy) Valente as told to Garrison Keillor—which filled the window of the Lake Wobegon USA store. I had seen the indoor roller coaster, the giant inflated Snoopy, the plaque marking the old home plate of Metropolitan Stadium, even the lone red chair hanging high on the wall above the log ride, signifying the terminus of a historic Harmon Killebrew home run. I'd had a lunch in the food court of walleye and cheese curds. But nothing surprised me more than the Lake Wobegon store. Yet two more opposed ideas.

Inside were T-shirts, mugs, tapes, books. "We'd like to sell a lot more stuff," the shop assistant said. "But Garrison torpedoes every idea we have. He doesn't get into the commercial end."

I passed on the book and bought a couple of the postcards. They showed a small town Main Street, circa 1950, with the salutation at the top: "Greetings from Lake Wobegon, Minn."

# PART FIVE

## *Nothing to Declare but My Wonderment*

My passport—bent, scuffed, rotten with falsehoods—has seen its last country.

It still has seven months to go before it expires, but it has no more empty pages. For the first time in my life I have filled my passport up with stamps.

The sense of accomplishment I feel fluctuates between the thrill of the trick-or-treater who has stuffed his bag with candy ("Thank you, Mrs. Guadeloupe"; "No, Mr. Israel, I'm not a terrorist, I'm a tourist.") and the relief of the undergraduate as the last page of his exam book fills with ink.

I could get some pages added in an awkward accordion insert—I'm not the first person to use up his passport, you know. But when I asked about this at the local office the woman told me it would be simpler just to apply for a new one. So I will, sending the old one in as proof of previous passportedness. But I'm going to insist they send it back.

It is my personal CD (compact document) of the last ten years of my life in motion, each cold stamp (*thwump!*) provoking—like Proust's *madeleine*—a crush of heated memories.

On long flights or boring train rides I sometimes wander idly through my passport. Just flipping through the pages produces a pleasing jumble of colors—smeared reds, blurred blues, double-visioned greens—and dancing geometric forms. The most popular of course is the rectangle (rounded at the corners by the Brits at Heathrow). But there is also an Israeli circle, a Spanish ellipse, a Guadeloupean hexagon, an old Polish octagon, and what can only be described as a Belizean lifesaver. Argentina's decorative design—aqua for incoming, violet for outgoing—must be the only stamp in officialdom that hints at Art Nouveau.

Affixed to the top of page fifteen are five Egyptian stamps—bas-reliefs and Nubian monuments—that look as if they belong on a letter. Another page is thickened by a glued-on pink Hungarian visa (No. 926921). The two Polish visas—

while stamped in—still take a page each with their consonant-drunk dictums.

This passport also has become a handy if sometimes puzzling lexicon of foreign migratory terms: *innreist* (printed in the soothing green of Norwegian *passkontrollen,* obviously a branch that keeps track of trolls), *salida, flughafen, terytorium, police nationale, servico de fronteiras, ulazak-izlazak* (which I believe is what I did through Belgrade), *népköztársaság* (I haven't the faintest idea, though it happened in Hungary).

People, too, keep popping up: names of consuls, immigration officers with squiggly signatures, men—such as Phillip S. W. Goldson and Silvio Pettirossi—now best known as airports (in, respectively, Belize City, Belize, and Asunción, Paraguay). Even my father—who died a few years ago—appears, cruelly, as the person to contact "in case of death or accident."

You see now how outdated and ultimately misleading my passport is. The DDR, or German Democratic Republic—which it says quite clearly here I entered on September 13, 1990—cannot be located on any current map. The hatless Polish eagle on page eleven suddenly appears with a crown on page twenty-three. How valuable is this faint black lozenge-shaped imprint bearing the name of Hong Kong? Where, now, is the officer whose initials fly so confidently through the 1992 stamp ushering me into Haiti? And would somebody please tell me what happened to that young man who peers out from the picture in front?

# 18

## *Cartoon Dinner*

There are countries where you float gently along on a cushion of smiles (Mexico, Thailand), and others that numb you with a sullen indifference that seems all-pervasive until you somehow break through the chill and receive the traveler's divine revelation.

At a little before six on a warm June evening I arrived at the Astoria Hotel in St. Petersburg, Russia. It had been a typical tourist day in the former Soviet Union: jostling with the masses on Nevsky Prospekt (your guidebook gives you the word for "excuse me" because nobody else does); entering buildings where ancient functionaries still sit mournfully at desks waiting for the opportunity to say "*nyet.*"

Now I stood on Voznesensky Prospekt because in the morning I had received an e-mail: "I shall meet you at Hotel Astoria at 18:00 at an entrance and we are farther together we shall go to workplace the artist Victor Bogorad. The Hotel Astoria is city center, you will find it without effort. How you concern to Russia vodka?" It was signed, "Slava."

I had never met Slava. Several months earlier, he had sent a letter and some cartoons to our art critic who, knowing I was headed to St. Petersburg, passed them on to me. The drawings were very good, engaging in social rather than political commentary, and subtly subversive. Adding to their universality was the fact that they had no captions; the picture was the joke, which occasionally took some thought to decipher. I wrote back, saying our paper was not in the market for cartoons, but I would nevertheless enjoy meeting him when I came to town.

In the meantime, I checked the Web site that he shared with two other cartoonists, Victor Bogorad and Leonid Melnik. They worked in a similar vein, but each man had his own distinct style, which I now found personified as they emerged from Slava's Opel.

Victor wore a shaggy mop, Leonid a trim moustache, Slava boyish bangs. They looked less intimidating than they had in their self-caricatures, but still, I greeted them with mixed emotions. Tourists in Russia are warned against getting into taxis already carrying one passenger; there is nothing in the literature regarding private cars with three cartoonists.

I looked in vain for Slava's wife. The evening of my arrival, when I had called his apartment, he had put her on the phone because she spoke the better English. She also had an attractive laugh. Helpless, I climbed in the back seat for an evening with the boys.

My spirits lifted as we turned onto the embankment and glided past the tour groups staking out the Hermitage. There is nothing like a ride in a car for a tourist who's been doing all his exploring on foot. It's not just the speed, and the sudden opening up of new vistas, but the sight of your fellow travelers still plodding along like Cro-Magnons.

Inside, we pooled our languages. The closest match, after Slava's English and mine, was my Polish and their Russian. We did a lot with place names. Miami. Warszawa. Slava said that he had spent part of his childhood in Vilnius; I thought I caught something about an exhibition in Munich. We crossed the Neva.

I kept one eye out the window, trying to memorize landmarks. We were not far from the center, in a neighborhood of mausoleum housing and bunker markets. After about the third turn I conceded to myself that I would never be able to find my way back alone. Tipperary.

Finally we pulled up in front of a shop, and Slava mentioned the word "vegetables." Then he and Leonid went inside, while Victor led me toward the nearby high-rise. A derelict foyer, gained through a tightly locked door, and then a flimsy elevator to the sixteenth floor. More keys, more grim halls, and then into the studio of Victor Bogorad. I took off my shoes as he locked the padded door.

It was a standard, one-bedroom, socialist apartment, circa 1980, that looked more like a home than an atelier. Sofa and lamps made themselves comfortable in the small living room, the kitchen still possessed a table, the bedroom a bed.

But the walls of the living room, I now noticed, were hung with paintings. Victor walked me through, waiting patiently with a smile that consolidated (congratulated?) my often tardy grin. In one, a man stood peering down philosophically at the edge of a cliff. It had a Sempé-esque, Little Tramp quality. Then after a few seconds I discovered the six descending dashes at the bottom, and the man's hands gathered in the vicinity of his fly. It was one of Slava's, chez Victor. Generosity and absurdity on the sixteenth floor.

In the bedroom, dozens of paintings leaned against the wall. I sat on the bed as Victor displayed them one-by-one. He did this not, as I had feared, with the pitch of a salesman, but with the delight of a maestro. There were countless gems: The nesting doll opening to reveal a bottle of Stolichnaya; the road sign depicting Sisyphus. My favorite was one of his own, and I asked him to go back to it as a sign of my admiration. A bespectacled man sat in a restaurant, a palm tree growing out of his head, and gazed longingly at the woman sitting alone, a cruise ship sailing through her hair. It seemed the ideal painting for a travel editor, or hopeless romantic: the perfect marriage of palm tree and cruise ship sabotaged by the eternal incompatibility of rootedness and transience. I wished to buy it, but didn't want to introduce business into what was turning out to be an extremely cordial evening.

Dinner was coming along nicely. Leonid stood at the table slicing peeled cucumbers directly into a bowl (I was starting to see everything as a potential cartoon) while Slava fried potatoes in a thick black pan. Leonid eventually moved on to tomatoes and green onions, sprinkled the whole with parsley and dill, and then poured in the contents of a small carton of kefir. Slava vigorously shook some powder, almost ritualistically, over the potatoes.

We took our seats, I under Leonid's painting of a soldier wandering into battle bearing a cake. From the living room wailed the voice of Memphis Slim. (Russia providing the perfect setting for the blues.) A bottle of Five-Star vodka, like a still life, was proudly presented.

"*Za zdorovye!*" we said, clinking our glasses. Slava, the driver, lifted his Coke.

My plate was piled with marvelously greasy potatoes stuck with tiny bits of pork and the most amazing salad that had ever passed my lips. I wondered if the rule about food tasting better when eaten outdoors also applied to food eaten with cartoonists. Slava magnanimously refilled our glasses.

"T-o-m!" Victor said earnestly, somehow managing to give each of the letters equal emphasis, before an eruption of Russian.

"He say," Slava interpreted, "when sex scandal, Clinton popularity go down in U.S. In Russia, it go up. Clinton great sex man. Yeltsin great drunk.

"Victor work for *St. Petersburg Times,*" he continued, "and *Moscow Times.* He do five cartoons a day. Leonid maybe one day nothing, next day nothing, and then . . .," suddenly, Slava turned himself into an animated character, demonstrating "a great flurry of activity."

"T-o-m!" Leonid followed. I liked the way they said my name, and then spoke to me in Russian. I was amazed at how much fun I was having conversing with people I couldn't understand. "*Govoril nevestoj razshevennoj tomostnie blizosti.*"

"I am in army, in Moscow," Slava went on regardless, sketching his own story. It seemed nothing was being left unsaid, but a lot was going un-resaid. "I know of Victor. He is famous during 1991. People cut his cartoons and put on wall. I call him. Then he working as engineer." Victor nodded. "On nuclear bomb." Victor shook his head, smiling. Slava, newly animated, had now become Victor, fictitious munitions man. "Not talk now," he said hurriedly into an imaginary phone, before going back to touching up his bomb.

"T-o-m!" said Leonid. "*Mosno kasej slezami neposlushnyj i chudakovatyj?*"

"We work in different papers," Slava said, returned as Slava. "But we make group to show work. Our name is Nuance. It is easier as group. We have show on Nevsky Prospekt in October."

"T-o-m!" said Victor. "*Vzmaxom voobrazhenija legkim skladki istoshnym koldovstvom chasy nerazborchivee zabav polusmeshnykh.*"

Slava sat silent for a few seconds, then shook his head. "Too difficult."

"T-o-m!" said Victor. "You like Addams?"

"Yeah, I love Charles Addams. And Sempé? Do you know Sempé?" (Cartoonists had replaced places.)

"*Da, da,* but Steinberg—Steinberg . . .," he wagged his head in an admission of unapproachable genius. Then he got up, returning shortly with a large album of the work of Saul Steinberg. "He buy when he in New York," Slava said. "One hundred dollar."

As I paged through the book, they each took turns drawing my caricature.

"T-o-m!" Victor said smiling, while Leonid worked the pen, and Slava readied to interpret. "He say cartoonist is funny profession. You say . . .," and he made a universal gesture with his middle finger, ". . . to country, and you take money for it."

We stood on the balcony, sixteen stories high, looking out over St. Petersburg as Memphis Slim sang. Though it was getting near midnight, the sky was still bright. The moment had an exquisiteness that went well beyond vodka.

Gradually, we put on our shoes and headed downstairs. As Slava drove through the quiet streets, I thought about what Victor had said. It was true, but he had left out the fact that, in Russia at least, the work demanded a particular type of courage. Not necessarily political, for now there was a certain degree of press freedom, but in terms of a more fundamental matter: how one deals with reality. In a doddering, dolorous country, these men had chosen laughter over despair. You could argue—*they* might argue—that it was simply their way of making a living, but that didn't negate their contribution as a minus sign in the national arithmetic of pain.

We stopped by a bridge and dropped Victor at his apartment house. In the lingering light, it looked old and imposing, Stalin to his Brezhnev studio. Then we headed back across the Neva, past the Smolny Convent to Nevsky Prospekt. I jumped out at Marata Street and bumped into a woman out walking her terrier.

"His name is Melville," she said unexpectedly, with only the slightest trace of an accent. "I brought him from Virginia. In Russia people would never name a dog after a great writer."

"*They* would," I thought, as I waved to the two figures grinning in the Opel.

# 19

# *"I Must Upgrade My Husband"*

I met Sara standing under one of Penang's colonial porticos—we were both seeking shelter from an afternoon shower—and before the rain was over she had given me an invaluable lesson in love.

I had arrived on the island the night before, taking the ferry from Butterworth. After the crush of Kuala Lumpur, I was looking forward to a weekend in the place that had actually been dubbed "the pearl of the Orient," even though I knew that its principal city, Georgetown, was now Malaysia's second largest.

On the ferry I had struck up a conversation with a young Chinese woman, a schoolteacher, returning home for the weekend from her posting in the highlands. It was her first job, the students were obedient, the climate was cool, she missed Penang.

At the dock she had told me to wait while she called her father; he would drive me to my hotel. I was sure he'd be thrilled. He pulled up about ten minutes later in a sleek BMW; without a kiss or hug, without even a pat on the back, his homecoming daughter got in the passenger seat. I slipped in the back with my bag. We drove past crumbling high arcades, around a clock tower, along a green (the *padang*) and then turned down a well-lighted street to the Towne House Hotel. I thanked the father and said good-bye to the daughter and walked into my homey lobby.

Another empty room. Not a single light worked until I realized that I had to slip the key holder into a slot on the wall next to the door—then the place came ablaze, including the TV, which was showing an Indian musical. Ululations for the lonely.

Downstairs in the restaurant, just before closing, I got a plate of soggy spinach and a bowl of rice. With my chopsticks, I airlifted the greens onto the rice and then up to my mouth, where the delicious brown sauce stung my lips.

Then I went out to walk the streets.

A few young Tamil men sat on the railing outside the cinema, looking at girls and waiting for the late show. Across the way, the *roti* vendor stretched elastic dough atop a flat iron stove under a bare light bulb. In front of the Oriental Hotel, the trishaw drivers slumped in their carriages; a few napped, curled up like children on the sidewalk.

The cross streets were quiet and lined with Chinese shop houses: the closed-up store on the bottom floor, the family quarters atop, extended over the tiled entranceway and supported by two square pillars that made artless colonnades that stretched into the darkness. On many of the pillars hung bulky red shrines, their joss sticks forming anorexic bouquets.

When I got back to my room, the musical was still going.

Saturday broke hot and sticky. I took the bus south out of town to the Snake Temple. According to legend, poisonous green snakes turned up mysteriously at the temple as soon as it was completed in the middle of the nineteenth century. I had visions of snakes dangling from trees and slinking underfoot, but they had all been penned in or domesticated. Two show snakes curled motionless in leafless bonsais atop the altar, anesthetized, the guidebooks say, by incense. In a side chamber, caretakers draped de-fanged serpents over giggling tourists who then posed for pictures. I took the bus back to town.

Even the most dedicated sightseer flags after a week; I am a lackluster tourist to begin with and had already been on the road eleven days. I'd lost count of the temples. Back on the *padang,* taking pictures of the sugary Anglo-Victorian buildings, I felt purposeless and small. Then it started to rain.

The portico of the old town hall offered the nearest escape. Even before I reached its safety I noticed the young woman sitting on the steps. She was dressed in a green-and-white patterned tunic over loose green trousers. Sandals wrapped elegant, molasses-brown feet. The Muslim convention of hiding the female form meant that I was now finding women's feet highly attractive.

The tunic was short-sleeved and had a modest décolletage. As I approached, thin red lips opened into an unexpected, gleaming white smile.

"Where are you from?" the woman asked me as I stood above her. Her English was soft and assured. Her thick black hair, parted in the middle, fell to just above her slender shoulders.

"The United States," I said.

"What are you doing in Penang?" The tone was not accusatory; it was all wonder and sweetness.

"I'm writing about Malaysia. For my newspaper in Florida."

"Malaysia is changing," she said. "It is taking more things from the West."

"Do you think that's good or bad?"

"If we take from things like technology, then it's good. But other things, like the breakdown of law, are bad." Then, abruptly, "Can I see your notebook?"

I took it out of my bookbag and opened it up. She examined the pages as if they were sacred script. I noticed that she held a black folder on her lap.

"What do you do?" I asked.

"I do interviews about secrets."

"What?'

"I have to go up to people and ask them if they smoke one brand of cigarettes. And if they listen to advertisements about the cigarettes."

"You do marketing strategy," I said.

"Yes, that's it." It sounded better as "interviews about secrets."

"Do many people smoke?"

"Yes. I would say 90 percent."

"Women?"

"No. Except women who work at night. I mean in bars. They smoke." Her two lush eyebrows rose in unison.

The rain fell harder.

"My name's Tom."

"My name is Sara."

"Do you like your work, Sara?"

"Not really. But I have to work because my husband is very poor. We live with his in-laws in Jelutong. It is the poorest part of Penang, and my in-laws are probably the poorest people in the village." She said this calmly, without emotion, as a simple statement of fact. She smiled as she said it.

"My husband's father was a fisherman. One of his brothers is paralyzed and one of his sisters just divorced from her husband and came back to the house with her three children. I would like to finish my studies. I studied biology for two years—I was working with, what do you call them? . . . parasites—but my husband can't pay for my studies now because he has to support his family."

"What does your husband do?"

"He works in a factory. My parents don't accept him because he is poor. This isn't a problem in the United States I think."

"It can be," I said.

"So they don't talk to me now. They have cut me off."

"Do they live in Penang?"

"No. They live in Perak. Do you know it?"

"I'm going there next."

"They live in a town near the sea. They are both schoolteachers, but they have land—a hundred acres from which they make palm oil. They are very wealthy."

"Do you have any brothers or sisters?"

"Yes, but they don't talk to me either. My parents tell them that if they meet me they will disown them. So they don't."

"It's not a question of you and your husband being of different religions?"

"No, we're both the same."

"Which?"

"Muslim."

"But you don't wear a head scarf."

"That's only some Muslim women. I don't go by the dress codes. I don't pray five times a day. Maybe once a day. I'm not a good Muslim." She laughed, showing her excellent teeth again. "And I don't have the money to go to Mecca."

"Do many Malaysians go to Mecca?"

"Oh yes. Especially older people. I think maybe when I get older I will get more interested in religion. When I'm young I want to be open to many things. I'm twenty-five."

In the same, even tone she said: "I wonder where my husband is? He was supposed to meet me here and take me home on his bike."

"He won't mind me talking to you?"

"No, he's not like that. He likes foreigners. But he can't speak English, only Malay. He's a very good man—he is caring, and has a good sense of humor."

The rain was letting up, but I didn't want to leave. I wanted to meet the man for whom this beautiful woman had sacrificed her family, her studies, her inheritance. I pictured a hungry, chiseled worker in the heroic socialist mode: a dark-hued Tom Joad.

"How long have you been married?"

"One year. He wants children but I'm not ready. Not the way things are now. I don't want a child and not to have milk for it."

She thought for a minute, her black brows furrowed. "I must upgrade my husband. Then my parents will accept him. We cannot do it educationally, so we must do it financially. I would like us to start a business, and then maybe go into antiques. You have to see what the market is like."

Her intelligence, and her steadfast determination in the face of novel adversity, impressed me deeply. And her total lack of self-pity.

"Ah, here's my husband," she said, getting up from the steps. He had arrived not, as I had imagined, on a motorcycle, or even a scooter, but on an ancient black bicycle. Though his helmet suggested a larger vehicle, its smooth white sphere accentuated his sallow moon face, his drooping shoulders, his little potbelly, a small diamond patch of which peaked through his shrunken cotton shirt. As we went up for introductions, I noticed that he was a head shorter than Sara.

She explained me to him in a lilting Malay. He offered a soiled, pudgy hand while under his helmet broke a guileless smile adorned by two gold teeth. So this was her husband. I looked at Sara. Her graceful features revealed no trace of awkwardness, no hint of apparent discrepancies. This was simply the man she loved. The man she was going to upgrade. Added to intelligence and grit, I saw, was saintly devotion.

We said our good-byes—Sara wishing me a safe journey home, her husband (I never got his name) grinning sweetly. Then I watched them mount their rickety bicycle and pedal off together toward Jelutong.

# 20

# *Croatian Rock*

Darkness fell as I entered Split. An unknown quantity now cloaked in shadow.

The airport shuttle—a huge sightseeing bus carrying me and another guy—loped past twinkling sheets of socialist housing before dipping into leafy confines halved by immemorial walls. Bare bulbs under awnings illuminated the playlet of a night market, and then a dark opening of water appeared.

We pulled into a space at the water's edge. I gave the driver the name of my hotel—Bellevue, pronouncing it, as an old Croatian hand had coached me, "Bellevie"—and he pointed to the other end of the harbor. I rolled my bag into the dimness of a palm-lined promenade, passing pensioners, families, and grills pyramided with blackened ears of corn.

The hotel—thin neon lettering and Venetian windows—occupied the front of a boarded-up square. It bespoke, even at night, a history of better days. On the first landing a timeless tableau—two dusty potted plants and the letters R E C E P C I J A coupled with a slightly askew arrow—transported me back to communist Poland.

I climbed the last steps with trepidation. I had called a month earlier to make a reservation and a deep, lethargic voice at the other end had responded: "Just give me your name and dat will be dat."

The man at the reception desk took in my name, and then we performed the old-fashioned exchange of passport for room key. I couldn't tell if this was the result of a written record or of a chronic availability of rooms.

Mine had a bathroom light that took fifteen seconds to illumine. When it did, I found that the maid had left a dirty mop in the tub. On closer inspection, I discovered it was a spot where the enamel had worn off. I walked past the two single beds, a thin white sheet folded barracks-like at each foot, and opened the window. In rushed the smell of the sea, and the sounds of the music festival directly below.

There is nothing like Croatian pop for getting the jet-lagged travel writer out of his room. I fled the vicinity, weaving my way through slippery stone streets that opened eventually into a smoothed stone square. Shuttered stone houses faced off across from a crenellated round tower. I slid through more right-angled alleys that deposited me into an hallucination: a sunken square hemmed in by antiquities.

The delicate remains of a colonnade filigreed one side, and the skeletal façade of a temple, now buttressed by brick, classically filled in the back. (And above this weighty space rose an illuminated campanile.) Spotlights dramatized the age-blackened columns, giving the scene a crumbling magnificence, while the café tables spread across the peristyle provided a jarring contemporary note. Welded onto the indoor/outdoor motif—niches and statuary under the stars—was the even more compelling juxtaposition of ancient and modern: teenagers flirting on ruinous walls; couples drinking in the shadow of the gods. It was like stumbling upon a cocktail party in the Roman Forum.

I had found my way into Diocletian's Palace. The guidebooks all told of this marvel: a massive edifice built at the edge of the sea by the retired Roman emperor. Diocletian had had an impressive career. Born of slaves in nearby Salona, the capital of Roman Dalmatia, he so distinguished himself as a soldier that he eventually rose to the rank of emperor. Calling it quits at the beginning of the fourth century, after a robust persecution of Christians, he returned to his homeland with the desire to grow cabbages. Swords into plowshares.

Yet, his final residence belied any delusions of simplicity. It was less a palace than a small walled city. (Covering nine and a half acres, it takes up, on contemporary maps, half of Split's old town.) The façade alone contained fifty Doric columns. Within the gated borders were not only imperial suites but temples, streets, public buildings, baths, courtyards, galleries, a garrison, a domed vestibule, and a mausoleum, which housed Diocletian's tomb for nearly two centuries (before his body mysteriously disappeared) and which, in a sweet revenge, was turned into the town cathedral.

But what really distinguishes the complex today is not the size or symmetries of its architectural splendors, but its fantastic utilitarianism. It is not just that people now gather where Praetorian Guards once strolled, but that they also live here. In what must stand as one of the world's, if not first, at least most spectacular instances of adaptive reuse, the citizens of Split blithely built their dwellings within the palace, grafting humble residences onto walls and filling in arcades with bedroom windows. Just as weeds sprout among ruins in other lands, here it's houses. (It is almost as if, after the Cultural Revolution, the Chinese had erected apartment blocks in the Forbidden City.) In the coming days I would stroll the grounds shaking my head in wonderment at the curtained front doors next to erstwhile temples, the soccer balls sailing past toppled pillars. I could not walk along the waterfront promenade without staring up in amazement at the stately columns embedded in the condo façade, and occasionally book-ending sagging lines of wash.

But now I needed to sleep. Back at the Bellevue, a new receptionist rose for my room number.

"*Dwieście dwanaście,*" I told him.

"What godforsaken language is that?"

"Polish," I said. "I thought it might work."

"Nothing ventured, nothing gained."

I tried a simpler way, number-by-number: "*Dwa jeden dwa.*"

"We are very proud of you," he said sarcastically, reaching for the key to 212.

The waiters in the dining room wore embroidered vests that reminded me of the wallpaper in the corridor. If I drank coffee, I would have thought it strange to have the cup delivered by someone not wearing a black T-shirt. Tea seemed to work better with the wardrobe.

After breakfast the palace always beckoned (you never really tired of the juxtapositions), but one morning I headed off in the opposite direction, through Veli Varos—a neighborhood of twisting lanes and chock-a-block houses that is regarded as the proving ground for the city's humor. (The writer Miljenko Smoje had grown up here, and the TV series based on his stories, *Our Little Town,* became the most popular comedy show in Croatia.) I climbed winding alleys that carried familiar Mediterranean echoes—Spain, Greece, Italy, Turkey—but held something slightly off kilter, an indefinable otherness, a Croatianness I assumed. And it wasn't just the architecture. Locals passed—men often in shorts and sandals—and I greeted them with good morning ("*Dobro jutro*") to no effect. I took it personally, but then noticed that they were equally aloof with each other. In this sunny picturesqueness, a grim introversion.

This was disheartening because I had seen Veli Varos (the very name makes you smile) as my last hope. Downtown, simply trying to get basic tourist information (not daring to hope for some deeper insight), I had found most personal encounters unpleasant. It ranged from the sullen regard of shop assistants to the brusque, unsmiling replies of the ferry representatives to the hostile glare of the harridan occupying, of all things, the city tourist office (out of which I staggered like a schoolboy after a run-in with the principal).

There were a few exceptions: the man in the fabric shop who walked me several blocks to an elusive restaurant; the woman in the grocery store who found a bruise on my orange and went and got me another. But even these acts were performed with a hardened helpfulness. One morning I woke up in my hotel room and thought for a brief instant (as I have in very few places in the world): I don't want to go out there again.

I walked back down the hill, and then along the sea, pondering civic mind-sets. The war, no doubt, had played a part, as had the crippling economy. (The government of the late President Franjo Tudjman had lifted millions of dollars out of the country, which now was experiencing 25 percent unemployment.) But what disconcerted outsiders was that, while the moodiness was all too apparent, its sources weren't. The city showed no signs of wartime devastation (the fighting, of which Split saw little, ended in 1995), and it contained no real pockets of poverty. Even the most identifiable mark of idleness—young men filling cafés in mid-afternoon—had an untroubling, *dolce vita* cast. People were struggling more than suffering, and struggle is a private, invisible process.

And the struggle, perhaps, was not just with the present. In 1993, in *Granta* magazine, the writer Michael Ignatieff described a visit to Jasenovac, fifty miles east of the Croatian capital of Zagreb. This was the concentration camp where, during World War II, 40,000 Serbs, Jews, Gypsies, and Croatian Communists were murdered. That is the Croatian estimate; independent researchers put the number closer to 250,000.

"When Croatia declared its independence in 1990," Ignatieff wrote, "it made one central mistake, one that may have put the new state on the road to war: It failed to disavow publicly its fascist past, to disassociate itself from the Ustashe state and what it did at Jasenovac." Had it done this, he suggested, "the local Serb leaders would have had difficulty persuading their Serb followers that the new Croatia was the fascist Ustashe come again."

He went on to write: "The wartime Ustashe state was Croatia's first experience of being an independent nation. It has proved impossible for Croatian nationalists to disavow that nationhood, even if it was also a fascist one. Instead, they evade the issue. They dismiss tales of Ustashe atrocity as Serbian propaganda; they airbrush atrocity into crime by playing statistical sleight of hand with the numbers who died."

I found a walkway down by the water, which led me past rocky inlets and leathery bodies. Matrons spilled from bikinis, their pendulous breasts and life-preserver stomachs warming unapologetically in the sun. I wondered what the widow in black walking in front of me was thinking until she removed her blouse to reveal the top of a two-piece. People took to the water with a naturalness that reminded me of Australia—where swimming appears to be less a recreation than a basic human need—but that here, in this Catholic land, seemed to have a deeper, almost sacramental quality. The morning dip as spiritual cleansing.

"Ours is a lost generation," Sonja said almost sunnily. She sat with her math book in a courtyard of the palace, a pretty woman with a clean face and dull teeth and the long legs that seem the happy prerogative of the Dalmatian female. I had stopped by her sign advertising portraits and asked why the young women selling souvenirs in the passageway were so listless.

"It's the end of the season," she had said laughing. "They don't have to be nice anymore."

It was a joke. "There's a word—*fiaka:* It means laziness, and it's used to describe the feeling in Split."

There were also problems with drugs. "It's a big drug city," she said. "We have drugs and football. Two extremes."

"And a pop music festival," I said.

"I don't listen to that music. You hear one song, and all the other songs sound just like it."

Sonja had spent the war in London, where many of her friends still lived, where she had first gotten up the courage to sketch people's faces in public. And she was moving soon to Zagreb, to resume her studies, this time in computers.

"I wish I could study what the Greeks did," she said. "Mathematics, philosophy, music. The highest things." But not, clearly, the stuff for interrupted students of a struggling young nation.

I asked if she would miss her hometown: the sun, the sea, the quality of the light.

"It's nice to be nostalgic about Split," she mused. "Because it means you're somewhere else."

Parishioners filed down the steps of the Franciscan church on Trg Gaje Bulata. With its box shape and square columns, it had looked the first time I passed it like a socialist ministry, but now, after Saturday night Mass, it reverted to form. The congregation thickened at the doorway and seemed to flow back into the fresco behind the altar.

It filled the wall: The risen Christ looming above a long green land sprinkled not with trees and houses but with hundreds of people in regional dress. Some of the figures stood cluelessly, arms akimbo in black vests; others strode daintily with drooping heads, while a bull, a lion, and an eagle flew symbolically above. In the morning I had seen the sharp-nosed figures of the sculptor Ivan Mestrovic—"there is something very distinctive about Mestrovic's faces," Sonja had told me—and had been awed by the power of his art. Yet this strange vision of Ivan Dulcic was, in its soberly whimsical piety, even more moving.

The Bellevue was still being besieged by pop. It was, I had concluded, the hotel where Rebecca West had stayed while researching her classic book on Yugoslavia, *Black Lamb and*

*Grey Falcon*. In one of the chapters on Split, she describes looking out her window at three men talking in the square, and her husband's observation that, "These people are profoundly different from us. They are not at all sentimental, but they are extremely poetic." I was glad she wasn't here for the music festival.

The handsome, white-haired receptionist greeted me in English. Vladimir had spent twelve years in Australia, where he'd gone in the 1950s to avoid military service. "I didn't want to carry a rifle around for three years. And it was very hard-line here then. We sang songs to Stalin and Tito, about how they were going to rule the world."

He returned in the 1970s, when a general amnesty was declared. I told him that he lived in a beautiful city. He gave a noncommittal shrug.

"It was built by the Romans. We don't have much regard for our antiquities. There's a place not far from here—Salona—with an amphitheater, ruins. In any other country it would be protected by a fence and they would charge people to see it. Here there are sheep and goats wandering about."

He agreed that the city had a problem with drugs, but insisted it hadn't led to crime. "This is one of the safest places in the world. We don't have muggings, robberies, hold-ups—it's not in our tradition. I work here all night by myself, and I leave the door open downstairs."

A haggard woman appeared and unleashed a pitiful whine, which Vladimir countered with gruff, helpless appeals. I thought perhaps she rented rooms from her home, and had a business bone to pick; then Vladimir turned to me and said, "This woman is complaining about the condition of her room. But there is nothing I can do. I told her: When the state runs a hotel, it is already a bad situation. When that state is Croatia, it is catastrophic."

The tone turned more sedate, and the woman retreated. Vladimir explained to me that for about four years, two-thirds of the Bellevue had been occupied by refugees. "All the hotels had refugees. They'll have to do millions of dollars of renovations. The way those people treat property. They were from rural areas; many had never been in a hotel before."

I asked what part of the country they came from.

"Many from the northeast. Did you ever hear of a place called Vukovar?"

I nodded gravely.

"I was brought up to believe that everyone is the same," Vladimir said. "I am not racist. But the brutality that the Serbs have shown, the utter barbarity."

He went on talking, about the "madman" Milosevic, the old Serbian desire to rule all of Yugoslavia. "They say wherever there is a Serb living, that is Serbia. Which is preposterous. Their military is one of the largest in Europe. Before the break-up, 85 percent of the officers in the Yugoslav Army were Serbs. They didn't want to give up power."

He scoffed at demands that Croatian war criminals stand trial. "That's like calling the Allies to answer for bombing Dresden." His was a perfectly clear, undoubting, one-sided view, which I didn't challenge, partly out of deference to the first Croat who'd opened up to me, and partly out of an already (after only three days) profound sense of futility.

Upstairs, the sounds of Croatian pop filled my room. I turned on the TV in hopes of drowning it out and got a station that was broadcasting the festival. It was a strange sensation: hearing from the tube the same cloying music that was coming through my window. And then switching it off, and finding it still going strong. The sheet was too thin to block it out, so I tried the pillow, with little success. But even as I moaned, I knew I was getting a valuable lesson in the meaning of the word "inescapable."

## The Ferry

I stood on the top deck of the *Petar Hektorovic* overlooking Split on a brilliant fall morning. For three days I had gazed at these gleaming white ferries until the word *JADROLINIJA*—the company name emblazoned on the side in giant blue letters—had become in my mind a synonym for escape. It had something to do with Split, but also with a personal restlessness. On almost every trip I take I am reminded of the perceptiveness of the man who wrote that his two favorite things in the world were arriving in a new city and leaving that city.

A few cars on the quay silently started their engines, moved forward in unison, then one by one disappeared into the hull. (It was the middle of September, the end of the season.) The foot passengers—having already risen in the elevator—staked out seats in the sun. They were mostly young backpackers, of indeterminate nationality. Three of them stretched out on the hard benches with a heavy weariness that suggested either an unbridled nightlife or a callous indifference to their surroundings (or both). The city laid out beneath us—with its palm-lined promenade, its signature campanile, its jagged mountain backdrop—was just a faceless way station on their progress toward another. But maybe not. Perhaps they were the exhausted Hvar chess team coming back from a weekend competition in Zagreb. The thing about being a traveler is that you just don't know.

I turned back to the city, so innocent and inviting, so suddenly likable from the deck of a ship. Still, I couldn't wait to move. A young woman came and stood to my left, a few feet away, also taking in the scene. Normally I would have hesitated to speak, but the long weekend of solitary wandering had made me recklessly bold. I didn't even wait to come up with something clever.

"Nice view."

"Yes, it's pretty," she said softly. "But I didn't like the city. The people were very sad. And I couldn't eat the food—it's so heavy. Everything's cooked in oil. There were no vegetarian restaurants."

She had a noncommittal attractiveness and a resolute, clear-eyed gaze. Her long, straight brown hair and flowery, ankle-length dress gave her an air of hippie Puritanism. Her accent was vaguely German.

"I'm from Switzerland," she said. "Near Basel. I arrived here by bus yesterday. It took twenty hours, but it was better than flying. I don't like to fly."

"Have you been to Hvar before?"

"Yes, I was there in July. It's so beautiful. In the summer you smell the lavender, and the pine trees. And the water is so clean and clear."

I asked about hotels in the town of Hvar; as usual, I hadn't made a reservation.

"I'm staying at a friend's house, but I don't think it will be a problem now that the season is over."

The engines began rumbling, and we inched away from the pier. The wind picked up as we turned in the harbor and Split receded into miniature.

"I guess the war had an effect on people's moods here," I said. "Perhaps on the islands they're more removed."

"Yes, a little I think. But my friend never wants to talk about the war. He had family in Sarajevo."

A male. When she had mentioned the house, I had pictured a villa overlooking the sea. Now I imagined a tall, dark Adonis, a black lock of hair bouncing over his forehead. Hvar is sometimes called Croatia's Saint-Tropez. I asked what she did in Switzerland.

"I was a kindergarten teacher. But I was fired because I didn't teach according to the program. I also paint and write—poetry and small stories."

"So you're going to Hvar for inspiration?" I was still hopelessly curious.

"It's more than that," she said thoughtfully. "I need to decide what I'm going to do. And I'm pregnant, so that changes things."

She looked somewhat relieved by the revelation, which came down like a curtain on our conversation. My curiosity was now sated; I couldn't think of anything else to say. We stood in wind-whipped silence for what seemed like minutes.

"If you don't mind, I'm going to sit down," she finally said. "I'm starting to feel a little . . ."

I stayed put. The wind had calmed as we entered the channel between Brac and Solta, the same one Hektorovic had passed through in the summer of 1555. At the age of sixty-eight, consumed with the construction of his manor house in Stari Grad, the poet decided he needed a change of scenery. *Abandoning all, I thought to take a trip.* He asked two local fishermen, Paskoj and Nikola, to take him to sea, and for three days he watched the men's labors and listened to their songs and, on return, depicted the journey in a narrative poem. *Fishing and Fishermen's Conversations* became the first, really, in a still-kicking line of philosopher-angler books (though titles have improved with time) and as such was hailed for its originality and its role in helping to break down the destructive barrier, through its sympathetic portrayal of the two fishermen, between aristocrat and commoner.

*But, while they supped, I went away and sat*
*Beside the sea-shore and began to marvel*
*That there be so many simple people*
*Who, poor and ill-clad, yet possess a plenty.*
*For such people are possessed of reason*
*And sound judgment which they wear like clothes;*
*So virtue dwelleth in them sweetly,*

*As gold lieth hidden in the depths of the earth.*
*We think them less able than the sea slug,*
*Yet when they speak, they speak as do wise men;*
*Outwardly they seem but simple folk,*
*Yet inwardly they have a wondrous wisdom.*

Finally, I walked over to where she was sitting (I had learned her most intimate detail, but not her name) and asked if I could get her anything from the cafeteria. She said no, still mindful, no doubt, of oily Split. Down a deck, a lone bar was open, dispensing only drinks. End of season.

As I drank my mineral water, I thought about the varied fates these ferries carry. They seem so obvious, taking tourists to their vacations and islanders to their jobs. But there were breaches, anomalies, intertwined futures in the balance. Planted into the frivolous and the mundane was a subversive element of responsibility and beatitude.

Back outside pieces of island drifted close, with that irresistible improbability of things that rise up from the blankness of the sea. A lone house sat at the water's edge, the only sign of civilization in a world of rock and pine, though it looked almost as if the stones had rolled down and, over time, orderly collected themselves there.

We had entered the harbor of Stari Grad. In the distance we could see the dock and, farther in, the cluster of Hektorovic's town. As we turned to back ourselves in, she got up and joined me.

"My friend can give you a ride into Hvar."

"Are you sure?" I immediately imagined the look that would greet the mother-to-be as she stepped off the ferry with another man. "I can take the bus."

"No, it's no problem."

As we churned our way backwards, she searched the faces on the dock.

"He's here," she said, not excitedly, but with a pleasure that showed in her self-assured smile.

I didn't ask where. I moved slightly away, not wanting to damage his view. As we picked up our bags, she said, "Please do not say anything about my pregnancy. He doesn't know yet. I didn't want to tell him over the telephone—it was not the right means."

We stepped off the ramp and through the sparse gauntlet of a welcoming party. He stood at the head, in black T-shirt and jeans, a short, stocky man with a bulbous nose and a shocking mane of unkempt hair. He threw out his arms for a sporting hug, and then kissed her decorously on each cheek. His surprise at seeing me seemed completely lost in a still percolating astonishment at seeing her.

We piled into a car with a shaved head at the wheel. "My car no good," her friend explained. "It catch on fire." Luggage and foreigners were piled in the back. Turning around in the passenger seat, he asked, "You have good trip?" And when she said yes, he immediately returned to a conversation with the driver.

We set off, to the sound of impassioned Croatian. They spoke as if they hadn't seen each other in days. I felt so bad for the woman that I couldn't bring myself to look at her. I stared instead at the two heads in front: one shaggy, one bare—hirsuteness and its opposite. In the confusion of arrival, I hadn't gotten their names, so I thought of them as Paskoj and Nikola: Two unsuspecting locals made to share their vessel. But I couldn't yet detect any redeeming qualities.

We drove past forests of pine as the men in front continued their discussion. I sat silent in the back, wishing I'd taken the bus. This was faster, but much more painful. I thought about kicking the passenger seat just to get the dumb father to turn around. I kept thinking of her back on the ferry, quietly anticipating this long-awaited reunion. Or perhaps I was thinking of her imagining it as I had. Yet she, at least, had had some idea of what was awaiting.

Finally, the sprawl of a development acned a hill. We rolled down a bumpy street and stopped in front of a half-finished house. Construction equipment littered the dirt yard.

"We get out here," the man said, now turning to me. "My friend take you to town."

I thanked him for the ride, and said good-bye to the woman. Then I watched them walk, one after the other, into a hefty privacy.

## Hvar

Hvar half-cups its harbor in oatmeal tones. A cozy spill of sun-warmed stone around a shimmery liquid center. Fishing skiffs bob and sleek sailboats nuzzle, their white masts dwarfing the regimental palms. The scent of lavender rises from vendors' vials and, in stepped alleys, Slavic susurrations echo. A walkway winds out along the harbor, past the fifteenth-century Franciscan monastery and the circle of bikinied schoolgirls batting a ball over transparent water.

Cafés sprinkle the waterfront promenade and amble into the cathedral square. A Venetian arsenal hugs a corner, its top floor housing Croatia's first theater, one of the oldest in Europe. It sends a note of real artifice into the prevailing atmosphere of suspected theatricality, bolstered by the last-minute appearance, high atop the hill, of an ancient citadel.

The extras filling the stage in late September are mostly bargain-hunting Easterners—Poles, Czechs, Slovaks, Hungarians, with a handful of Brits, Italians, and Germans. They stroll the promenade and study the blackboard menus (an endlessly repeated chorus of fish and spaghetti *frutti di mare*). They walk out along the sea path and throw down beach towels on unclaimed rocks, the Germans sometimes shedding every stitch of clothing in the conquest. Imagine the Little Mermaid grown up and flabby.

In the evening, concerts enliven the monastery courtyard—a touring Czech choir, a pianist from Zagreb—after which people quietly make their way back along the water (so close they can stoop and touch it), the lights of the town dancing helplessly on the surface.

Hvar, at least at the end of the season, has the feel of a languid idyll. It appears as that rare thing: an exquisite place devoid of pretension, like something out of the pre-Attitudinal Age. The occasional native indifference is the result not of disdain but an ingrained fatalism (the malaise of a people with a long history of being ruled by others, and then communists). The teenager perched on the wall outside the monastery alerts you to a darker side: warring mafias, rumbles at the discos. "Hvar is a cross between Sicily and Jamaica," he says in excellent English, and you are struck not so much by the harshness of his imagery as by the worldliness.

Hvar is the belle of the island of the same name, while the venerable statesman is Stari Grad. It horseshoes its own less crystalline harbor with houses that are somehow not quite as spruce. But what it lacks in charm it makes up for in character. For it was here, around 385 B.C., that Greeks from Paros first settled, calling the place Pharos (which the arriving Slavs pronounced as Hvar). And it was here that Hektorovic lived and wrote.

Just up from the harbor, his house—Tvrdalj—still stands, with its famous fishpond and Latin inscriptions: *How beautiful Faith and Truth are! Alas, the days flow by like waves and do not return.* And, above the entrance to the lavatory: *Know what you are, and then how can you be proud?*

I visited the house on a sunny Tuesday morning, and then walked through quiet stone streets narrowed by ancient stone houses. In a stone square I found a stone stairway, at the top of which stood the door to Maja's.

"We were just talking about you the other day," she said, having recovered admirably from the shock of my presence. She looked unchanged from the Fourth of July picnic in Fort Lauderdale (our only previous meeting): long thin arms and thick head of hair, the Israeli boyfriend still smoking in the background.

It was a little past noon and they had just gotten up. (The life of an artist.) The apartment had a makeshift air, as some of their belongings had not yet arrived from Miami, where they'd spent the last year. And they had just bought a house, which they would show me. But first we had to stop at the Lampedusa Café.

"This is where we come every day for our coffee," Maja explained, pointing to the terrace along the waterfront.

A friend was waiting: a large man with a bald head grinning peacefully from behind lozenge-shaped shades. He wore the loose white clothing and the three-day beard of a man of leisure.

"Aldo works in the cultural center," Maja said as we took our seats. "He can tell you everything about Hvar. The only problem is, he doesn't speak English." So she interpreted, starting with the Greeks, then the Romans and Byzantines, the grand entrance of the Slavs in the eighth century, followed by the Venetians and the period of Austro-Hungarian rule. Even our café had a story: Its name was taken from the island off of Sicily where, in the late 1800s, many men from Stari Grad went to fish and, in a few cases, settle.

Recent history was less remarkable. "Nothing happened here during the war," Maja said. "Two or three times a month the Yugoslav army blockaded the harbor, so we couldn't go to the mainland. Their planes flew over the island regularly. Once, they destroyed the two planes that took tourists on little sightseeing tours. That made people really mad."

Two young women came over to say hello. Mira was an athletic-looking blonde who spoke English like a Dutch woman; Ivana was short and fashionably bespectacled, frizzy brown hair falling onto a skimpy mauve dress. She sounded a hundred percent American.

"I just graduated from NYU," she said, "with a degree in archaeology and art history."

We all walked to see Mira's new house. She was an artist, who had moved here from Zagreb. How she had bought it, I hadn't a clue.

"This is the street where they found a mosaic," Ivana said.

"It's a shame it's covered up," I said.

"That's the best way to preserve it. What I'd like to see them do is unearth it again and put a Plexiglas cover atop it. But of course there's no money for that."

Mira's house stood at the corner of Srednja Kola and Vagon, two glorified passageways seemingly carved out of stone.

"Srednja Kola used to be the main street," Ivana said, "because the Riva [waterfront promenade] was too windy. Now people meet on the Riva, but it's not as nice as in Hvar. There the water is so clear it just invites you to jump in. Here we have a sewage problem—a few people have already gotten sick. They're trying to do something about it."

We entered a dusty darkness. The first floor had no windows; by the light from the open door we could make out a vast cavity in the front room, its bottom a jigsaw of mostly intact mosaic.

"I was just cleaning it this morning," Mira said. "I'm going to live upstairs and turn this room into a gallery. What I'd love to do is put pillows around and have people come and sit, just like in Roman times. Make it a kind of meeting place for artists."

Then she said casually: "The Greek street's in the next room." And moving through the doorway, with help from Aldo's cigarette lighter, we saw the large squares of cut stones purposefully placed. This was the first house I'd ever seen in which not just the décor but also the era changed from room to room.

"There are many more finds in this neighborhood," Aldo said through Maja.

"Yeah!" cried Ivana. "My sister just bought the house next door!"

"You know what I missed in Miami?" Maja asked. "Stones."

We were outside again, navigating a maze of oatmeal walls with green and brown shutters. The remark carried a little of the mystification of the pet rock craze (I can see missing your language, or even the particular blue of the water), but the more I thought about it the more sense it made. Here stone walls enclose rock-strewn fields outside of stone villages. Along the sea, stone houses sit above stone steps leading down to beaches jagged with boulders. In missing stones Maja was missing her world.

"Did you see the fishpond?" Ivana asked as we neared Tvrdalj. "The story was that whenever a fish died, Hektorovic didn't eat it, instead he buried it. They do that today."

In the cultural center, housed in an old sea captain's house, we found more artifacts, here under glass and informatively labeled. Aldo went into his office and returned with a paperback.

"For you," he said in English, handing it to me. It was a copy, in Croatian and English, of *Fishing and Fishermen's Conversations.*

"I was editor," he said proudly.

On the way to Maja's new house, we stopped at St. John's Church and examined more mosaics. To show us the fine acoustics, Maja sang a few lines of "Ave Maria." I asked why, in such a small town, there were seven Catholic churches. (Earlier I'd seen St. Lucija, with its poignant stone relief of the resurrected Christ above the doorway.)

"They're dedicated to different saints," Maja said. "St. Nikola, for example, is the saint for sailors, and travelers. Most of them are only open a few times a year, like for the saint's day."

"Are young people religious here?" I asked.

"A lot of them believe in God, but they don't like organized religion." Though Ivana said she had gone to Rome to participate in World Youth Day.

Down the street stood Maja's house, catty-corner from St. Stephen's Church. Its Venetian campanile filled the bedroom window.

"The bells start ringing at six in the morning," said Maja.

In the garden, Aldo picked almonds and figs from the trees.

"We also have tangerines, lemons, plums," said Maja. "We're going to fix the place up and then rent it out."

But not this afternoon. A visitor had arrived, from far away. The figs were ripe, and lusciously sweet. And the days flow by like waves and do not return.

"This is a terrible car for Hvar," said Maja, as her boyfriend negotiated the narrow lane in his ancient Mercedes. She sat in the backseat with Vanda, another artist who had joined us for a ride after the others had drifted off. If Hektorovic were around today, I thought, his great work would be titled: *Art and Artists' Conversations.*

"I know something special about the island," said Vanda, who had been silent, searching for something with which to impress me. "The Easter procession. There are five villages that people walk to, one after another. When they get to a church, they sing in an indescribable way. It is like crying."

"There's a local men's choir," Maja said, "that put out a CD called *Following the Cross.* They're famous all over the world now."

We passed a truck packed tight with grapes; a sweet viscidity filled the air.

"Wine is one of the major industries on the island," Maja said, "along with olives and lavender."

It was almost dark when we got back to Stari Grad. After a drink at Café Antika—"we usually sit outside on the benches and watch people go by"—we walked a few yards to Jurin Podrum.

"This is where everybody gathers in winter," said Maja, taking a seat at a corner table. "It's run by Aldo's brother."

A rustic simplicity: stone walls, wooden roof beams, two small flags (Croatian and American), and a snapshot of a man with a maniacal expression. "That's the cook," Maja said with satisfaction.

We ordered: salad, fish, grilled squid, and red and white *bevanda* (wine mixed with water). Then I asked Maja what it was like here in winter.

"There is so much time in twenty-four hours you can't realize it. But it's good for contact with nature. You go for walks and you find wild asparagus, wild cabbage. It's more interesting to spend hours collecting than to buy. And in winter we drink young wine."

I asked if she took the ferry into Split very often. "No. You don't go to Split with only one reason. You need five reasons to go to Split. There are people on the island who have never been to Split. They know nothing outside the island."

A rotund man with a mustache entered.

"He has a popcorn concession during the summer," Maja told me. "Last weekend he said: 'That's it. I'm on vacation.' He's on vacation till next season."

"People here live very simply," the boyfriend said. "They get by with only the basics."

Our salads arrived, beautiful presentations of tomatoes, lettuce, arugula. Maja picked a leaf out of hers.

"This is a weed. It's what you find growing in walls. Hey, Vlad, what's this doing in my salad?"

"I wanted to remind you of your new house."

Aldo and his wife sauntered in, taking the table next to ours, followed by Mira and her boyfriend. Then the man I had met in the morning in the yard of St. Lucija. It was like a tourist edition of *This Is Your Life.*

When the entrees arrived, Maja said: "My fish is delicious. The head is full of white meat, and I don't usually eat the head."

She and her boyfriend insisted on paying, and driving me back to Hvar, though I said I'd be happy to take the bus. No, they said, it would give them an excuse to visit the town.

"Hvar is big business now," Maja said. "It attracts some people who are not so nice."

I asked about the shooting the other week, which the teenager at the monastery had told me about.

"That was very unusual. And it had to do with mafia," she said. "It doesn't affect other people."

We found a café on the waterfront just down from my hotel. Almost immediately, a young woman stopped to talk to Maja.

"I used to be in a rock group," she said, after the woman had gone. I wouldn't have imagined her in any other kind. "It was called Gego's Band—Gego was a nickname of the leader. I played electric guitar. And we had one hit, "Mama, I'm Crazy." It was the Number One song the summer of '94. Every station played it, and every island wanted us to come play. We would take boats to the islands, and all these people would come along. Many of them were drunk even before they got on the boat.

"On the mainland was war. Here was crazy time. I think it's always like that—you need balance. In America during the Vietnam War you had the hippies."

I asked if it was possible to get a copy of "Mama, I'm Crazy," and Maja said no, even she didn't have one. The recording had somehow disappeared from the earth. Which was a shame, for it would have gone nicely with my Hektorovic.

The next morning, walking through the main square, I saw the woman from the ferry. She was sitting at a café table while her boyfriend—in the same outfit, with the same bluster—was reaching for something: a menu, a lighter, possibly the umbrella to shade their table. I walked past quickly, so as not to be spotted, but before I turned the corner I seemed to detect a knowing half-smile on her face.

## Dubrovnik

He occupied the bench, just outside the city gate, like an office. It was, you knew immediately, his bench; public property subverted to a private shabbiness: mussed hair, graying beard, rheumy eyes, untucked shirt stretched by bulging stomach. Your reward for climbing the staircase alleys to escape the tourists.

I quickly turned around and walked back through the open gate, back into the proper, rehabilitated old town. Stone carvings—crosses, gargoyles—sat behind bars in a hollowed-out space in the fortress wall. They had the beguiling air of art from a distant, naïve age. I entered the gallery on the corner to inquire.

"Oh, those are Pero's," the owner said, coming to the doorway. She wore a sleeveless black blouse over an ankle-length skirt and had a refined, attractive face. Her voice, like those of many of the Croatian women I'd met, was slightly hard: It seemed to go with the black hair and the dark eyes and the beleaguered past. Her name was Nina.

"He lives just up there," she said, pointing up the street. "Do you have a special interest?"

"I'm a travel writer, writing about Dubrovnik."

"I can tell you about Dubrovnik. Why don't you come by this evening, around seven. We can talk then. Ah, there he goes now. Pero!"—she called after the vagrant risen from his bench—"this man would like to meet you."

The two of us trudged up Peline Street, between the stone houses and old city wall.

"During war I cannot go to army—too much kilos," Pero said, lovingly patting his stomach. "I patrol this part of city. I have key for door—I control who go in and out." (Later I learned that the keys were kept elsewhere, but it was a good story.) "I patrol in this dress—he tugged at his loud shirt—"and with hunting machine for chickens. When they come down mountain, we shoot back." And he laughed at his tale of the out-of-shape sculptor turning away crack soldiers.

He stopped in front of a trellised terrace. Dappled light fell onto the stone figure of a female nude squatting toward the street. She had large breasts and a folk-heroic mien. Pero went and turned a spigot, transforming the statue into a fountain, the flow of water emanating from between the legs. Two passers-by looked on in amusement; Pero asked if they'd like a picture, then leaned over lustily to take a drink.

"I do sexual and sacral objects," he said, wiping his mouth with his hand and leading me onto the terrace. In a niche of the house stood a smaller, robed figure. He wore a long beard and held up a ball with a disproportionately large right hand. The piece had an endearing originality, conjuring whimsy from the hard reality of stone.

"This is St. Blaise," Pero said. "He help Croatia to take first gold medal in handball. When was Olympics in Atlanta, I walking with friends after match, we were drunk, and the next day I make this.

"I make 500 kilo St. Blaise," he added, "for Dubrovnik hospital. I make sculpture of pope that is in Munich. My family is good Catholic for 500 years. Every Sunday I was go to church when communists was in Yugoslavia. But now church is full of communists, I don't go."

He walked over to a bust, a more conventional work that still possessed a distinctive flair.

"This is Stjepan Radic, great Croatian leader. He say, 'We not be free if we no have Croatian guns on Croatian shoulders and Croatian money in Croatian pockets.' Now Croatia is free. We no have money but we have guns." And he allowed himself a rueful chuckle.

"This," he said, pointing to another bust, "is my friend who was killed in war. He was engineer, he work in government company, but he was first to help. You want drink?"

It was about ten in the morning. We walked into the dark house, through rooms empty of furniture but filled with stuff; it looked less like an abode than a cross between a studio and a storage space. In the kitchen Pero picked up two equally unwashed glasses—from among a thick forest of empty bottles and glasses—and poured some brandy. He plopped into a chair that had a clear view out into the street—his chair; I unearthed my own from under a dusty, nameless clutter.

"This my first sculpture," he said, grabbing a small, rudimentary piece. "I am nervous one day. My wife say, 'Why you nervous?' I say, 'Problems. Much problems.' She say, 'Why not you take stone like your father and work with it?'"

He leaned over for a very long stick, like an enormous ruler, and aimed it at a switch on the wall. "When I see tourist outside I turn on water," he said, looking out happily to gauge the reaction. "More people take picture of woman who pish than take picture of cathedral.

"When I was younger I have discotheque. I name it 'Yellow Submarine.' Very popular. Then communists say, 'No can be private.' They broken it up."

He reached behind him for some papers; the disorder, at least here in the kitchen, was localized enough that it obviated getting up. Pawing through a pile, he pulled out an old student ID. In idealistic black-and-white gazed a clean-shaven, clear-eyed Pero Miljkovic, history major.

"Everybody call me Pero Limunada," he said. "I had limunada business. I had restaurant, too, up on hill, but now it has no top of it."

Old alarm clocks, I noticed, helped populate the kitchen. "I collect. But get up as I like. If I have inspiration, I work three day and night. If no have inspiration, I no work." Today apparently was muse-less. And life, it appeared, now wife-less.

"Tourist only looking for souvenir, for little money. I no working souvenir. Before the war we have rich tourist. Now we have cheap tourist."

A few minutes later a young man walked in and said in a German accent, "I'd like a red wine for me and a juice for my girlfriend." Then, looking around, asked, "It's not a bar?"

"If you want," said Pero, rising slowly from his chair to get them drinks.

When they were gone, he said: "I show you house."

Down a short flight of steps to two more disheveled rooms. "House has three hundred years. Here," he said, entering the room on his right, "will be degustation vino." It had little to recommend it except that, here and there, a stone in the wall had been chiseled into a witty shape. Rock doodles. Modern cave carvings.

"This my grandfather telling me story," Pero said, pointing to two small figures dwarfed by a Thurberesque house.

"I am on the TV and journalist ask me, 'Pero, are you naïve artist?' I say, 'No, I not naïve artist. Naïve is only those who buy from me.'" And then the furry, gotcha grin.

We walked back outside, into the late morning sun.

"Here come my doctor. He going to tell me not to drink. But I must to drink. Hello, doctor," he said, clasping his brandy.

"Living in old town very bad. To change something on house, complications. To get satellite dish, complications. Garbage—we no have man who cleans; all people cleans.

"Like one big family, but most old people. Young people go and study in Zagreb, or go out of old town to live with car, in modern apartment."

Yet it was impossible to imagine Pero not here, at the near-summit of all the ancient alleys, the tragicomic epicenter of this stone-strewn world.

Nina passed by on her way home for lunch.

"I wanted to her make love," Pero lamented loudly. "But she don't want."

"Maybe," she called back sweetly, "when we are on pension."

At 6:45 I climbed back up to the top of the old town. Nina was waiting in the doorway of her gallery; I followed her up a winding staircase and took a seat on a sofa draped with a protective white cover.

"Do you prefer black tea or green? Perhaps you'd like to try some local brandy?"

I picked up one of the books on the end table: poems in French of Jacques Prévert.

"I am translating his oeuvre," Nina said. "In the old Yugoslavia all the translators were Serbs; their syntax is different. I translate all the poems and then the publisher picks only certain ones. They cannot publish them all, for it would make too big a book and nobody would be able to afford it. People used to have a lot; now they have very little."

She handed me the cup of tea.

"And it happened just like that."

She passed me a snifter of brandy, followed by a plate of grapes. Then she sat at the opposite end of the sofa.

"But people are proud. Even if they're suffering financially, you don't see it. They may live with grandparents; grandmother makes the clothes. People put on a good appearance."

The bombardment of her city began in early November 1991; Nina took her two boys on the second boat out and sailed to northern Croatia, where her sister lives. During the seven-month siege, four shells landed on her house. "But they didn't explode."

After eleven months, she returned. Now, eight years later, the city was for the most part physically repaired (patches of new roof tiles unnaturally brighten overviews) but far from being psychologically healed.

"People are anxious—that's what they are. They're not happy. They used to be happy, but not now.

"In the old days," she said, changing the subject, "there were tanneries up here, and prostitutes. This was where the poor people lived. The houses down below were for the noble families.

"I almost never leave the old town. I have everything I need here. In the morning I walk down to the green market and the fish market. There's a bakery nearby. There are things to do. Concerts. Exhibitions. The French, Austrian, and Italian cultural institutes have programs. It's not boring. It's a very easy place to live. Easy," she sighed, "except for the money problems."

Marija stopped and pointed to a design in the macadam: a round indentation, like the imprint of a bowling ball, wearing a halo of smaller dents.

"That's the trace of a shell," she said. "Or as some people call them: 'a Serbian rose.'"

I had been given Marija's name by a friend in the States. She had short black hair and an Italianate face with an indefinable Slavicness. We were walking from my hotel down the fragrant street high above the pebbly beaches.

"See that tree?" she asked, pointing behind us to the crest of the mountain as it bent toward the sea. "That's where they had their heavy artillery. Then up in here," she moved her arm closer to town, "there were snipers. This stretch where we are now was right in the line of fire."

Just inside the Ploce Gate she led me to a map with a legend. I had passed it every morning without looking, assuming the triangles and circles identified churches and monuments. Now I saw that they had a more martial purpose, indicating roofs damaged by direct impact, roofs damaged by shrapnel, direct hits on pavement, and facilities burned by fire.

"Sixty-nine percent of old town roofs were destroyed," Marija said, in the insider tone of the travel agent she now was. "Nine palaces burned down. Most have been rebuilt by now. By palace I mean a place that was built as the home of a noble family.

"They put sandbags on some monuments, but not a lot. People didn't think anything was going to happen. We had the French occupation, the Austrian. Then World War II. Nobody damaged Dubrovnik." Throughout my trip I had heard this refrain, which seemed to lift the city out of the category of mere magnificence and place it, like Varanasi, or Lourdes, in an inviolable realm of sacredness. And to demote the Serbs to an unprecedented level of callousness.

"On October first they cut our electricity and water. They wanted as many people as possible to leave town. I thought my arms would grow from being stretched by carrying buckets back from the wells outside the old town. Still, I went to church, in a freshly pressed blouse.

"I think attacking Dubrovnik was their big mistake. When people around the world saw what was happening to Dubrovnik, they finally reacted to what was happening all over here." Dubrovnik crucified, so that Croatia might live.

"Three hundred and sixty people were killed, one hundred of them civilians."

We had entered the Stradun, the central promenade of stones so smoothed by centuries of footsteps that it has the look, and in wet weather the feel, of a frozen canal.

"There were fifty-two craters up and down here," Marija said. "There were no windows left—in the shops or in the apartments above. Everything was boarded up."

So much of the appeal of the Stradun, as of Paris, is in the regimentation: the repeating arched doorways, the mirrored rows of forest green shutters; it was painful to imagine it all blown asunder.

"For Christmas the artists of Dubrovnik painted the boarded up windows," Marija said. "Some political pictures, some funny. It helped lift people's spirits.

"We had one and a half years of curfew. I read every book I had; did every crossword. We ate dried foods, like pasta, and canned things. We had bread—our bakers worked all through the bombardment—but no fresh fruits or vegetables. The first meat we got was chicken. And then it was chicken, chicken, chicken, chicken. For safety, some people moved to St. John's Fortress, which houses the aquarium. But they didn't eat the fish.

"People started to walk differently. Even after the bombardment, when I walked down the Stradun I would still look up to where the artillery had been. And I stayed close to the north side of the street, the safe side."

We stopped for a drink at the Trubadur Caffé, taking two of the large wicker chairs set in a row outside in the alleyway. A quartet played contemporary jazz; directly opposite, the walls of the cathedral showed shrapnel scars.

"I don't hate the Serbs," Marija said firmly. "But I don't like them." She took a magnanimous sip of her wine. "I feel sorry for them."

Nina's red shoes descended the steps to Prijeko Street and then turned into Rozarij where they disappeared under a white tablecloth. A pink fish arrived on an unadorned platter, she gave her OK, and it was promptly whisked back to the kitchen for grilling.

"We used to have a lot more restaurants," Nina said. "Now, on this street, there is only one other place that really knows about cooking."

She took a puff of her cigarette. "There's no professionalism here. I know a woman who became the director of an institute with absolutely no qualifications. But her son died in the war, so she's a hero."

The fish arrived in pools of olive oil. Nina picked up a small cup and drenched hers in more.

"I think we should become a city-state again, like Monaco. People from Zagreb never used to come here. They went to the northern islands. People from Belgrade came—we used to get *la crème* from Belgrade. But they don't come now; they're afraid. Now people from Zagreb come because it's Dubrovnik, it's," she made an unjingoistic frown, "Croatia!"

After dinner I walked her home, back up the steps in the balmy autumn air.

"Summer here is busy," she said in a suddenly softer voice. "You almost look forward to September. November is a little sad, when the weather turns. But in December there's St. Nikola's Day, when we exchange presents. And then Christmas and New Year's.

"By the middle of January I can already smell spring. The mimosas are in bloom; you see the yellow in gardens when you walk outside the old town. At the beginning of February we have narcissuses, and St. Blaise's Day, when all the almond trees are in blossom. In March we get the freesias, anemones, and tulips, which last till the end of April. Roses come in May, with the flowering orange trees." All the welcome explosions.

"This is my house," she announced suddenly, just before we reached the top of the hill.

We said our farewells and then I finished the climb, turning to follow the city wall along Peline Street. The fountain was silent, though Radic gazed mischievously over his mustache, and St. Blaise was still triumphantly holding up his handball. And through the open front door I could see deep into the dark house to the lighted kitchen where Pero sat in his lookout chair, fast asleep.

# 21

## *Spoken to the Heart*

The street was spinning—a roofless carousel mounted with motorbikes. They roared up the boulevard that leads down to the river, zoomed by the balloon vendors at the foot of the square, swung in front of the gingerbread Hotel de Ville and careered past the glass-doored entrance of the Rex, where I stood on the steps—my first evening in Saigon—tired and transfixed.

Some bikes carried entire short-sleeved families, others single, determined young men, or pairs of watchful trousered girls (giving the scene the feel of a *paseo* in a small Mexican town, only motorized). They circled an animated crowd of bubble blowers, picture takers, shoeshine boys, dried-squid vendors, and Sunday strollers all taking the air under the towering billboards of Panasonic and Konica. The cyclo drivers—slumped headachy in their bulky contraptions—seemed the only living things still stationary in the city, aside from the geckos stuck to the walls of the old town hall.

I took a long walk, and when I returned the parade was still going on—a humid, spontaneous swirl of noise and color. It would have inspired a Vietnamese Chagall, or even a sales rep from Coke, but it was daunting to anyone who held the slightest hope of entering into it.

I had a few names of people to contact in Saigon (nobody calls it Ho Chi Minh City). The first, Esther—an unlikely name for an English teacher in postwar Vietnam, even an American one—called on Monday and invited me to sit in on her class at the university. She told me to take a cyclo and not pay more than 4,000 *dong*.

Already I knew how my appearance on the steps of the Rex would arouse the drowsy cyclo drivers. They were like those Disney figures that spring to life as soon as your train enters their world, and then, after you pass, return to rigor mortis. One arm would shoot up, in the classic schoolboy cry for attention, and a look of unbearable joy and expectation would fill the face. Then, as you shook your head and walked away, the arm would drop dejectedly and the eyes glaze over with hurt and despair. Refusing rides from cyclo drivers gave me, I thought, an idea of how the last helicopter pilots must have felt leaving those people behind on the roof.

It was a long pedal to the university. At Tran Nguyen Hai Circle we drifted into a dense flow of bicycles, motorcycles, motorbikes, cyclos, and cars. Riding slightly above tire level in an open seat through the wanton crush—there are few stoplights in downtown Saigon—I felt invigorated. I marveled at how the man pedaling behind me would, with the finesse of a gondolier, aim for a spot and then glide my seat over (against the current, just missing a slowly departing wheel) with a well-timed touch on the handlebars. Though sitting on that cushioned throne—excessively large in a country where so much else seems made for children—I could never ward off a feeling of colonialism.

The university branch where Esther taught was an unprepossessing cluster of concrete buildings. Students rolled up on bicycles, the young women fetching in hats of felt or straw and, occasionally, opera gloves to protect their skin from the tropical sun. Esther arrived by cyclo; she exuded a youthful, optimistic American spirit, though I knew that she had at least one grown son.

Her classroom was locked, her director AWOL. "This is the thing that gets to me here," she said cheerfully. "The disorganization." It was too early for me to tell if this was a feature of Vietnam or communism or a combination of both. When a key was finally located, it unlocked a high-ceilinged room with bare walls and inoperable fans. The heat was oppressive. Lectures from neighboring classrooms came in through paneless windows.

After class, we walked to the student canteen. "I have to get a portable microphone," Esther said. "All last semester my throat hurt from talking so loudly." We drank soda from glasses crammed with crudely cut ice, and I asked Esther, "Why Vietnam?"

"I could say something New Age, like 'I think I lived here in a previous life.'" (Didn't we all? I thought.) "But there was something about the place that spoke to my heart." She had first come a year ago, on a solo backpacking trip through Asia. "I hated Thailand. I thought the country had sold out completely to tourism, that there was nothing genuine or authentically Thai left in the place.

"I live next door to a family, and they've sort of adopted me as 'the older sister,'" she laughed. "That's what they call me. And I like that system of being part of an extended family. It cuts into your privacy. They have no sense of personal privacy the way we do. And some of your self-determination. But that's OK."

As if on cue, several of her students arrived and asked if they could join us. "Tom's an American journalist," Esther introduced me.

"What is the difference," one of the boys asked struggling, his ability to pronounce lagging behind his capacity to think, "between a journalist and a correspondent?"

Leaving, I complimented him on his English. "When an American or an Englishman tells you you speak good English," he sculpted the words as roughly as the waitress had our ice, "you can deduct 50 percent as untrue."

"There is nothing to see in Saigon," Marie da Silva told me the next morning. "NOTHING! It is an industrial city."

Da Silva was a Frenchwoman who, for the last eight years, had run a successful silk business out of a small shop on Dong Khoi Street. "Everyone comes to see me now," she said. "This store is like a consulate. A man came in the other day connected with oil. I know nothing about oil, but I can tell him how to do business in Vietnam."

"How?" I asked.

"You have to love the Vietnamese."

Da Silva was correct that—except for a few pagodas—Saigon offered little in the way of architectural pleasures. But for the Westerner it has a number of literary and colonial landmarks. On my walk that first night, I went looking for the Hôtel Continental, on whose open-air terrace much of the action in Graham Greene's *The Quiet American* takes place. The hotel gleamed with a fresh coat of white paint but the famous terrace—dubbed "The Continental Shelf" by journalists (correspondents)—seemed as long gone as Pyle and Fowler and Phuong. The Continental was the writers' hotel; André Malraux lived in it after getting booted out of China. The Caravelle across the street was the journalists' hotel (Eric Sevareid used to read his nightly reports while standing on its roof) and the Rex, just down Le Loi Boulevard, was the American officers' hotel, site of the press conferences known forever as "The Five O'clock Follies." The military had now been replaced by businessmen, though memories of their presence still lingered in the hotel rules posted on the back of my door.

> 7. *Guests are not allowed to use their rooms as liaison offices, nor to displace or move the furniture and equipment from one room to another.*

This part of Saigon, especially Dong Khoi (Rue Catinat in the days of the French), I thought of as "The Graham Greene

Quarter." Street kids here peddled *The Quiet American* to tourists, a tribute that would have delighted Greene probably as much as the Nobel Prize. At night, painted young men in long white dresses rode enormous black motorcycles up on the sidewalk, blocking your path and blinking false lashes. This, too, would have amused the author.

Today's itinerary, a little to the north, covered what I called "The James Fenton District." Fenton, an English poet, stayed around for the fall of Saigon (April 30, 1975), writing stories for the *Washington Post* and, later, a wonderful book with the equally wonderful title, *All the Wrong Places.* Here he tells of entering the American embassy that fateful morning: "Some people gave me suspicious looks, as if I might be a member of the embassy staff, so I began to do a little looting myself." And of hitching a ride on the first tank to reach the Presidential Palace. He notes that the palace gate, contrary to some newspaper accounts, was not knocked to the ground by the tank but opened by a civilian guard.

I headed up Nam Ky Khoi Nghia, thrilled, as always, by the street life. Everything (almost) was done outdoors. Babies were bathed, children wrote homework, mothers took naps, deftly folded into their tiny chairs. The Vietnamese have a feline ability to make themselves comfortable in the most confining space; walking one day through Ben Thanh market I was startled to find at eye-level a young woman in pajamas coolly reclined among the avocados. A barber shop was any wall a man with a chair and a pair of scissors could find to hang a mirror. A store was a table with items atop it. The Vietnamese gave new meaning to the term "sidewalk café"—the pavement serving not only as dining room but kitchen, with the smoke from charcoal fires joining the street exhaust, and the suds from hand-washed dishes flowing to the gutter. I had been warned about beggars and cripples, but when you got off the main tourist paths, the hard-bitten citizens of this clamorous city were laden mostly with smiles.

The gates of the former American embassy, on Le Duan Boulevard, were locked, the grass behind growing wild around a couple discarded oil drums. A black stain dripped down from the roof. The famous roof. If you looked hard enough, you could almost see the crowd of people on the steps leading up to the helicopter.

A woman approached and tried to sell me postcards. Phalanxes of schoolgirls passed on bicycles. They all wore white *ao dais,* the traditional dress of flowing trousers beneath a long-sleeved tunic. The tunic is slit up each side to just above the waist, allowing freer movement and revealing a soft triangle of forbidden midriff, a design that ingeniously manages to be both modest and sexy. Each girl held one corner of her tunic up at the handlebar—to give her legs more mobility?—while the back part floated out behind her. Strands of long, straight hair fell beneath their hats like licorice waterfalls. I watched them for several minutes, dazed by their impeccable posture and ephemeral air as they rode cool and pristine through the humidity and dirt.

Then I rounded the corner and found a side entrance. To my surprise, a car sat in the driveway. A man on the steps told me the embassy now housed the offices of PetroVietnam.

From there it was a short walk down a wide, treelined avenue to the former Presidential Palace, now Reunification Hall. It had the same period look as the embassy (1960s) but less of the feel of an abandoned bunker (it was now primarily a museum of executive excess). Downstairs an photograph exhibit documented the taking of the palace on April 30. I looked in vain for a bald English poet.

Tuyet had a broad young face—made even wider by her frequent smile—and the best English I'd heard in Vietnam. I just wished she wouldn't keep turning around and using it on me as she steered us on her motorbike. It was Tuesday evening rush hour and I was, I noted, the only man in Saigon being moto-ed by a woman—the cousin of a Florida friend, as if that counted. Still, I felt pretty good. The wind in my hair—you don't get that in a cyclo—the wind in her hair, her hair in my face. We made a sharp turn and came up to the square in front of my hotel. I looked over and saw myself still standing on the steps, scratching my head and saying: "Hey, what the hell's he doing on the back of that thing?"

After about twenty minutes of life-threatening intersections, we barreled down a side street and came to a stop in front of a small wooden case of shampoo and cigarettes. "Well," said Tuyet smiling, "we're home."

Her mother stood up from behind the case and warmly invited me into her house. It was completely open to the street and had a concrete floor. I sat in one of several wooden chairs set in a row against the wall. The red lights of small shrines glowed in the back.

Tuyet worked for an American company. "Anyone who has knowledge of English and computers can get a job now," she said, as motorcycles roared past a few feet away.

She had studied English at the university; her first job had been as an English teacher, but she left the profession due to a chronic sore throat. At school she had read *The Quiet American*—"about an Englishman and his love for a Vietnamese girl"—and *The Old Man and the Sea*—"my friend compared it in his final exam to a lizard losing its tail."

Her mother returned with an enormous plate of spicy beef sprinkled with peanuts, potatoes, and salad. "Sorry," Tuyet said laughing, "no high-tech spring rolls." Then she went out to buy me beers. They both watched sadly as I failed to finish the plate.

"You sure you can't eat any more?" Tuyet asked. "I don't want a call from my cousin saying 'How come Mr. Tom Swick left your house not full?'"

She said things were changing now, life was gradually getting better. People weren't afraid to talk to foreigners anymore, students no longer had to study Russian. But the idea of going to America to visit her cousin, whom she was dying to meet, was an exorbitant dream. She handed me a carved turtle—symbol of longevity—to give to her when I got back.

She asked if I'd learned to bargain with the cyclo drivers. "Many of them speak good English, you know. We call them 'cyclo hi-fi's.'" When I said I'd better get back, she called her brother to give me a lift. "Take care of him," she ordered. "He's VIP."

And I felt like one too, riding to the hotel—the streets were darker now but also less crowded—on the back of a motorcycle. The man pulled up in front of the Rex, shook my hand, then sped off back home. I looked over at the cyclo drivers—hoping they'd noticed my suddenly improved station, my entry into the swirl—but they slouched as listlessly as geckos in the humid night.

It took me days to get to the train station. I kept putting it off, like a visit to the doctor. Saigon was not nearly as rough as I had been warned—in fact, it had a kind of scruffy sweetness—but it was populous, and experience had taught me that if the streets are chaotic the train station is bedlam.

Ever since getting barked at in Madrid in 1976—my ticket agent's contemptuous Spanish ricocheting unintelligibly off the window—I have had a mild fear of foreign train stations. Which is a sorry affliction for someone who loves trains—like an oenophile being terrified of corkscrews.

So I tried alternate ways to get a ticket. The travel agents and hotel staff were unfailingly patient, courteous, accommodating, and wrong. None of the information one person gave me matched the other's, and all of it was at odds with my guidebook. Part of Vietnam's appeal is that there are few countries where you can be led astray so charmingly.

Then one morning I steeled myself and climbed onto the back of a motorcycle. We picked our way through crowded alleys and came to what looked like foundry gates. Beyond, surrounded by an empty expanse, loomed the station.

Inside, it was surprisingly hushed. At the first window a woman motioned me to the center of the hall, where, in a small, protected space, a desk sat with a vase of plastic flowers atop it. Next to the flowers was a sign that read: "Foreigners Information." It seemed an exceedingly thoughtful arrangement (surely not a legacy of the French)—the equivalent of access ramps for the linguistically impaired. I took a chair as if waiting for my teacher.

She appeared shortly, a plump woman in an embroidered *ao dai*. She pulled out an enlarged timetable, came around the desk to go over it with me, and explained the intricacies in careful English. My only regret was that I didn't have an apple to give her.

The evening of the following day I got a taxi in front of my hotel and took one last tour through the multiwheeled circus of Saigon streets. Inside the nearly empty station, a young woman in an *ao dai* graciously pointed me toward my train. High above her, a large portrait of a waving Ho Chi Minh bid me farewell.

I was the first in my compartment, followed by a ragged parade of street urchins insisting on my need for a cheap paper fan. I declined, though the evening was still and humid. Then I safely deposited my bag in the cupboard of the topmost bunk.

All the Vietnamese I met, when they heard of my plans to take the train to Hue, told me not to. "You're not going by yourself!?!" Tuyet had said, before translating the news to her mother, who shook her head woefully. "Because you are a friend of Meri, we feel protective of you. We don't want anything to happen to important American citizen. Why don't you fly?"

I said I wanted to see the country. Who, I asked, had ever written an interesting story about an airplane ride? And, I reminded her, Miss Vietnamese Safety, the planes were still Russian.

Foreigners were of another opinion. "Compared to what happens on European trains," said a young Swiss man who'd spent a month in the country, "they're asylums." (I assumed he meant this in the sense of sanctuaries.) Esther said that, as everywhere, you had to keep an eye on your things. Once she'd been in a compartment when someone hanging down from the roof had reached in the window and snatched a suitcase off the middle bunk—which is why she recommended I take the top one.

I was depressing the fan vendors with variations on the English negative—Nah, No, No-o-o-o-o-o-o, No-no-no, NO!!—when Dr. Nguyen walked in. He, too, was going to Hue, where he worked as a cardiologist in the Central Hospital.

"When I was boy, I study French. In school, English. Then Russian." He said this in a weary, unfinished way, as if wondering what was next. A frail, elderly man entered, followed by a middle-aged woman in silk pants and horn-rimmed glasses. She bought us a round of paper fans. We were all flapping them rhythmically when the train pulled out a little past seven. In minutes, the noise was deafening.

Very soon Dr. Nguyen looked at me and then up at my bunk, signaling that that was where I was to go so that he—who had the lowest berth—could stretch out and sleep. I obeyed. I was sorry not to see the last of Saigon, but that would have been difficult anyway. The window had a metal shutter that was pulled down several inches from the bottom. The view through the remaining space, which even the Vietnamese had to stoop to look through, was further obstructed by thick chicken wire. No suitcases were going to disappear through this window.

Upstairs I was happy to find a thin white mattress, like a pad, stretched across my wooden bunk. I had tried to book a "soft berth"—like a European couchette, with four to a compartment—but had had to settle for a "hard berth"—six to a compartment—which I was afraid meant exactly what it said. The padding came as a welcome surprise.

Still, it was a restless night. The guidebooks had all talked about the berths, the views, even the food, but not one of them had mentioned the noise. It was, without question, the most rackety train I had ever been on. The open windows everywhere—necessary because of the lack of air-conditioning—contributed. But there was a particular quality to the clamor. The constant background noise made it seem as if all the people from the Super Dome were somehow sitting in our compartment during a goal-line stand. This was punctuated, for long periods, by a piercing roar, rather like that of a C-130 taking off. When the plane finally departed, and we were left with only the 50,000 fans, life seemed almost tolerable. But the plane always returned.

Around six, I crawled down from my perch and peered through the slit at sunlit scenes of pastoral Asia. It was all there: the rice paddies, dotted with eternally bent figures in rolled-up pants and conical hats; the water buffaloes being led down dirt roads or bathed in lakes; the domestic cluster of thatched gray huts, snug against a grove of palms; the green-carpeted hills in the distance; the sky a beatific blue above. And seeing it live the first thing in the morning made me quiver.

A young man and woman dressed in loose-fitting railway shirts dropped by with breakfast: cold noodles and chewy bits of beef in plastic containers. No chopsticks, but a thick spoon as if for hot and sour soup. Then the woman returned with a plastic bag of thick slices of white bread and another bag containing fatty gray lunchmeat of unidentifiable origin. Esther had warned me that foreign passengers are given what the Vietnamese think of as "Western" meals; I feigned ignorance of this, theoretically, considerate custom and spooned my noodles.

Dr. Nguyen had stripped down to his sleeveless undershirt; despite the constant breeze, it was still stifling. He had short, muscular arms with beautifully smooth skin. He had just been to visit his daughter at her technical school in Saigon. I tried to imagine an American physician taking the train to his daughter's college. He said that his hospital in Hue, with 1,000 beds, was the third largest in the country, after Hanoi and Saigon.

The woman who had bought us fans now passed out green oranges. She sat with me and the doctor on the one lower berth, while the elderly man lay motionless on the other. "He's sick," explained the doctor, pointing to his own stomach. I avoided the old man's hollow gaze. Americans—crippled us with their war, now joy-riding on our trains. I felt sad and spoiled and excused myself.

The best place to get a view, since the corridor windows were as armored as our compartment's, was by the doors at the end of the car. Here the windows were left so untouched they didn't even have panes. The eastern one, with occasional views of the sea, was occupied by one of the young conductors, who sat on a child's wooden stool. I took the other, first squatting (which the Vietnamese can do for hours, I for maybe three minutes) then kneeling, which was OK because the overflow from the flooded toilet (hole in the floor) had yet to seep beneath the lavatory wall.

After about an hour the elderly man shuffled by on his way to the bathroom, smiling when I looked up to see whose slippers these were. Then he shuffled back. A few minutes later, he returned. He had found a wooden stool for me to sit on.

We reached Danang in the middle of the afternoon. I stepped outside for a walk along the platform, my ears still ringing. Soon after leaving the city we started climbing into lush vegetation and tracing the shoreline—falling ever farther beneath us—as we went. The scenery moved from merely beautiful to sublime.

Window seat east was still taken, now by an unusually hefty passenger. I moved my stool over next to him. The groaning ascent greatly reduced our speed, and also the clatter, but the slant unleashed a whole night's worth of urine. So just as my ears were getting relief, my nose was assaulted.

My shoes were in it (I held my bag in my lap), but I could not leave. Each new ascent revealed another deserted cove, where sandy white crescents gave parentheses to turquoise waters. We edged onto a promontory and, looking down, saw three graceful wooden boats in the spotless sea, their fishing nets anciently draped in front of their bows. I remembered that Paul Theroux, in *The Great Railway Bazaar,* had declared this the most beautiful of all the landscapes he'd seen in his journey from London. When I first read that, I thought he was just trying to shock (he was traveling during the war), but now I was convinced that he had been telling the truth.

We continued climbing, hanging precariously, the sea waiting below; other times, we plowed through jungle that seemed, with all its buzzes and electric greens, to have invaded the car. (Often I was tempted to reach out and pluck a frond.)

And then, after another hour, it was over. We were back on a level surface, and rumbling over a bridge that traversed a river promisingly named Perfume.

At the station on the other side, I shook hands with Dr. Nguyen, who gave me his business card ("Head of Intermedical Department C, Central Hospital") and urged me to call if I needed anything while I was in town. I said I hoped I wouldn't. Then I smiled farewell to the elderly man, and the bespectacled woman, and walked out into the early evening heat of Hue.

Our long wooden boat puttered down the Perfume River. Feather duster palms waved from shore, a pagoda rose in seven stories of ever-diminishing octagons. Spools of cotton puffed the sky, turning the distant mountain from emerald to tar and back again.

"My girlfriend," Diep said, "she have many boyfriend."

We sat side by side in small wooden chairs under a low roof. It was not yet ten in the morning and the sun was murderous. Rivulets of perspiration ran beneath my shirt; Diep—in her long-sleeved, high-collared, powder blue *ao dai*—sat like a dewless flower. It would have been a moment of exquisite romanticism if she hadn't been my tour guide.

"She very tender," Diep said. I gave her a long look.

"You know," and then she sang softly, hardly above the roar of the motor: "Love me . . . ten-der, love me . . . tru-u-ue."

I had heard that in Hue you could hire a woman to sing to you on a boat on the Perfume River, but I hadn't expected an Elvis impersonator. Which in a strange way black-haired Diep—in her shades and powder blue pants suit—vaguely resembled.

I had heard a lot of other things about Hue (say "Who-ay" fast, so the "a" ambushes the "u"). It was the rain capital of Vietnam, though for the past three days the sun had been relentless, the air thick with dust. It was a strongly Buddhist city, the center of Vietnamese nationalism—still on display behind the Thien Mu Pagoda is the Austin sedan that the monk who immolated himself in 1963 took to Saigon. The city had been the training ground for the nation's leaders: Quoc Hoc Secondary School counts among its alumni former South Vietnamese President Ngo Dinh Diem, General Vo Nguyen Giap, and Ho Chi Minh.

Hue was the former Imperial Capital, its temples and pagodas now bearing the scars of the Tet Offensive but its legacy of culture and refinement still intact. It is the reputed home of the finest cuisine ("Hue is the Lyon of Vietnam," an American food writer had told me) and the most beautiful women in the country. And its streets are filled with melancholy.

In Saigon I had gone to see Trinh Cong Son—a legend for the songs he wrote of love and politics in the 1960s and 1970s. It was a failed encounter. He was small and anorexic-looking, even for a Vietnamese, and answered every question with as few French words as possible. I felt, for the first time in Vietnam, unwanted. Leaving, I told him I was taking the night train to his hometown.

"It is a sad city," he said gravely. "*Triste,*" he repeated. And the word seemed to carry in its sound not only sorrow but rain.

* * *

An exultant sun was setting the evening I arrived. The shopkeepers along Le Loi Street, standing in their open-fronted showrooms beneath fluorescent lamps, gave me smiles that transcended salesmanship. And it struck me again how a traveler in Vietnam, when feeling low, need only take a walk.

I drifted down a side street that resembled a tunnel. The only light came from hodgepodge houses hidden behind trees. Phantom bicycles rolled up suddenly; shadowy forms passed in cloaks of tonal whispers. A café arose on my right, its patio candles flickering through a trellis. A few feet past, I felt a presence.

"Are you American?" a voice behind me asked carefully. I turned. Two faces—bright-eyed and boyish—beamed in the darkness.

"Yes," I said.

"You have coffee with us? We want to practice our English."

Hai and Nghi were, despite their tender looks, students at the university. Hai was pimply and prying; Nghi, pretty and silent; they complemented each other perfectly. On their table sat two well-nursed glasses of iced coffee.

Hai came from the north. He had chosen Hue because the cost of living was lower than in Hanoi. He was an only child, his father "died in the war." Back in the dorm they slept twelve to a room, mosquito nets draped over the beds. Hai studied English but didn't want to teach; he wanted to become an interpreter or work in tourism, something that would allow him to travel. He had never been to Saigon; in six days I had seen more of Vietnam than he had in eighteen years. He was rabid with curiosity.

"What means: 'He is smart as a whip?' 'She is a tomboy?'" He gave a look of almost prurient intensity at my definition of the unfeminine girl. "What is difference between Old Testament and New Testament?" he asked. "Catholic and Protestant?" "I think if necessary," he said when I had finished, "I choose Protestant."

He asked me to tell him the story of the Virgin Mary—"Which religion think very well of Mary?"—Jesus Christ, Adam and Eve. And he listened to each with a slightly forbidden eagerness.

Around ten, exhausted, I got up to leave. Hai asked if I could meet them here tomorrow. Then they both straddled the same bicycle and accompanied me back to Le Loi Street.

"The moon," Hai said looking up, "is waxing, yes? Waxing and waning." He smiled with satisfaction at the lesson practically applied. Then, leaning close, he said with great seriousness: "I hear there is a beach, somewhere in the world, where everybody is naked. Is it true?"

Back at my hotel, I stepped into the lounge. Behind the bar stood a petite young woman in a yellow *ao dai.* Her name-tag carried one of the few Vietnamese words I knew (names in the language always have a meaning): *My,* the word for "American."

A party of Parisians traipsed in and My—with an unhurried ineptness—began filling their orders. It took forever. When the drinks were finally done, her wrists looked too frail to carry the tray. But she walked with such stately grace that I wondered who in this room should be waiting on whom. I assumed it was her first week.

"Three month," she told me when she returned. "Not good job. Always . . ." and, lacking the word, she made the expression: a split-second smile.

She had majored in Russian, she said sadly, before dropping out of the university to earn money for her family. Now she wanted to learn English, but it was difficult. Aside from everything else, most of the tourists who came here were French. She asked if I would stop by tomorrow.

Mr. Buu's house hunched one street over from Hai's café. It was a cramped, cluttered warren. We sat in what would have been, in a more prosperous country, the side vestibule, but here was a combination of living room and dining room open to the street. Our teacups listed on a wooden table pushed up against a concrete wall. Even though I'd already been a week in the country, I still expected a little more from the home of the head of the university French department.

Trinh Cong Son had suggested I look up Buu Y, saying that they had been friends since childhood and adding that he was descended from the royal family. (I recognized the name Buu as the same as that of a well-known Hue artist.) He was, if possible, more petite than the songwriter, with flowing, shoulder-length hair streaked with gray (the longest hair I was to see on a man) and delicate features. It was easy to picture him reading Baudelaire to a roomful of lovesick undergraduates.

One of his children ran by; I asked her name. "Vu. It means rain. It is not a common name for girls, but I chose it because when people think of Hue, they think of rain. This," he said, looking out to the sun-drenched street, "is very unusual."

With prompting, he spoke of his life—getting drafted, deserting, teaching in Saigon without papers, writing for reviews—in elegant French. He did not write much now, he said, because of the demands of teaching and administration; also, the quality of the journals had declined dramatically. His wife sat next to him, smiling during the silences (which perhaps only I found awkward) and maternally pushing more cakes on me.

Vietnam was changing fast, he said, "Hue not so fast." Then, after a pause: "Happily."

His wife whispered something to him, and Mr. Buu translated. It was an invitation to dinner tomorrow.

Two days in town and my calendar was fuller than it is at home. Back at the hotel, I stopped by the lounge to say hello to My. She was entangled in orders—the Parisians had multiplied—and asked if I could meet her for coffee on Monday morning.

In the evening I walked down the dark street and came to the café. Hai and Nghi were already installed. "Can you please tell me," Hai began before I had taken my seat, "something about your Civil War?"

At Mr. Buu's the next afternoon I produced a Bordeaux I'd bought on Le Loi.

"No, no," he grieved. "You shouldn't have spent your money. Wine—that is a great luxury for us. We will," he said, now smiling and placing the bottle atop the refrigerator, "use it for décor."

His wife began the long process of serving the meal. There came a bowl of sticky rice; another of rice mixed with ground-up shrimp; a plate piled with snow-white rice paper spring rolls stuffed with shrimp; an enormous platter of long strands of chicken ("cooked in water," Mr. Buu explained, "with mint, onion, pepper, salt, and lemon, and," he added importantly, "shredded by hand"); two small dishes of sauce: one piquant, from fish brine; the other sweet and sour. Then, with impeccable timing, his sister arrived with a large salad of shrimp, figs, sesame seeds, peanuts, and oil—to be eaten, Mr. Buu informed me, with the spring rolls.

Tasting, with eyes closed, I could have imagined myself a guest of the emperor in the Forbidden Purple City. To wash it all down we drank tall glasses of Huda beer—brewed in Hue, as the billboards said, "with Danish technology"—that Mr. Buu frequently replenished with ice.

I expressed concern about the trouble and expense.

"These are everyday dishes," Mr. Buu assured me. "Nothing expensive here."

"No expensive," his wife insisted, smiling. "No expensive."

We talked between bites. Ever since I'd arrived in Hue, I'd been haunted by a statistic: Ten thousand people—most of them civilians—had died in the city during the Tet Offensive of 1968. Delicately, I raised the subject.

"I was away in Saigon," Mr. Buu said finally. "But the brother of my stepmother was killed." There followed one of our frequent silences. Later, I expressed astonishment at how graciously I'd been treated throughout my stay.

"War is war," Mr. Buu said quietly. "Peace is peace."

Then they asked me to come again for dinner.

The boat tour on the Perfume River came as a relaxing break from the whirl of social rounds.

At seven that evening I had another appointment with Hai and Nghi. They were not at their usual post. The proprietor came and led me to a side door, behind which a loud, honeyed music blared. Opening it, we found both of them sitting tightly on a sofa with two young women. A video screen carried a fuzzy picture of lovers walking on a beach. (No, not that beach.) Hai was holding a microphone and singing into it extremely badly. So, they had another side to them, if slightly arrested. I felt as if I'd just barged in on a grade-school party of spin the bottle.

"Tom, you like karaoke?" Hai asked, breaking off in mid-song. "Here our girlfriends." Space was made for me in the middle of the couch. I felt positively large. Hai's girlfriend put her face up to mine, nearly touching my nose, and shouted above the music, "Hello! How are you?" It was the extent of her English.

The lovers—young Vietnamese—had moved off the beach and into a fountained courtyard. Short incomprehensible words—whiskered with accent marks—flashed across the bottom of the screen. All that was missing was a bouncing ball.

"Can you tell where this filmed?" Hai asked, while Nghi now sang.

"Spain?" I guessed.

"No, California. Can you tell what songs about?"

"Love," I said.

"Yes!" he said, and the room convulsed in giggles.

★ ★ ★

My was an hour late the next morning. It was so pleasant at the Song Xanh café—sipping my tea on the bank of the river, watching bicycle traffic on the other side (Hue going to work)—that I didn't mind waiting. And my train wasn't till the afternoon.

When she finally appeared she was accompanied by a girlfriend, another hapless Russian major. My ordered two glasses of milk and asked if I would take a letter to America. She pulled it carefully out of her bag; I had never seen the name "Sacramento" written so delicately.

"He just friend," she said emphatically. "Not boyfriend."

I put it in my bag with the package of oranges and cookies the Buus had given me.

The café was waking up. The tables downriver from us had filled with students; someone had fed a cassette into the tape player. The music hypnotized with a lovely, piercing, Oriental melancholy.

"That Trinh Cong Son," My said. "You know?'"

I said I'd been to his house. She displayed no surprise, asked no questions about how he lived, though she was obviously enamored of his songs.

"He write about love." She paused. "Not just love. Love and . . ." she looked out towards the river, wordless.

Loss, I knew, but didn't say it because I wasn't sure she'd know it and because she seemed already deep in another thought. There was a heart-rending incompleteness about her: the interrupted studies, the half-awake bartending, the unfinished sentences. Who knew what else?

After an hour she said they had to get going. Errands to run. My insisted on paying. Then she asked me to write. The last invitation.

"My," she said, as if I wouldn't remember. "Bar tender," she added, pronouncing it as two words, the accent on the second.

# 22

# *Tourists and Guests*

A little before midnight our Air France airbus swung out across the Sea of Marmara, hovering low over the tenebrous water. On the right, the filmy orange lights of Istanbul appeared in the distance; below us stretched a freighter. As the plane floated carpet-like toward shore, I thought of other cities I had arrived in at a late hour. It seemed a more rewarding pursuit than worrying if the hotel still held my reservation and wondering how much the taxi would overcharge me to find out.

Guidebooks will tell you it is never a good idea to arrive anywhere in the dead of night. You can't see well, things get obscured. The confusion of the new—the resonant free-for-all of an international airport—is only heightened by the dimness and drowsiness of the hour.

As is, of course, the mystery. Streets are quiet, windows shuttered, cafés closed, citizens dreaming. The riddle of the foreign is amplified by the enigma of night. Two insomniacs argue in the yellow pool of a street lamp, and no matter how many days you stay, or what wonders you see, you will always remember those men bickering as you sped by in your taxi. Like many of life's irrational acts, arriving late is graced with profits.

My first nocturnal arrival in a foreign city occurred in France. On a crisp, October afternoon in Paris I boarded a train (this in the days before TGVs) and arrived many hours later in Aix-en-Provence, an elegant university town in the south that is not the type to inspire dread unless you are young and shy and coming for a year to study the language. Outside the small station the only sound was the trickle of water from a distant fountain—a more soothing note I could not have thought of myself.

I got my first taste of the Caribbean after hours, arriving one warm winter night in Pointe-à-Pitre, Guadeloupe. The yellow headlights suggested France; the sultry air, something else. In the morning I turned the corner outside my hotel and banged into a market—perspiring women in brilliant headscarves hawking unnamable fruits—that would have been much less revelatory had I not arrived in concealing darkness.

Cities, I think, can be grouped into day and night in the same way that Ned Rorem, in his diaries, has divided the world into masculine and feminine. London you should arrive in during daylight hours (preferably for breakfast), while Paris is at its best after sunset (a glass of burgundy). Singapore's a day city; Hong Kong, nocturnal. San Juan light, Havana dark (the better to hide the deformities of age). Chicago is day; New Orleans night. New York I would classify as the timekeeper's version of bisexual.

Sometimes a city can surprise you. Cairo, which I had always thought of as diurnal (have you ever seen a photo of the pyramids at night?) wrapped me in a fervid orange murk and a blur of swishing robes as I descended at midnight from my Tel Aviv bus. It had seemed the least desirable hour at which to arrive, yet now, having done it, I can't imagine a better one.

The same goes for Istanbul. At the airport I bought a visa under a portrait of Ataturk (looking like a more focused Uncle Fester) and breezed through customs out to the late-night line-up of mustachioed cabbies. I surrendered to one who soon zipped along the water, swerved up a hill, and then broke into an open expanse of empty streets and umbrella-less terraces. To the right I glimpsed—with the *frisson* of a hiker coming upon an angel—the darkened outlines of Hagia Sophia.

My pension sat just behind it. The receptionist greeted me by name. A young man took my bag and led me up a cobblestone street lit by old-fashioned lanterns and stilled by an almost village hush, punctured presently by the plangent cry of a Bosporus ferry.

In the morning I walked back down the cobblestones, the houses now in bright hues of mustard and beige. Past the tour buses, metal-and-glass chariots idling along the ancient hippodrome, and along Divan Yolu toward the university and the Covered Bazaar. Nikes gave way to dusty black loafers. A great arch, with a flurry of green and gold Arabic script, rose at the top of a sloping square. A guard stood underneath, checking IDs, while a dozen policemen loitered inside.

"What's going on?" I asked a young man carrying a Turkish translation of John Maynard Keynes.

"Nothing special," he said. "The police are always at the university. The situation is tense. There are fights almost every day between fundamentalist students and those on the left."

"What are you?" I asked.

"I'm on the right. I love my country. The others don't. They want the Kurds to be free, to have their own state. Why can't they live with us?"

Farther along, I wandered streets lined with cheap clothing shops—leather jackets, fur-collared coats, pre-washed jeans—and noisy with Cyrillic signage. Restaurants promised borscht and piroshkis. Occasionally a name with Roman letters would pop out—Myovich, Mlynarczyk—readable (if unpronounceable) and from the same post-communist neighborhood. I had overshot the Covered Bazaar and entered the modern Slavic one.

I retraced my steps and finally got to the more famous mall. The maze had been sanitized, with paved floors and well-lighted passageways, but it still had the unventilated feel of a place of banished sunlight. In one atmospheric café, where mustachioed men played cards under murals of camels, the air seemed of another century.

Outside the side entrances stretched more warrens of shops, including Mustafa's pillared house of carpets.

"Where you from in U.S.?" He was a bald, wiry man in a bushy gray mustache, neat gray slacks, and sporty black turtleneck. "I been to Florida. Cocoa Beach. Vero Beach. What it called—Tamp?"

"Tampa."

He shook my hand. "Sorry. Wet. I come back from prayer. We must wash before we pray. We must be clean for God. I been to church in America. I never see anybody wash."

"We do at home, before we go."

"You go only one week one day. We go one day five times. We very much love God. Listen," he said, clasping me in his gaze, "you love people, they love you. You lie, you cheat, you lose." He gave this simple axiom a catchy rhythm, making it sound like a popular jingle.

I asked the age of the fountain opposite his shop, which was set into the wall of the neighboring mosque.

"Three hundred years. And still standing. Old Turk, great man. New Turk, not so great." His face expressed unhealed grief for a lost empire.

"What about Ataturk?" I asked.

"He's dead."

"But he was a new Turk."

Mustafa smiled. "He was a great man. He beat eight armies—Greek, England, New Zealand, Australia, France, Austria . . ." He lost track. "England, Greek. Eight armies. Eight Turks come fight you. Can you beat them?"

I shrugged.

"Turk army very strong," he continued. "I was in Korea with America. America never win war without Turk. America soldier just want to smoke, drink whiskey." And then, abruptly: "You love people, they love you. You lie, you cheat, you lose."

Saying good-bye I headed across the street and down a hill, plowing through more markets. Merchants in dark sport coats pushed carts piled with melons, porters bowed at right angles under the weight of bulging sacks, idle boys spit pistachio shells. I began counting how many men passed before I spotted a woman—fifteen, thirty-four, the highest I got was sixty-seven. An old man sitting on a stoop greeted a friend by bringing his fingertips together at his lips, then opening the hand and raising it to his brow for a swift salute—the whole gesture conveying, in one fluid motion, affection and respect.

I reached Kumkapi, its fish restaurants spilling onto the sidewalks with white-clothed tables and wicker chairs. Then a street opened up to the Sea of Marmara, where small wooden boats bobbed in rows, each flying the red flag with the white crescent and star. Families strolled along the sea wall, and thirty yards out teenage boys—three in swim trunks, four in underpants—dived from the rusted hull of an upturned freighter. I walked along happily, humming to myself:

*You love people, they love you.*
*You lie, you cheat, you lose.*

A few hours later, dressed in coat and tie, I hailed a taxi to the Pera Palas. It had long been on my list of great hotels to visit, and what better time, I thought, than on the evening of my birthday?

The Pera Palas was built in 1892 to continue the pampering of passengers who arrived on the Orient Express, and it soon became—like Raffles in Singapore, Shepherd Hotel in Cairo—THE place to stay in Istanbul. Agatha Christie wrote *Murder on the Orient Express* while staying at the Pera Palas, and bellmen will tell you the number of the room in which Ataturk slept. In one of her lapidary travel essays, Jan Morris wrote of entering and finding the place "still faintly fragrant of Ottoman cigars and ancient omelettes."

I reflected on all this while sitting in my first Istanbul traffic jam, which also seemed, in its way, de rigueur. A snake of cars, motionless but not hornless, waited impatiently to get onto the Ataturk Bridge. Istanbul is famously divided, by the ferry-churned Bosporus, into two continents: Europe and Asia. But the city's more pertinent division, for the majority of visitors, is the one created here on the European side by the Golden Horn. This smaller body of water splits the Occidental city into the old monumental part, symbolized by the historic cluster of the Sultanahmet, and the "modern" commercial part, epitomized by the shops and clubs of Beyoglu (to which I was headed for a celebratory drink). It is, almost literally, like the difference between day and night.

We finally crossed the bridge and sped up a steep hill crowned by the faded evergreen walls of the Pera Palas Hotel. Inside, poking around the birdcage elevator, I was dazzled to catch a distinct whiff of omelettes. Soft guitar music drifted out of the bar, where I took a seat against a peach-colored wall. It was all I had hoped for: mirrored columns, lace curtains, high ceiling, carpeted wood floor. The waiter brought my glass of *raki* and I sipped it slowly, trying to feel more cosmopolitan than middle-aged.

On leaving, I walked up the street and noticed the decorative gray façade of the Grand Hôtel de Londres. It appeared to be of the same generation, if not the same class, as the Pera Palas. Inquiring at the reception desk, I was told a single room went for sixty dollars a night. The lounge, off to the side, had the look of a once exclusive men's club, with its overstuffed armchairs and antique radios perfectly arranged in a perpetual dimness. Parakeets chirped from a cage on the windowsill. I made a reservation for when I returned.

★ ★ ★

The next morning I took a taxi to the airport for the flight to Cappadocia. Stepping from the departure lounge onto a bus, I asked a young woman seated with her mother if this indeed was the bus taking us to the plane destined for Kayseri. What I actually said, in my best Turkish, was: "Kayseri?"

The young woman, with straight black hair falling onto a black cardigan, smiled and said, "Yes." Then, also in English, she asked where I was from.

"The United States."

"We know that," she said, smiling at her mother. "Whereabouts?"

They were Americans, of course—mother from Boston, daughter living in New York—heading to Goreme, a town not far from Urgup, where I was staying. Before we reached the plane they offered me a lift in the car they were picking up in Kayseri.

I had always tried to avoid tourists when traveling; it seemed one of those unwritten rules of the road, like getting out of the way of trucks. Those chummy backpackers bonding with their kinsmen along the now worldwide chain of Lonely Planet-approved hostels always made me wonder why they ever left home. Tourists, especially Americans, not only presented an unwelcome reminder of the place I'd just left—I don't want to hear about botox in the Anatolian steppes—they constituted a threat to the uniqueness of my experience. Travel, like many worthwhile endeavors—work, love, sport—is a competitive act. Other tourists are your enemies.

On board I was pinned next to a window by a merry band of Japanese housewives. Well, I thought, Turkey has always been a crossroads between East and West. The woman next to me ventured a few words in English, informing me that she and her friends were on an eight-day tour of Turkey without (giggle) their husbands. I mentioned an interest in Japan. She quietly opened her purse, extracted a piece of colorful paper, and, after a few minutes of meticulous folding, presented me with a delicate swan.

At the Kayseri airport Amy and her mother picked up their numerous bags—I was already beginning to question my acceptance of a lift—and the three of us were driven to a car lot for the dreaded sweat over the incomprehensible rental agreement. Once on our way, Amy's mother calmly related her first encounter, while the negotiations had been going on, with a Turkish toilet.

"You what?!?" asked Amy.

"I squatted," repeated her mother. "You have to, dear. It's just a hole in the floor."

"But I've never done that. How do you do it? Like, which way do you face?"

Amy stopped the car and we all got out to watch a shepherd shearing sheep. I would never have done this alone. The grizzled shearer and his helper greeted us amicably and kindly posed for pictures. Amy's mother went back to the car and returned with a carton of Marlboros.

"The gift of cancer," sniggered Amy.

A little farther along we saw our first cave.

"Look at that!" gasped the mother. "People live in there!"

"Mom," Amy chastened, "do you know what that would go for in Manhattan?"

This wasn't travel, I knew; I was no longer in Turkey, but I was still having a wonderful time sprawled in the back seat munching Pepperidge Farm Milanos, my pretty new sister happy at the wheel. The sign announcing Urgup appeared like a verdict sending me back into solitary.

By my second morning in Urgup I felt as if I had already established a routine. I walked downstairs to the lobby, plopped my anchored key on the reception desk—with a thump and a "*gunaydin*" (good morning) to the owner watching TV—and headed out into the sunny courtyard, past the cushioned banquettes set into arches along the side of the hotel, to the little canteen at the base of a sheer rock wall. There, the owner's daughter brought me breakfast—a plate of sliced cucumbers and tomatoes, olives, *beyaz* (Turkish feta), and a basket of bread and jam—and then hovered timidly, offering more bread and shooing the cat as her wavy black hair fell thickly onto her gray cotton cardigan.

I was the hotel's only guest. The first day I had felt awkward; today, almost regal. It was helpful having a routine in a place as strange, as troglodytic, as Cappadocia. Driving from Kayseri—practically the geographic heart of Turkey—we had started out in a landscape resembling Wyoming, minus the sagebrush but with the same scrub-covered mountains rising gradually from the plain. Then we came upon some stone outcrops and the cryptic mouths of a few tantalizing caves. Urgup, as we descended from the mountain, appeared like any town in the distance, with modern apartment blocks ribboning its sides, but as we entered we saw that the place curled around a centerpiece of rock. It was like walking into someone's living room and finding the sofa abutting a boulder.

The streets looked quite normal, but going out from the main square we found the houses retreating into rock, some actually crunched under overhangs. What could have been a dreary petrified aspect was relieved by the organic wholeness. Everything consisted of stone, and had the stone's unifying khaki hue; it was difficult to tell sometimes where geology ended and urban planning began. You almost wondered if the town had not been built but had instead been chiseled, house by house, out of a blanket of rock, with the sculptors leaving, for some unknown reason, a large unfinished chunk in the middle.

As astonishing as the scenery was the gradual discovery that this harmony—of boulder and building, man and nature—survived in the contemporary lives of the inhabitants. That first afternoon, the hotel owner, Orhan, led me to the rock face punctuating his backyard where, up some steps of stone, we entered a bar he had established in a cave. Handsome kilims hung on rough-hewn walls and beautifully embroidered cushions softened molded banquettes. In the middle of the ceiling, a narrow chute, with thin metal handles, led dizzyingly to an upper level.

It was the coziest cave I had ever seen. I had always admired the Mediterraneans' talent for transforming the mundane—the way they can take a bit of sidewalk and throw down a couple tables and hang a few light bulbs and create an ambiance—but this domesticating of caverns seemed to take the art to a whole new level.

Below, Orhan led me into a second grotto, the walls still thick with troughs (in the past, animals were kept on the ground floor while people lived upstairs) and then down a dank tunnel that emptied into another cave, this one built with a four-foot-high retaining wall that held back a pool of collected rainwater. (We could hear a slow, steady, *drip, drip, drip.*) This Orhan, explained, kept the garden prospering in the dry summer months.

"My English," Emel said apologetically, grabbing the cat off the table, "vedy little."

"What are you reading?" I asked her, miming a reader. When I had come out for breakfast she had been sitting on the banquette, engrossed in a book. She went out to retrieve it. The cover read: *Olmus Ruhlar,* Nikolai Gogol.

"*Dead Souls,*" I guessed, and then turning inside, saw that I was right. "It's a wonderful book."

"Yes!" she said. "Wonderful!"

"You like books?" I asked.

"Yes, I like. Flaubert, Tolstoy, Goethe. American, I not know."

"Mark Twain?"

"Oh yes, I know." Then a pause. "Dostoyevski—American?"

"No Russian. Rooski."

"Oh, vedy good. I like."

I showed her the novel I was reading, *The Black Book,* by the Turkish writer Orhan Pamuk. "Yes," she said. "Vedy good. Vedy good."

Emel had finished high school, I learned, but had not gone on to college. Now she spent her days working at the family hotel and reading classics among the rocks.

The minivan filled quickly: a family from South Africa, an Australian woman, two young Canadian men in voluminous shorts, two couples from Hong Kong, another from Singapore, one lone American. Children of a vanished empire, convened at the crossroads of East and West. Our guide's name was Mustafa.

We headed out into the countryside, which was like no countryside any of us had ever seen in our disparate homelands. Vast ridges of erratic rock imbued the landscape with an unearthly beauty, a dreamy tumble. Stones erupted in fantastic contortions, smoothed and buffed like Henry Moore sculptures. A few miles away, an army of behemoths occupied Goreme, so that instead of a village with rocks, you had rocks with a village. There were high-rise caves all in a row with wind-carved roofs that looked like thatch turned to stone. A grove of pinnacles and cones appeared, each thrusting a rounded rock into the sky, the top-heavy caps turning the lot into a sex-shop shelf of Brobdingnagian dildos.

"This is called Love Valley," Mustafa said. "Thirty million years ago three volcanoes erupted in Cappadocia: Erciyes, Melendiz, and Hasan. The volcanic ash carried rocks along with it. The ash hardened, but not as hard as the rocks, so over the years it erodes much quicker. We call these formations 'fairy chimneys.'"

The place was vaguely reminiscent of South Dakota's Badlands, but on a much larger scale and with an ancient culture. The Hittites lived here in 2000 B.C., mixing with the already settled Hatti; they were followed by Lydians, Phrygians, Byzantines,

Greeks, and Romans. Each group in its turn bred horses (the name Cappadocia comes from the Hittite for "land of pretty horses"), farmed the fertile soil, and tunneled into the malleable rock, some of them creating not just homes but churches (whose frescoes are still visible), monasteries, and entire underground cities. When the Arabs arrived, the Christians found this burrowing lifestyle a veritable godsend.

We drove west to the Ihlara Valley, where we took a walk between a bubbling brook and a sheer cliff dotted with still more caves. At one point we heard a shout, and turning around saw a peasant woman coming up fast on a trotting donkey. She pulled to a halt so we could take her picture. The trees flecked the air with a scent strangely reminiscent of pepperoni.

Back in Urgup, I stopped to admire a truck adorned with an illustration of a man with a mustache so long that it curled up under the noses of two tickled bystanders. A Turk had told me: "In some villages still, you're not a man until you grow a mustache."

"It's lovely, isn't it?" a female voice behind me asked. I turned and found a young woman sitting under a willow tree drinking tea. She had black, close-cropped hair; a dusky complexion; small, perfect white teeth. "It's by the cartoonist Coplu. He does work for the *Turkish Daily News.*"

Sara was from Sydney, and like a lot of Australians was traveling slowly. In fact, she had decided to linger for a while in Urgup. "I must have gone dotty in the head to settle in a place where women are relegated to such low status," she said. But she was diligently learning Turkish, and finding virtues. "The people here are intellectually curious. They don't have a peasant mentality." I thought of Emel.

"What is your background?" I asked, curious.

"Bitsof, as we say in Australia. Bits of this and bits of that. Portuguese-Indian on one side, Burmese-Malay on the other. Oh, and I can't forget my Scottish grandmother."

The thunderstorm broke just as I got back to my hotel. It sounded as if all the rocks of Cappadocia were being tossed into the Ihlara Valley. After forty-five minutes, it was over.

I walked out to find that the street had become a river. At the first intersection, I had to jump across using little sandbars left by the flood. Downtown, shopkeepers threw buckets of water over the sidewalk tiles and then, with wide brooms, vigorously swept away the silt. It was the most active I had seen the town.

I stopped into a wine shop. I had heard about the white wines of Cappadocia, and wanted a taste, but the merchant sold only bottles. No matter. He took one down, popped the cork, and poured me a glass as if I were a long-absent friend. We sat on opposite benches; he offered me an open bag of Doritos. He did not speak English. We sat in companionable silence, which was broken only by the muezzin's call to evening prayer. Finishing the wine, I got up and reached for my wallet. The merchant brought his right hand to his heart and made an obeisant bow.

"Hello my friend, where are you from?"

It was the carpet seller's tired line, but I was in a good mood, walking along the still wet streets and passing the shopkeepers schmoozing on their stools.

"I've been to Cocoa Beach, Gainesville, Jacksonville. I took Greyhound to Atlantic City. I like Florida better."

He was a short, bald man with intelligent brown eyes and a thin Roman nose. His name was Remzi. "Like the king. This is my friend Mustafa—he's visiting from Iran—and Huseyin."

"But not Saddam," Huseyin said laughing.

"There's a slide show in five minutes over in the town center," Remzi said. "You want to see it?" If this was a pitch for a carpet, it was the most elaborate one I had come across.

Huseyin stayed to mind the shop, while Remzi and Mustafa and I headed over to the center. This is Turkey, I thought, hangin' with the guys.

The auditorium was empty; a man on the stage called down to Remzi. "The show's tomorrow," Remzi said. "I got it wrong. But he says we can watch them getting it ready. He's a local archaeologist."

We took seats in the front row, Remzi sitting proprietarily in the middle. "That's Zelve Monastery," he said to me as the first slide appeared to the accompaniment of liturgical music. "That's Uchisar, the houses climbing up the face of the rock. That's Love Valley. Those are frescoes from the New Church in Goreme—Byzantine art from the tenth century. You enjoying it, Mustafa?"

After about half an hour, the rehearsal ended, and we headed back to the shop. "Hello, how are you doing?" Remzi called to the merchants sitting out along Kayseri Street. "How's business?"

He turned to me. "I love to speak English to my friends. I teach in the evenings—a lot of shopkeepers like to learn English. It helps in their business. I'm also a tour guide. But my real job is as an agricultural agent. I'm a very busy man."

Back at his shop, Remzi invited me in for tea. Here goes, I thought. I confessed that I was a travel writer, uninterested in shopping. He understood, perfectly. The tea arrived in its tiny, tulip-shaped glass. His assistant rolled out the first brilliant rug.

"You have these in Iran," he said to Mustafa. "All the dyes," he said, turning to me, "are natural. The blue comes from the juice of grapes. The red from apricot blossoms. The green from pistachios. The brown from walnut husks. The pink from rose petals."

I took out my notebook, to demonstrate my scholarly interest. More carpets were presented. The assistant picked them off of rolled piles and unfurled them with a taciturn, Ta-DA! flourish, one atop another in a growing mound whose purpose seemed to produce enough guilt in me to buy at least one so he wouldn't have to go and pick them all up. I couldn't tell if I were dealing with Remzi the teacher or Remzi the businessman.

"This is an undyed carpet," he said, showing one in white, brown, and black. His assistant brought over a photograph of a flock of sheep exhibiting the same three hues. "You see this only in Urgup."

"Who makes these carpets?" I asked.

"Peasants—women mostly. They make them in the winter, when there's nothing to do in the fields. One or two will work on a carpet, more for the bigger ones. They sit around and gossip and sing."

"Well," I said, finishing my tea. "That was very educational."

Remzi looked pleased.

The next morning I waited at the hotel for Azim, a friend of a friend whom I had called out of the blue and who said he would drive down from Ankara—about one hundred fifty miles—to meet me.

He was three hours late—a lanky young man with wavy black hair and a gentle expression. He had brought his girlfriend, Tulay, who had long blond hair tied in the back and an irrepressible smile. (Her mother, I would learn, was German.) Despite the late start, we repaired to the canteen, where Emel brought us tea.

It was decided that we would drive to Hacibektas, and then back to Ankara, where I would stay with them for a few days. Before we left, Emel insisted on showing them the caves. At one point I noticed her talking quietly with Tulay.

"What was she saying to you?" I asked her when we got in the car.

"She asked me how she could learn English."

Hacibektas sits at the northern tip of Cappadocia, across the Kizilirmak, the longest river in Turkey. It takes its name from the Sufic philosopher Haci Bektas Veli, who settled in the area in the thirteenth century and developed within Islam a radical system of belief. One of his more famous sayings—reflecting a sentiment that Ataturk would embrace seven centuries later—was: "A nation which does not educate its women cannot progress."

"I like the Bektasi," Tulay said, as we walked to the monastery. "They are more open, more tolerant, and more inquiring. They read a lot."

"They allow women and men to be together," said Azim. "They even have dances in which the men dance with the women. This is very strange for Islam."

We entered a room thick with sepulchers. The tomb of Haci Bektas was draped in a green cloth squirted with Arabic script and protected by a clear plastic sheet. A middle-aged man was slowly making his way around it, stopping at each side to kiss the sheet, touch his forehead to it, kiss and touch again.

From the courtyard we entered a room bordered by a wooden platform that was raised only a few inches off the ground and divided into twelve sections. "There are twelve imams," explained Azim, "like the twelve apostles. And there are other similarities to Christianity. The use of alcohol, for example—the drinking of wine is important. The number three also has significance.

"The Bektasi don't go to mosque," he said. "There are no mosques in town. They believe you can talk directly to God; you don't need a building. They have houses where they meet sometimes."

On the way out, we passed a bust of Ataturk. I was surprised, knowing that he had closed the monastery after taking power in 1923. "He closed all religious schools," Azim explained. "And he couldn't make an exception. But they like him all the same. Because they are for democracy. The Bektasi and the military are the two forces we have in this country to keep the fundamentalists in check." Mystics and generals.

Back in the car, we headed north toward Ankara. The road was straight and level; rock fantasies gave way to featureless plains. The world, physically at least, had returned to normal.

One-minaret villages pricked the fabric of the sky, bordered by fields where women wrapped in copious skirts bent under the sun in timeless postures. They made me think of the Irish leader Charles Stewart Parnell, who once during a campaign told the worker who rushed up to greet him: "Calm down, old man. Whether I win or lose you'll still be breaking rocks."

Yet the situation in Turkey seemed to loom larger than most political squalls, touching the very soul of the country. The power struggle between the military and Prime Minister Necmettin Erbakan, leader of the Islamic Welfare Party, was fundamentally a philosophical confrontation, pitting the secular against the religious in a battle for control over public life. Similar battles had been lost by secularists elsewhere in the Islamic world, and the irony of this was that Turkey, once viewed by the West as the invading infidel, the primary threat to its values and beliefs, was now being looked to as the crucial defender of some of its most cherished ideals: democracy, justice, the division of church and state. Turkey's cultural identity had matched in confusion its geographical position—European or Asian? Western or Eastern?—and as a result the country was providing the ideal setting for one of the most significant dramas of the modern era.

"Erbakan never says, 'I am a man of Turkey,'" Tulay said, as we sped past a truck. "He always says, 'I am a man of Islam.' And everything else he says is vague—he hates saying anything direct."

"He's a politician," explained Azim. "Though his profession is engineer."

"How did his party come to power?" I asked.

"The poor people," he said. "The Welfare Party promised them money and things if they got elected. Also, some people thought: 'We haven't tried them yet. Let's see what they can do.' There are a lot of poor and uneducated people in Turkey."

We soon came upon clusters of houses growing on treeless hills: the outskirts of a steppeland capital. Over the rise there spread before us a kind of survey course on modern apartment house construction: several faceless gray blocks in a sixties' socialist mold, their edges softened by allocations of trees; a few colorful towers with wrap-around balconies, some still in the works and rising out of dirt lots; and down in the vale, a tony walled compound of two-story houses.

"That's the parliament," Azim said. "I mean, it's where the members live."

"They all live together, with their families?" It seemed an odd arrangement for such a volatile group, like building a condo for Southern Baptists and gays.

"Yes. I used to go out with a girl who lived in there and it was terrible, getting checked by the guards all the time. They mark down when you leave and what time you come back," he sighed. "They know everything."

Azim lived in one of the gray blocks. The foyer was stark, but his apartment, one floor up, was warm and spacious, the corridors rumpled with rugs, the large windows of the living room giving onto a pine-scented yard. We dropped my bags and headed out for lunch.

The restaurant—tiled floor and wooden chairs—occupied the corner of a modern building in a nascent neighborhood just south of downtown. Period photographs of old Anatolian families hung on the walls; a pair of young professionals ate by the window. We talked about the fundamentalists.

"Since Erbakan came to power," said Azim, "they have gotten stronger. They get families to send their children to Muslim schools, which, you know, are supposed to be for training imams. Now there are many more students than there are positions for imams. And only men can become imams, but women go to these schools too."

"And the women say that they want to become doctors," said Tulay. "But their religion forbids them to touch men. So how can they treat patients? It's ridiculous."

"What's the situation with public schools?"

"Right now, students only have to go up to the fifth grade," said Azim. "After that they can go to religious schools. The military wants to make secular education mandatory until the eighth grade. Because then students are at an age when they are not so easily brainwashed.

"It's funny," he said. "When I was a student, I hated the generals. I was a bit leftist. Now I like them, because they are for democracy."

Our lunch arrived: meat chunks sandwiched between thin pancakes smothered in a yogurt sauce, an orange rivulet of oil dribbled across the snowy surface.

"You're both Muslim?" I asked.

"We were brought up Muslim," said Azim. "I used to be an atheist. Now I'm not sure."

"I think Islam needs to grow," said Tulay. "Like Christianity did, with new groups like the Protestants. Islam is stuck in the past. If you steal, they cut your hand off. That doesn't work today. We have civil laws.

"It is an Arab religion," she continued. "I don't think it's for Turkey. Keeping men and women separate. Covering the face. Turkish women want to present themselves, to use lipstick, make-up, to look good. They like to dance," she smiled brightly, "to express themselves. Under Islam, you can't."

We drove downtown and dropped Azim at his TV studio. Ankara, as befit a modern capital, was awash in wide boulevards and Western brand names, heavy-set buildings and purposeful crowds. It had a clean, swept, contemporary feel, especially after the shadowy warrens and layered grime of Istanbul. I found it hard to imagine fundamentalism taking hold here, but then I recalled a description I'd read of 1970s Teheran. Around a corner we drove past some stone banks with arched windows that Tulay described as "Ottoman style of the Ataturk period."

Kemal Ataturk was the father of modern Turkey, the founder of the republic in 1923 and its first president. (The surname, the use of which he introduced into Turkish life, means "father of the Turks.") Born in Salonika, in the waning days of the Ottoman Empire, Ataturk developed into a military genius—defeating the Allies at Gallipoli in 1915 and then driving out the Greeks seven years later—and an unrepentant progressive and admirer of the West.

In his sweeping drive to modernize Turkey, he changed everything from the country's language—replacing the Arabic alphabet with the Roman—to its dress: Men were no longer permitted to wear the fez, and women were encouraged to drop the veil. They were also given equal educational opportunities and, in 1934, the right to vote. He closed down all religious schools, creating a void that many people see as the source of the current fundamentalist resurgence. All of which makes his transfer of the capital from Istanbul to Ankara look rather tame.

Yet when Ataturk took power in 1923, Istanbul was still, after 2,000 years, one of the world's great cities; Ankara was a backwater of 20,000 people, most of whom had no electricity or running water.

We were headed toward the original settlement, which at the turn of the century was still called Angora, after the valued goat's wool of the region. Tulay weaved masterfully through darting traffic and turned under a large equestrian statue. Atop the horse sat Ataturk. "You see one of the figures at the bottom is a woman," she said. "They helped a lot in the war, carrying food and supplies."

She zipped up a steep hill, parked, and led me along the ramparts of the old Byzantine citadel. Mortared in with the brick were odd bits of marble balustrades and pieces of classical columns; it was like finding Homer and Thucydides on a shelf of paperback thrillers. "They used whatever materials they could find," Tulay explained. "I think it was good. Because if they hadn't, these nice pieces would be lost today."

We found an opening in the wall and, walking under an archway, entered not an embalmed fort but an animated village. Boys kicked soccer balls along cobblestone streets and mothers and daughters formed knitting circles in front of whitewashed houses. Tulay stopped by a stately couple seated on a bench—the woman in a headscarf, the man in white beard and brown cap—and while she chatted a neighbor slipped into my hand a warm disk of bread. "She wants you to have it," Tulay interpreted, and I was so moved I forgot the Turkish word for thank you.

We climbed more carless streets, tugging at the delicious loaf and peeking into courtyards. Schoolgirls passed in argyle socks and pleated navy skirts. A strange serenity hung in the air, the product not only of elevation—we had risen far above the brio of the city—but of antiquity.

In a restaurant courtyard we sipped apple tea. On our way out, we stuck our heads into the dim kitchen where an ample-skirted woman was plucking small loaves out of an old-fashioned stove and piling them neatly on a white cloth she had spread across the stone floor. We could have been in some old Anatolian village. Tulay introduced me, and the woman, securing the last loaf, straightened to address us.

Outside, Tulay said: "She told me to tell you to write good things about Turkey. She said people often hear the bad things and that discourages tourists. And she said that tourists are important because they are like neighbors. And we all need good neighbors because we depend on them."

On our way home, we got stuck in rush-hour traffic. A patrol car sidled up next to us. I asked about the reputation of the police, and Tulay confirmed my suspicion that it wasn't good. I remembered the ones at the university in Istanbul, and the stories of confrontations.

"There was a comedy skit on TV," Tulay said. "A policeman was having an argument with his daughter because she wanted to go to university and he refused to let her go. She kept asking him 'Why, why can't I go?' And he said, 'Because I have never beaten you.'"

"They showed that on television?"

"Oh, yes."

Back at Azim's apartment, we spent the evening in front of the tube. "There have been such rapid changes in Turkey," Azim said, surfing with the remote. "In 1984 we had one channel in black and white. Now with satellite I get thirty."

He often watched international programs—he was a TV journalist—but for my sake he stayed with the local fare. I got my first look at Erbakan, leading reporters down a hallway. He looked like a portly grandfather in a business suit, with none of the ayatollah's ascetic, black-browed fury. His round cheeks and wispy white mustache gave him the air of a well-fed rabbit. His vague remarks were followed by an update on the Kurdish situation.

"My brother's wife is a Kurd," Azim said. "She's OK. But the PKK [Kurdistan Workers Party] has changed my feeling about Kurds. Many Turkish soldiers have died at their hands."

He thought a bit. "Those are really our two big problems: the PKK and Islamic fundamentalists. If we can solve them, the economy can take off. And then Turkey can become like America—maybe in one hundred years."

"All people talk about now is religion," complained Tulay. "While nobody does anything about the economy."

As if on cue, we came upon an interview with a young woman who had married a shaman because he had told her that God had instructed him to take her as his wife. A couple of clicks brought us to a smuggled documentary showing bearded men in turbans marching with machine guns. A few of them broke ranks and beat to the ground a dummy of Ataturk that had been hung in effigy.

"That's in Germany," Azim said. "A lot of the money for the fundamentalists comes from Turks who are working there. They live in tight, closed communities and are very conservative. There are a lot of them—about three million. We don't have to worry about becoming a member of the European Union," he joked, "because we're already there."

Religion didn't seem to be faring very well on television. "Are there any Islamic programs?" I asked.

"Two or three," said Azim. "Families like to watch them because there is no sex."

"Or violence?"

"No, there is violence."

An attractive, sobbing woman appeared, hounded by reporters. "Oh, she's a model," Tulay said. "A policeman dressed like a normal person offered her five thousand dollars to sleep with him and she accepted."

"But prostitution is legal," I said.

"But you can't sell your body if you don't have the papers that say you can." She laughed at the logic.

"In the States," I said, "we have policewomen who dress up and arrest men who want to have sex."

"That's interesting," she said. "In Turkey it's always the woman who is punished. I must tell my feminist friends."

The next morning Azim went back to the studio and Tulay—who was between jobs—took me to Anit Kabir, the national shrine to Ataturk. At the entrance, a young soldier in fatigues asked in a polite American accent to check my bag. I expressed surprise. "I went to high school in Virginia," he said.

We walked up a macadam grade lined with linden trees that gave off that peculiar scent of pepperoni. A low colonnade of square brown pillars crowned the hill; a towering flagpole, flying the star and crescent, rose in the middle. Arriving at the top, we entered a vast square, shimmering in the sunlight and penned with thin lines of blue-frocked schoolchildren. There was an unmistakable grandeur in the sweep of the place, yet a forbidding ponderousness in the blocky architecture, as if the Mall in Washington had been redone in socialist realism.

"In school," Tulay said, as we stood near the flag, "every day before the lesson begins students say: 'I will work hard and honor Ataturk. I am glad to be a Turk.' You do this until about the age of eleven."

I thought of the portraits of George Washington—the father of my country—that had hung in my old school, and wondered: What if he had died in 1938?"

"About six, seven years ago," she said, "people would be very sad on November 10, the anniversary of his death. Many people cried. I cried when I was a little girl. But then we said that he did great things for Turkey and we should be glad of that." A Turkish woman, I had read, had declared at his death: "Turkey has lost her lover and must now settle down with her husband."

"There was a time," Tulay said, "when there was too much about Ataturk—all the time you heard about Ataturk—so people didn't really appreciate him, they took his work for granted. But now, with the rise of fundamentalism, he has become very important to us again."

Ataturk's cars sat parked outside the museum: curvaceous black Lincolns from the 1930s, a Cadillac limousine. Inside, his personal effects were displayed: gifts from world leaders, ceremonial swords, cigarette cases, shaving kits. In a far room we came upon his wardrobe: tweed jacket, plus fours, winter overcoat, a long tapered pair of still-polished shoes. "Very handsome man, I think," said Tulay, looking at a picture of him in a tailored suit. "Very masculine." Along one wall stood a wax figure of the president dressed in white tie and tails.

Leaving, we walked up marble steps into the neoclassical mausoleum. Far ahead, in front of the grave, stood a class of high school students—a slack jumble of faded denim and dark hair. Coming up beside them, I saw that each face was numbed by a look of veneration and solemn pensiveness uncommon to teenagers. For several minutes no one spoke or moved. The great hall was silent, the future at stake.

My bus sailed south across the Anatolian plateau. The young conductor went from passenger to passenger, squirting each pair of cupped hands with a lemon-scented potion that was then rubbed vigorously into the pores, the men sometimes slapping it onto their necks and cheeks. The picture windows filled with fields and minarets that shrank as quickly as they had grown. I was taking the long way back to Istanbul.

Azim and Tulay had seen me off that afternoon. Waiting for the van that would take me to the bus station, we sat at an outdoor café where Tulay was the only woman.

"A leftover from Ottoman times," she said matter-of-factly. "The men meet here and the women stay at home. In Europe the men are at home, I think. My grandmother, who lives in Germany, hates that. She wants my grandfather out of the house."

"You don't see each other," Azim said smiling, "you have no communication, you have no problems. But the men deceive the women."

"And the women the men," said Tulay.

"Really?" said Azim, looking surprised.

The van was waiting when we sauntered up to the stop. Azim said something to the driver as I climbed in, then he and Tulay stood on the sidewalk and waved good-bye. It is the way every traveler wants to leave a place—saluting new friends, the momentary sadness simply verifying the affection.

When we pulled up to the station, the driver motioned for me to stay seated, then he drove a few yards to the second entrance, where he said something to the man getting off first, who then led me through the cavernous hall and out to the berth with the bus to Konya. I was a bead, passed along a self-perpetuating thread of Turkish solicitude.

Konya sits 150 miles south of Ankara. It is an important pilgrimage site for Muslims, being the adopted home of the Sufic mystic and poet Mevlana (Our Master)—better known in the West as Rumi—who founded the Whirling Dervish sect. It was also the stronghold of the Islamic Welfare Party. Some of the Turks I'd met had painted a portrait of a grimly conservative city—my guidebook noted that several years ago a man was severely beaten in the street for smoking a cigarette during Ramadan—and claimed with a certain pride that they had never been to the place.

The bus pulled into the station in late afternoon. I took a taxi to the Belikcilar Hotel, a four-story concrete block that stood across the street from the fluted turquoise dome of the Mevlana's tomb. The two made a very convincing case, at least in architecture, against modern secularism.

The Belikcilar, at forty-five dollars a night, was the best hotel in Konya. There were dervish postcards in the lobby and, on the TV in my room, a program of dervish whirling. I sat on the bed and watched, knowing this would be the closest I would get. (The dervishes appear publicly only once a year—the week preceding the anniversary of the Mevlana's death on December 17; it is easier to catch one of the monthly performances at the Galata Mevlevihane in Istanbul.)

Half a dozen dervishes spun in place on a wooden floor. Each wore a towering camel-hair fez and a flowing white skirt. A small band off to the side played flutes and kettledrums. There was none of the wired frenzy Westerners seem to associate with the dance, as when they tell their sugar-rushed children they look like whirling dervishes, but rather a steady, graceful, ceaseless twirl, effected by the positioning of one foot as the pivot and the other as the thrust. (A guide in the museum the next day would explain that after a few days of practice, during which dervishes sometimes suffer from upset stomachs, they can spin like this for hours.) Each man held both arms out at his sides, keeping one hand pointed up, the other down (toward heaven and earth), and repeating under his breath a chant of remembrance. Each revolved in a private, conical reverie—the outstretched arms facilitating balance while intimating openness—that produced an ethereal fluidity, a corporal poetics for communing with God.

Saturday morning I walked across the street to the Mevlana's tomb. A clutch of moon-faced young women stood by the sixteenth-century fountain, their hair hidden under head scarves, their thin coats falling to their shoes. They looked like novices from a monastery; but they were college students from Malaysia, engaged—one told me in gentle English—in Islamic studies in Turkey.

I followed them inside, feeling slightly unworthy in my jeans. Yet the Mevlana was a liberalizing force in Islam. Like Haci Bektas, he promoted the station of women, understood (clearly) the value of dance, and stressed the importance of humility and tolerance. A quatrain from one of his poems had been posted at the entrance:

*Come, come again, whoever, whatever you may be, come,*
*Heathen, fire worshiper, sinful of idolatry, come.*
*Come even if you break your penitence a hundred times*
*Ours is not the portal of despair and misery, come.*

At the entrance we were given plastic bags in which to carry our shoes. We walked across worn carpets past a corral of tombs that pointed upward like stone dervish caps. The Mevlana's stood by the far wall, fronted by a large crowd: peasants in somber sport coats, kerchiefed grandmothers, jogging-suited children, Nikon-draped tourists, heathens, idolaters.

"Hello my friend. Welcome to Konya. Would you like to have some tea?'"

"I'm not interested in carpets," I said. I was actually looking for a place for lunch along Mevlana Boulevard.

"Who said anything about carpets?"

I followed Mehmet into his shop. Carpets covered every inch of wall and floor—a velvety, burgundy retreat. I sat on the couch, Mehmet on a stool opposite. He was the first Konyan I had talked to.

"It's a good place to live," he said. "Good water. Yes, the Welfare Party comes from here, but people let you be. If you want to be religious, you be religious. If you don't want to, you don't. Nobody bothers you."

Two tulip-shaped glasses of apple tea arrived. "I didn't vote for the Welfare Party," he said, taking a sip. "But if they leave, who's better to take their place? Nobody on the left or right. We need somebody who is honest, not corrupt. So why don't you want a carpet?"

His sad brown eyes widened imploringly. I suddenly understood how a woman who comes up after a date wanting only coffee feels. In Mehmet's mind I had entered into the game and was now refusing to play by the rules. I was just another foreign tease, a carpet virgin. An expression of tedium slowly clouded his face; he answered my next questions in monosyllables. He was no longer interested in conversation. I recited my tired excuses, thanked him awkwardly for the tea, and walked out into the street and its invigorating absence of compromise.

A few doors away I found a travel office. Remembering Samuel Johnson's famous observation—"The grand object of travel is to see the shores of the Mediterranean"—I walked in and bought a ticket to Antalya.

The bus was almost full, another sleek, modern, clean-windowed coach. The conductor again made his way down the aisle—like a priest serving communion—with his refreshing potion. Then he repeated the trip, pouring each passenger a cup of mineral water.

Between sips I read about Antalya in my *Rough Guide.* "Turkey's fastest growing city . . . grim concrete sprawl . . . over half the vacationers are Germans." Azim had recommended Fethiye, described on page 384 as "a lively, Turkish-feeling market town." If I spend the night in Antalya, I reasoned, then I'll waste part of Sunday getting to Fethiye. And, after ten days on the road, I desperately needed to do my laundry. I began to feel a pull toward a town I had first heard of a day ago, and the intoxication of extemporaneous travel.

There is something about dramatic scenery that seems to justify the journey. The bus was climbing now, high into rocky mountains, and winding its way up torturous curves. Then, slowly, it started its descent and just before sunset we rolled into the most beautiful bus station I had ever seen. Looking like the surviving pavilion from a recent world's fair, two imposing, angular glass structures rose on a slight mound, connected by a skeletal framework high overhead, a polished marble expanse sprawling beneath it. I slid across the stones, looking among dozens of ticket windows for the one for Fethiye. Nothing I would see in this town, I figured, could compare with the station.

The next bus was leaving at 9:30 P.M. for the three-hour trip to Fethiye. After brief reflection, during which I pictured myself arriving in a boarded-up town in the middle of the night, I forked over 700,000 *lirasi* (about five dollars) for a ticket. Then I went upstairs to the cafeteria and fortified myself for the journey with a *pide*—a delicious Turkish pizza shaped like a flattened football and bordered by a plump braid of ambrosial crust.

As is often the case with late-night, overland journeys, it was a motley, masculine crew that boarded the small bus. I ignored the seat number on my ticket and staked out a window by myself. The trip seemed interminable. Then, a little before midnight, we pulled up to a roadside café. I was furious—thirty minutes from our destination and we make a stop. In my mind I saw the last hotel in Fethiye closing up for the night.

We didn't get into town until half past one. A single taxi sat in the vast station lot. The driver did not understand the name of the hotel I gave him—Se-Sa, picked randomly from the dozen in my guidebook—but I caught its sign ("*C'est ça!*") just as he was about to speed along the gulf and out of town. He careened into a U-turn and screeched up in front of the entrance where, as if having dutifully waited up for me, a bellman emerged to take my bag.

Sunday, I awoke late and took a walk along the waterfront, which began in front of the Se-Sa and curved around to the center of town. Sailboats lined the main promenade, their brown masts mottling the traditional forest of white. Many of them were beautiful wooden yachts for hire, with crew, their itinerary maps displayed on their sterns. The town itself, except for a few whitewashed alleys that wound back from the harbor, was not especially picturesque (partly the result of earthquakes, the most recent in

1957). But it had that languorous, dulcet quality of all seaside resorts. Strolling, on a Sunday no less, I felt as if I were on a break between classes: geology in Cappadocia, poli sci in Ankara, religion in Konya, classics coming up next in Ephesus. Yet, walking back to the Se-Sa to do my laundry, I looked up and saw the pillars of Lycian rock tombs historicizing the face of a downtown mountain.

In the evening Fethiye turned chic; it was like walking through a completely different town. The display windows of jewelry stores glowed and drab upper floors disappeared in the dark. Strings of lights illuminated trellises and alleys newly furnished with hubbubed tables. The only difference from Mykonos or Santorini was the absence of music blaring out of shops. Not for the first time, Turkey reminded me of a subdued Greece.

I plopped down at a place called Megri, where one of eight bustling waiters—ranging in age from twelve to thirty—brought me a cold bottle of Efes beer, a puffed oval of sesame-seeded bread (puncturing it with my fork, I felt a hot blast of air on my hand), a delicious eggplant puree, and a seafood kebab that accommodated calamari, octopus, an unidentifiable fish, potatoes, peppers, and two whiskered, bug-eyed shrimp, their armored shells holding in their succulent juices.

After dinner I took a stroll. Entering a sweet shop, I examined the glass case and pointed to a small piece of lightly dusted jellied nougat. The owner lifted it with tongs, dropped it in a plastic bag, then wordlessly added four more pieces of different varieties. "*Teşekkur ederim,*" I said. Thank you.

Nearing the Se-Sa, I heard music coming from a side street, followed the sound, and came into a school courtyard transformed into a wedding hall. A band played at one end, a young man pounding vigorously on an enormous drum tied to his waist, while women with silky movements circle-danced under a cord of light bulbs strung between two netless backboards.

A girl of about ten emerged from the pack and started dancing in front of me. Her black hair glistened and bobbed in its pageboy cut, her blue-and-white dress shimmied around her unformed body. She fluttered sinuously with the music, swaying low, then rising, puffing her chest toward me, her arms outstretched, her smile immense, her lucid brown eyes planted directly on mine. Then she began thrusting one bare shoulder forward and coolly slapping it back with the palm of the opposite hand—the smart smack of flesh on flesh adding to the beat of the drums—all the while keeping her girlish smile. I grinned just as helplessly, mesmerized by the body of a child executing the movements of a woman, this bravura display of innocence and knowledge.

I remembered Tulay complaining about the incompatible austerity of Islam, explaining that Turkish women like to dress up, to dance, to express themselves. This Fethiyean pre-nymphet was not only showing off for a stranger (astutely picking the only one here who would write about her performance), but also making, it seemed, an unassailable argument for secularism in Turkey. For how could the fundamentalists eradicate, or even subdue, a feeling so clearly innate?

Monday morning breakfast at the bus station café: *gevrek*—a thin sesame bagel—washed down with a bottle of mineral water. A man sat reading the morning edition of *Gozcu,* while a boy of about thirteen—in white shirt, black bow tie, black pants, white socks, and brown sandals—swept crumbs off the tables with a wooden-handled brush.

The bus for Izmir skirted the coast and then turned north through rock-strewn mountains softened by clumps of tenacious trees: geological jellied nougat. After two hours I jumped off in Selcuk, again at the recommendation of Azim, who claimed that Kusadasi—the traditional base for excursions to Ephesus—was a crowded, charmless city plagued by Kurdish mafia.

I made the pilgrimage to the Greco-Roman ruins—getting a ride from the young manager of my hotel in a car undulating with the songs of Sezen Aksu. And I then walked back down an avenue shaded by mulberry trees. In the evening I sat in the main square and watched the men mouthing at their café tables, the storks putzing in their nests atop the Byzantine aqueduct, while the sun slowly fell.

Nearby stood the train station, with its own café tucked under branches and a fountain where a girl, with a little red wagon full of empty plastic bottles, graciously motioned me to go ahead of her to get my drink. And here it was again: not just kindness, but that instinctive radar for detecting a stranger's need for it. I thought of the wine merchant in Cappadocia who opened a bottle to give me a taste, the woman in Ankara's old town who emerged from nowhere to hand me a warm loaf of bread, the van driver who made sure that I caught the right bus, the sweets seller who knew I wanted more nougat. Over hundreds of miles, the thread had remained unbroken

Turkey was proving my theory that there are countries that treat you as a tourist and others—often the less celebrated ones—that receive you as a guest. It gave me satisfaction far beyond the personal, for few countries have been stamped with such consistently negative associations as this one. "Turkey," Mary Lee Settle wrote as recently as 1991 in the preface to her book *Turkish Reflections,* "has the worst and most ill-drawn public image of almost any country I know."

There were, going back to the 1500s, the soldiers of the Ottoman Empire spreading Islam throughout southeastern Europe and inevitably earning the Turk (among Christians at least) the label of "infidel." A place of pilgrimage in Austria is the hill where the Ottomans were defeated in 1683 by Polish King Jan III Sobieski, henceforward hailed as "the Savior of Vienna and Western Civilization."

This image of swarthy adversary was not short-lived. In the 1800s, the English spoke of the "unspeakable Turk." In *The Innocents Abroad,* Mark Twain opined: "I wish Europe would let Russia annihilate Turkey a little—not much, but enough to make it difficult to find the place again, without a divining-rod or a diving bell."

Alexander Kinglake, journeying to the East at the turn of the century, said of his Turkish porters in his travel classic *Eothen:* "They looked as if they would have thought themselves more usefully, more honourably, and more piously employed in cutting our throats than in carrying our portmanteaus." World War I found Turkey allied with Germany, and added to the list of history's massacres a name as sobering as Antietam—Gallipoli. Around this time came the deportations and mass killings of Armenians. Ataturk, with his Western sympathies, improved the country's image, but centuries of prejudice and misconceptions were not erased. Popular culture soon took up where ethnocentric history books had left off. "The Turks I saw in *Lawrence of Arabia* and *Midnight Express,*" Settle wrote, "were ogrelike cartoon characters compared to the people I had known and lived among for three of the happiest years of my life."

Istanbul's old Sultanahmet Prison is now a Four Seasons hotel. Before its closure in 1970, it was said that you were not a real journalist until you'd spent a few nights inside. Today it is fun to watch foreign guests enter self-importantly under the inscription that says, in old Arabic lettering, "Murderers, criminals, and journalists together."

The hotel serves, of course, as the perfect metaphor for the country's journey, in the eyes of the West, from bullying heathen to gracious host. And it signifies not only Turkey's victory, but tourism's as well. For this global activity, often criticized (justifiably) for the harm it causes to cultures and environments, can also—as evidenced here—have a salubrious effect as a destroyer of stereotypes.

Returning to Istanbul, I moved into my room at the Grand Hôtel de Londres, whose neighborhood, Beyoglu, soon became my favorite. Old-fashioned streetcars chugged up the otherwise traffic-less Istiklal Street. The long avenue, leading to Taksim Square, shared similarities with Budapest's Vaci Utca and Lisbon's Rua Garrett—two other pedestrian ways at the fringes of Europe that are as much shopping street as urban promenade. The crowds that marched here were young, modern, mixed: There was an equal number of women, and few of them covered their hair with scarves. (Although this didn't make them any easier to talk to.)

In the evening, music from pubs undulated down the side streets, and I entered a smoky one crowded with young people. I was seated at a table with three other patrons, all of them men. The waiter brought us beers, and small bowls of chips, nuts, and Turkish plums, like tiny green apples, which my tablemates ate with sprinkles of salt.

Two musicians and a singer—students, one of the men told me—sat by the front window. Their instruments, a wooden flute and an *ud* (a sort of fretless lute), produced sounds that differed from the slick commercialism of Greek bouzouki music; they hovered somewhere between the histrionic ululations of Arab song and a profound Russian melancholy, as seemed appropriate in a country caught between the Black and the Mediterranean seas.

"Political song," the man who spoke English would kindly bellow across the table to me. Or, "love song." At one point he said, nodding to the other men, "They want to know where you from?"

I told him and he translated. Then he shook his head.

"They have bad idea of America." He seemed reluctant to clarify, as if doing so would compromise his ethic of hospitality. I insisted.

"They say America is imperialist."

"And the Ottomans weren't?"

He laughed. "You right." Then he translated, but got no response.

Suddenly the people around us started to sing. Everybody knew the words. For the next song half the room rose, men and women, and, holding hands, animated the aisle with two long, sinuously moving lines. I watched with pleasure and envy, awed by this youthful passion for a music that wasn't the product of a cleverly marketed trend but which sprang from a much older, deeper, truer source.

The following afternoon I met Senem and Harika in the courtyard of the Galata Mevlevihane, the old ceremonial hall of the Whirling Dervishes. I had noticed the book Senem was carrying—*Principles of Management* (in English)—and used it as an opening. I still had not spoken to a woman in Istanbul.

I asked if they'd care to join me for tea. They looked alarmed; then, after brief consultation, cautiously agreed. I immediately had second thoughts: Was I leading them into some terrible transgression? On the way, the young ladies asked my age and marital status, quickly establishing that they were in the company not only of a strange man, but one who was married and twice their age.

We found a table on the second floor of a nearby coffee shop. A waiter came and, undisturbed by our arrangement, took our orders. Senem and Harika, I learned, were university students, living with their parents out near the airport. They had come into town to visit the British Council (hence the book) and play tourist. Last summer they had worked—Harika as an accountant, Senem as a flight attendant for Turkish Airlines—but during this vacation they were taking it easy.

"What do you see in Istanbul?" Senem asked. Her thin pale arms, emerging from a sleeveless blouse, were wispy with fine black hairs. I went down the list: Blue Mosque, Hagia Sophia, Topkapi Palace, the cistern, the Covered Bazaar, the Russian quarter, the Galata Tower, the Pera Palas.

"My uncle worked there," said Harika.

"Did he like it?"

"No. They don't give him much money."

"You know the Hagia Sophia was first a church and then a mosque?" said Senem. "And then Ataturk made it a museum. I hope they make it a mosque again."

"I hope they make it a church again," I said, and they both laughed.

"Are you Muslim?" I asked.

"Yes," said Senem.

"And you go to the mosque?"

"Not that often."

"But when you do, you sit upstairs?"

"Yes," she said.

"And that's OK with you? To sit apart from the men?"

Senem nodded.

"You asked me if I was married, so let me ask you: Do you have boyfriends?"

Harika did; Senem didn't. I asked Harika who paid when they went out. "The man," she said.

"Do you live together before marriage?" I asked.

"No," said Senem. "Not in Turkey. The family is very important."

I told them about a young Japanese woman I'd met who complained about advances from Turkish men. "But I guess that happens with foreign women."

"With Turkish women too!" Senem insisted. "They go like this," she made a hissing sound as if calling a cat. "It's awful. We don't go out at night. It's dangerous."

I told them about the women in the pub last night, by themselves as well as with men. They were unimpressed.

"Turkish men are only interested in sex," said Senem.

I said they were not unique, realizing it jeopardized my own tenuous status.

"So you don't go out at all at night? What do you do?"

"Stay home," Senem said, with a touch of sadness. "Watch TV. Read."

An awkward silence followed. I felt bad, thinking that my cavalier questioning had revealed to them the limitations of their lives. The check arrived and Senem took it. When I protested, she said:

"You are our guest."

# 23

# *Our Gang in Havana*

The carcass of the city was laid out under a leaden sky. Houses and apartment towers fused into a brittle, deteriorating mass, a petrified settlement. A few moppish trees were all that subverted the stark grid of peeling surfaces and darkened windows. Some homing pigeons occupied one of the low flat roofs like lone survivors. It was a landscape of unparalleled bleakness (why have the names Beckett and Havana never been linked?) and, like a car wreck, horribly riveting. I could not turn away from my ninth floor window.

Where the concrete ended, the ocean pounded. It crashed against the seawall and fell in startled waves onto the empty street. Fluid, spacious, undefiled; no wonder so many Habaneros are drawn to the Malecón along its edge. Surely it is not just the mirage of America that attracts, or the cooling breezes, but the balm of an immaculate, blameless vista.

And the water is so close you can touch it (or be touched by it). I had never seen a city and an ocean in such fervid contact. Usually there is a beach (Rio) or a bay (Sydney) to cushion the blow; here the high seas swell outside your window. Looking down from my hotel room, I imagined myself on the bridge of a fantastic, decrepit freighter.

The flight from Miami had taken less than an hour. As soon as our Mexicana charter touched down at José Martí International

Airport, the cabin resounded with a small burst of applause. "They're clapping because they've come home," the woman next to me explained to her granddaughter. "It's always nice to be home."

Inside the terminal, long lines sprouted under mounted TVs showing music videos and slapsticky comedies. Nobody laughed. I glanced quizzically at the flyer I'd been given for Cohiba cigars, and then, opening it up, found on the inside pages my entry form for immigration. The wait to get through lasted longer than the flight.

Outside, a crush of eager faces stared. They displayed the heightened anticipation of people looking for loved ones carrying bags of necessities. One young woman stood out, her bright smile like a beauty contestant's, masking an inner anxiety. She didn't need to wear the organization's T-shirt; it was obvious she was our tour guide. "Welcome to Cuba," she said warmly.

The van pulled out into a tropical green countryside under a Baltic gray sky. Goats nibbled on a bank of grass and billboards advertised the revolution. People walked, or pedaled bicycles. The first vintage Chevy rolled past like a runaway photographer's prop. A flight measured in minutes had carried us back decades.

"Who wants their Cuba Libre without rum?" Silvia asked. No one raised a hand. We moved en masse to the Presidente bar, off to the side of the elegant lobby.

"Are you the man from the *Sun-Sentinel?*" a woman asked me. Her name was Vera; she was standing under a chandelier with Ruth, the grandmother from the plane. They were both from Tamarac. "I read the classical music critic, the theater critic."

"I'm the travel editor."

"Oh, I never read the travel section."

"Me either," said Ruth.

Twenty minutes later, after I stared out the window up in my room, we regrouped in the lobby for the ride to the restaurant.

"Do you have hot water?"

"We don't have any water."

"Our TV doesn't work."

Each failing was mentioned, surprisingly, in a tone of surprise.

The Centro Vasco sat a dozen blocks from the Presidente, a sad, hushed, tired establishment; a fluorescent rebuff to the joyous, blaring, fiery Cuba of legend. (One stereotype shattered in the first two hours.) I sat with Ellen and Sonia, two friends from college now living in California and Idaho. We ate canned fruit cocktail (in the tropics!) followed by a thin, tough cutlet of beef.

"Can we have some bread?" Ellen asked the waiter, in decent Spanish.

"You want more bread?"

"We never got any bread."

We ditched the group and headed back on foot. The streets were poorly lit, the houses maquillaged by darkness. Vedado had started as the western suburb of Havana, and in the shadows we could discern the traces of a once-elegant neighborhood: faded villas rounded by classical porticoes, ratty apartments fit with art deco edges. Pushing through the gates of one building, we gazed in at a family in a bright yellow room, watching their own wonders on a black-and-white TV.

Nothing bored us. There was not just the everytrip attraction of the new, but the jolt of hearsay made tangible combined with the thrill of the forbidden. It didn't matter that we were here legally, on a cultural tour licensed by the U.S. Treasury Department; or that I was closer to home than my home is to either Ellen's or Sonia's; what mattered was that we had made it to the source of exquisite rancor and nostalgia.

Waves were still plummeting onto the sidewalk, and now spritzing us with salt spray as we stood a block inland. Half a dozen teenagers walked along the seawall, disappearing every few seconds under another street-lit wave. Sonia said, "There were fifteen of them when they started out."

We headed up Avenida de los Presidentes (who could sleep?) and then turned down a leafy side street. A wrought-iron fence enclosed a gracious, white-pillared mansion; blue lights dripped from a banyan tree. The Union of Cuban Writers and Artists, its Blue Ferret club in full, al fresco swing. We paid five dollars, found a table in the courtyard and ordered *mojitos.* A woman sang *boleros*—soft, romantic ballads; an emcee recited poetry. I caught the name Neruda, and the lines, "*los versos mas tristes esta noche*" (the saddest verses this night). People milled around in the back, or sat at green plastic tables with a bottle of rum in the center. They were nicely dressed, and had the intelligentsia's universal look of superiority.

"This is lovely," said Sonia, as a breeze rustled the banyan leaves above us.

"It's good to get away from the group," said Ellen. "Already I'm feeling a little too much togetherness."

"I was sitting next to Phyllis on the bus in from the airport," said Sonia. "Have you met her? She said to me: 'I'm a complainer.'"

"What did she have to complain about so soon?"

"The reading list. She was upset there was no Castro biography."

"She's a librarian," said Ellen. "It's not like she couldn't have picked one up."

We left around midnight. Back out on the street, Sonia confessed that twice she had received taps on the shoulder, and meaningful looks from the admiring men.

"I'm hot in Cuba."

The hotel the next morning was surrounded by khaki. Students sat under the statue-less pedestal on the avenida, while others stood with their teachers in fidgety rows. Many of them carried flowers, in memory, we were told, of Commandante Camilo Cienfuegos, whose plane had disappeared into the ocean forty-two years earlier. A small band marched by and everybody followed it excitedly to the sea.

As soon as a wave splattered the street, minions would run and toss their flowers over the wall, then scurry back before the next spill. Or try to. Often, the sea rose up and drenched a unit right in the middle of its release. This caused the hundreds of spectators to roar with laughter. More students charged the wall, crisp and determined, and retreated dripping. Even the policemen were chuckling. It was a riotous, endlessly repeated scene of flying flowers, dancing spray, and clinging uniforms. I had never seen a more joyous memorial service.

On the terrace of the Presidente, Carlos waited patiently, enjoying the spectacle of us witnessing the impromptu and the patriotic.

"We read a poem by Che in our office, in honor of Camilo," he said, after we had all slowly filed back for the meeting. "It was our idea—nobody told us we had to do it."

We listened obediently, seventeen Americans, only a few of whom could not remember a Castro-less Cuba.

"We are a social organization," Carlos continued, "not governmental. So we tell you our personal views."

A man in a baseball cap that read "Genuine Antique Person" sat nodding his head in agreement with everything that was said. It seemed an unhealthy reaction to the words of a man representing the Orwellian-sounding Cuban Institute of Friendship with the Peoples.

"Tourists who come here sometimes say to me: 'Carlos, we want to meet real Cubans. And I tell them: you can talk to anybody you like. But remember: I am a real Cuban too. Silvia and Gustavo," he said, looking at our guides, "are real Cubans." And they were; young, nicely dressed—the next generation.

The Genuine Antique Person kept nodding his head in solidarity, and staring, it seemed, directly at me. Ruth and Vera looked much more skeptical, as did Ellen and Sonia.

"The only thing that is forbidden in Cuba is to be uncomfortable," cooed Carlos. "We want you to be comfortable."

The Genuine Antique Person liked what he heard.

Our van rolled along the sea.

"This is the U.S. Interests Section," Gustavo explained as we passed a stout office building. "During the week you will see lots of people standing around here, waiting to get in."

Next to it was a large stage.

"Political rallies are held here. It was built to welcome Elián back. Do you remember that boy?"

The van groaned a yes.

"And look—there is a statue of José Martí, holding a child in one arm, and pointing with the other. You see where he is pointing?" It was directly at the U.S. Interests section. He had an angry, accusatory glare, quite removed from the intelligent regard I'd seen in portraits of the refined poet and statesman. Dissing public sculpture.

We plunged through low canyons of tottering colonialism. We weren't in Old Havana yet, but there were arches and niches and weathered façades, all running together in a kind of symmetry of decline. The living conditions were abominable—cramped and airless, without any trees—but the overall effect was not as grim as the view from my window. The architectural flourishes gave everything a Neapolitan air of romantic squalor.

I was surprised at how grand the city was—not just in size, or in style, but in the combination of the two. I had seen a lot of pictures, and half expected that they had captured, if not everything, at least the finest things. How often have you visited a place, your imagination fired by photographs, only to find that they left little to the reality? Havana seemed the exception: It stretched outside one's expectations, and showed itself to be beyond the conjurings of a camera.

A large opening appeared in the form of the Plaza de la Revolución. It had that vast, vacant, portentous look (no place to hide) of public spaces in communist capitals. You thought of Red Square and, especially, Tiananmen Square, while the lack of traffic, the lazy roll of bicycles along the edges, reminded me of Hanoi. It seemed, too, something of a museum piece, with the famous steel frieze of Che branding one of the surrounding buildings. A living but timeworn dinosaur.

"The Pope had a Mass here," Gustavo said.

"Did many people come?" someone asked.

"Yes, because he's a personality. But Cuba is not a Catholic country. Most people believe in African saints."

We took our pictures and climbed back in the van, which dropped us off at a rum factory, right in the city, with a store conveniently situated on the second floor. Bottles lined the shelves and cigar boxes sat atop the counters.

"Do you smoke cigars?" I asked Gustavo.

"No," he said. "It's just old men."

Outside, I mentioned this to Sonia.

"I guess that whole retro thing," she said, "hasn't really caught on here."

"Well, when you're already living in the past . . ."

The Genuine Antique Person wandered up to me. His name was Bernie. "I like the people here," he said. "They have a vitality, a dynamic spirit."

I stood speechless. I hadn't seen it; I hadn't noticed anything remotely close to it. I am a travel writer; my job is to pick up on these things, to read the messages in postures and gaits, expressions and clothing. A woman walked by, carrying a bag. I looked closely and still could not detect a dynamic spirit. All I could make out was a kind of languid acquiescence. This is one of the reasons I hate traveling with a group.

Back in the van, Wanda from San Jose said: "The Cubans in Miami, they paint a different picture. They tell you people here are hungry, dirty."

"You don't see tattoos," said Chip approvingly. "Or graffiti."

Lunch was at the Café del Oriente opposite the Lonja de Comercio. I sat with Wanda, Daisy, and Parker, who was wearing a Puerto Rico sweatshirt and a Panama hat. Silvia came by and said we had a choice of beef, chicken, or fish.

"Polio," said Parker, making an attempt at Spanish rather than humor. "And black beans."

"They don't have black beans here," Silvia informed him.

"We've been in Cuba twenty four hours and still haven't had any black beans. Why don't they take us to real Cuban places?"

"I see Castro's doing everything to make the Cubans dislike us even more," said Daisy.

"How's that?" I asked.

"By making us eat in places Cubans can't afford."

I didn't tell her that almost any restaurant would be out of the price range of the average Cuban.

"That's why so much of the world hates us," she said.

"If I were independently wealthy," said Parker, "I'd come down here and get a place to live for a couple of months. I love salsa. I went to the Casa de la Música last night. It was great. There's something about salsa that relaxes me."

In the van, Gustavo had told us that "the housing problem is the main problem in Cuba today." He said that, after a year of marriage, he still lived with his in-laws, one of fourteen people in six rooms.

My fish arrived, along with a salad of tomato, cucumber, and shredded cabbage, the same combination I'd gotten in St.

Petersburg. I'd seen vestiges of the old Soviet friendship in the streets—Havana must be the only city in the world where you can find a '56 Pontiac parked next to an '81 Lada—but I hadn't expected to find them on my plate.

We strolled through Old Havana, around the leafy green Plaza de Armas and up to the blue-shuttered Plaza de la Catedral. Daisy accompanied me across the cobblestones, still moved by the morning's memorial service. "When have you seen," she asked me, "that much spirit in the United States?"

The van drove us in darkness along the Malecón. The sea was still raging, peppering the street with salt, and keeping away dreamers.

"Gustavo," Sonia said, "with all the old cars here, being a mechanic must be one of the best jobs in Cuba."

"The best job in Cuba," he said, "is to have a private business. People who rent apartments—they do very well."

"You're a capitalist," Sonia said laughing.

"No," he said. "I'm a realist."

We filed into La Zaragozana, just down the street from El Floridita. I wondered if the high-end tours get the old Hemingway hangout.

"You have a choice of pork, chicken, or fish," said Silvia.

We were the only people in the restaurant. A band materialized. It was our first hearing of "Guantanamera." Our first discussion, too, of the inevitable opening up of the country, and its subsequent ruination. People moaned about how Starbucks will come in, and then McDonald's, and how the place will lose all of its color and authenticity. Such talk always annoys me. It puts too much of an emphasis on externals, forgetting that what's important is not buildings but the people in them; and not how they look—now that louche is pretty much universal—but what they think and feel. More important, this attitude almost always ignores the best interests of the locals. There is something maddeningly haughty about being chauffeured in an air-conditioned van through crumbling streets to ample meals and then expressing the hope that things never change. It is a kind of anti-imperialistic imperialism, wanting to keep a place disfranchised, in stasis, just to satisfy outsiders' cravings for the antique. There is nothing more self-serving, and often destructive, than the tourist in search of a pure experience.

Over dessert, Silvia asked me about my job. I said my newspaper gives me money to travel and write about the places I visit. She had never been outside Cuba. The idea—of having not just the freedom but the means, in my case the *obligation,* to travel—must have seemed utopian to her.

"I would love to go to the U.S.," she said.

"But you have to get a passport—and visa."

"It's not that simple," she said.

"It's expensive," I suggested.

"There are other obstacles," she said cryptically, and then looked away.

The group headed off to the Tropicana; I took a right at El Floridita and walked down Obispo. The dark pillars of a bank rose up, their closeness, the street's narrowness, gave everything the slighter smaller-than-scale look of a movie set. It was easy to imagine the place in the 1950s—sailors, businessmen, honeymooning Americans. Music flowed through the open slats of brightly lit bars.

I turned down an empty, unlit street. A policeman stood at the next corner, his legs apart. I continued on and a jagged space opened up, a half block of rubble under the stars. It was like entering a bombed out city, breathing the same air of desertion and ruin.

Not far away, a card game bellowed on Plaza Vieja. A young woman greeted me with "*amigo*" as I got near. Her English was very good. She was from Santiago de Cuba, but lived here now. It was convenient, she said.

"And beautiful," I added, looking around the classical square.

She seemed unconvinced. "Do you want to see?" she asked, and then walked me under some scaffolding, past the card players, and into a courtyard. The classical quickly gave way to tortured tenement: four close levels of soiled walls and opaque windows, a rusting stairway seemingly hanging in midair. A man wearing nothing but a pair of gym shorts aimed a hose at the filthy pavement. I don't think I had ever stepped so effortlessly, and dramatically, out of the tourist's world and into the local's.

With pity, and relief, I retreated outside.

"We have to move," the woman said. "They are going to start renovations. They are going to send us to a place called Alamara, outside the city."

"Will you come back after the renovations?"

"I don't know."

I wished her luck.

"If you want somebody to show you around Havana," she said, "come by anytime—I'm always here."

Back on Obispo a young woman, walking arm-in-arm with her boyfriend, turned and said hello. She had a beautiful, surprisingly lingering smile. She asked if I was Italian, then French. Nobody expects Americans; Havana is the place to come if you want to be made to feel Continental.

"This is my brother," she said. I couldn't see any family resemblance. He was stocky and brutish (especially in his sunglasses); she was svelte and delicate, with darker skin. I was now seriously doubting my abilities as an observer.

"My sister is in dance school," the brother said. This seemed to make sense.

We walked along together. My Spanish, never stellar under the best circumstances, was struggling to follow a language emptied of

Ss. Then they asked if I wanted to join them for a drink. I started to doubt that the sister was a dancer; that they were brother and sister. I suspected that she was a *jinetera,* a jockey. It is the term for people, not just women, who offer foreigners services, not always sexual. What began meaning "prostitute" has been stretched to embrace "hustler" and even, considering the times, "entrepreneur."

We traversed the Parque Central (the capitol looming on the left, the brother pointing out landmarks) and headed down a street of closed-up shops and shadowy forms. Every few yards the brother would stop and shake someone's hand.

"My brother knows a lot of people," the sister said. "He was a famous boxer."

They led me to a darker, emptier street. When I hesitated, the brother cajoled me. "Nothing's going to happen. It's very safe here. Policemen are everywhere." His voice had a counterproductive vehemence. Exasperated, he took out his wallet, extracted a business card, and stuffed it into my shirt pocket. His sister pulled me forward; her palms were unexpectedly coarse.

Around the next corner, a glow appeared. The entrance to Chinatown: red paper lanterns and swarthy Cuban waiters in emperor jackets. We sat at an outside table and ordered *mojitos;* when they arrived, both brother and sister poured a little onto the pavement.

"For the *santaría* spirits," the sister explained. Then she took off her sweater, revealing a bandeau top and spilling her drink.

"The spirits will be very happy," I said, and they both laughed.

She ordered another. Her brother downed his and said he had to get going. It was a little after midnight. Surely, I thought, our bureau chief will now walk by.

"He is a very good brother," the sister said. "He comes by and plays with my son."

"You have a son?" I asked. She looked awfully young.

"Yes. He is ten months old."

"Where is he now?"

"With my mother."

She asked if I wanted to go somewhere. I told her she was very beautiful, but I had to get back to my hotel. We retraced our steps. On the way she pulled me into a dimly lit shop so I could buy her some cookies. As soon as we were outside, she tore open the bag and started eating, stuffing one into my mouth as she chewed and walked.

At the park we said our goodbyes. Then I climbed in a taxi while the young mother sauntered back out into the night. It was hard not to imagine her better off working at the Gap.

Monday morning I stood at my ninth floor window and watched the waves trip over the seawall. Then I dressed and walked to La Rampa—once known as the "Tropical Broadway"—to get my journalist's accreditation at the Centro de Prensa Internacional.

The receptionist told me to have a seat in the lobby. After about ten minutes a casually dressed man approached and introduced himself in careful English. Raúl had a friendly smile. As he opened the door to the corridor, he told me that his goal was to improve his English.

"But I would think that most of the foreign correspondents here speak Spanish," I said.

"That is my problem," he laughed.

In a windowless office, we sat on opposite sides of his desk and chatted. Raúl had spent some years in Madrid, and we reminisced about the nightlife. Then we talked about the food. Finally, he gave me a form to complete. Near the end I came to the question: "Have you ever written a book?" It seemed a little odd; I answered simply, "Yes."

Presently, an older man came in and sat at the computer, slowly typing in what I assume were my answers. Raúl and I talked a little baseball. Then he asked if I had a photograph of myself. I said I didn't. He pondered this failing, while I pictured myself being deported, and then said we could go to the shop and make copies of the one in my passport. The shop, conveniently, was just off the lobby. He handed my passport to one of the salesgirls while I perused the postcard rack.

After I paid, bringing my total morning expenditure to about sixty-two dollars, we returned to the office. The computer expert was still typing. Raúl and I talked about the Pope's visit to Cuba. (He had been in Madrid, so missed the excitement at the Centro de Prensa.) Finally, the other man left. We kept chatting for another ten minutes, until a woman arrived, took Raúl's place at the desk and started typing heavily on a manual typewriter. This, I assumed, was my accreditation card. When she was done, she handed Raúl the paper from out of the carriage. He excused himself and returned a while later with it nicely laminated. Smiling, he handed me my press credentials. All in all, it had taken three people about one hour to produce a document the size of a business card. Here, though humanized, was all of the old Soviet waste.

The group had already left on its day-trip to Pinar del Rio, so I strolled over to the Nacional—Havana's Plaza Hotel, with a view of the open sea instead of a city park. This was where Parker was staying; driving in from the airport we had dropped him off first, turning down the straight, treelined drive.

I hired a taxi to Centro Havana and visited a friend of a friend. Juan, a librarian, lived on the third floor of a dilapidated building; several windows on the stairwell had been punched out, not recently one guessed. We sat in the living room of his tiny apartment, which he shared with his son; I on the small sofa; he in the one chair. A stainless steel sink sat upright on the floor between two bookcases. Many of the titles, I noticed, were in English.

"They all were sent from the States," he said. "None of them were bought here. I don't even go in the bookstores here."

I asked if things had gotten better since the "Special Period," the euphemism given to the hard times following the collapse of the Soviet Union, and the drying up of aid.

"I won't say the Special Period is over until I can afford a month's worth of food. My monthly rations are usually enough for one week. Sugar can last a little longer, and for me, rice—I don't eat a lot of rice. But beans—the beans are not enough for anybody.

"I don't want a car," he said wearily, "or fancy clothes, I just want to be able to afford to feed myself."

He asked if I would like some tea. I said yes. Then he asked if I wanted it with sugar. I nodded, then immediately realized my faux pas. I tried to insist that I had misspoken, that I always drink unsweetened tea. I turned the subject to Castro.

"Sometimes I wish he were dead," Juan said. "And then I wonder if there will be anyone who can follow after him. He has such a presence. He is so tall. I watch him on the television and I am amazed that someone can lie so well."

He had entered the lottery for a visa to the States, for the first time. You had to have a degree, he said, and some other qualifications. Even if he won, he wasn't sure he'd go. "I can't take my son. And I am—how do you say, marked, branded?—by the socialist system. I don't like it, but I don't like capitalism either."

He apologized, saying he had to get to the hospital to visit his cousin. "When someone is in the hospital you have to spend a lot of time with them, help them. The doctors are good, but the nurses aren't. It's a strange country," he said, "you can get a heart transplant for free, but often you can't find any aspirin to buy."

Before leaving, I asked him if the sea was always spilling into the city.

"No," he laughed. "Sometimes it is as smooth as a lake."

★ ★ ★

In the evening the group was back. We went in our van to a restaurant in Miramar, the district just to the west of Vedado. Embassies and state institutes filled many of the old mansions, saving them from disfigurement. We pulled up in front of an open-air restaurant that looked vaguely Polynesian. A long table awaited us, along with a choice of chicken or pork, tonight with black beans. (Juan's lost portions, I thought.)

I sat at one end with Sonia and Ellen and Bernie. He was a retired psychiatrist. The discussion turned to 9/11. Bernie posited the idea that there is no such thing as "an innocent person." I suggested that children who die in a hijacked plane can be seen as innocents. He doubted the existence of moral absolutes; he wouldn't condemn, or even define, evil; he said was looking for a more "Aristotelian approach." Bringing Aristotle to Cuba, especially with some of this crowd, was fine with me: Look around you at what is, if you want to see the truth. But I didn't take to his linguistic calisthenics in talking about terrorism.

Back in the van, he seemed invigorated by the discussion. "So you don't think we should have fought Hitler?" I asked.

"Oh no, I do," he said. "If it were up to me I'd say 'Let's go into Afghanistan and bomb the hell out of them.'"

It had all been a game.

One of the beauties of travel is the release from routine, which is not as complete when you are with a group, seeing the same faces every morning, and is even more compromised when your group is in Cuba, where you can find yourself attending more meetings than you do back at work.

After breakfast on Tuesday, we arrived at the Cuban Institute of Friendship with the Peoples, just down the street from the Blue Ferret club.

"You are lucky," Carlos greeted us, "because now we're having an exhibition of photographs of Fidel and Che with children."

We took our seats on the side terrace, while Carlos warmed up for his boss, with whom we were to have "a friendly talk."

But first, he thought we would like to know about the structure of the institute. "There are five divisions," he said. "I represent part of the North American division. We also cover work with Canada. All the friends we have in Europe, we have a group taking care of them.

"Here comes my boss. Let me tell you, I have a lot of respect for him. One, because he is my boss." (Laughter.) "But also because he's my friend. He's a living history."

"He's going to have a good future," cracked the boss, taking the floor.

"It is very nice to have you here. It is very nice to have you here as friends. The experience we have with you is as a very friendly people."

I had never seen an institute so relentlessly living up to its name.

"Cuba is the safest place in the world for Americans," he said. "We don't see you as enemies, we see you as"—and he fooled me here—"neighbors."

He told us that he had traveled to Ohio, "a conservative state." And he said that the people there told him they wanted better relations with Cuba in the future. "They produce a lot of food. They want to sell their food to Cuba."

He was from the oleaginous school. "I always say the embargo against Cuba will not be lifted by law, it will be lifted by love."

On that note he opened it up to questions.

"A problem for the U.S. is that we see Castro as a dictator," observed Ruth from Tamarac. Immediately my heart went out to all the fractious, uncompromising, South Florida seniors.

The boss smiled. He had heard this before. He was smooth and practiced. He knew how to deal with friends.

"For you, what is a dictator?"

"Somebody who has absolute power."

"This is one of the questions we like to answer," he said. "Who is Fidel Castro? He is a man who since he was seventeen years old is fighting for the humble people of Cuba.

"There is a priest now living in Miami, who was one of Castro's teachers. Castro came from a very wealthy family. And the priest wrote that Castro is made of wood. It means he has guts, courage. Fidel once came to him. 'Father, is it possible to put a light in the basketball court? I want to have light to practice at night.' He got the light. Because he was the best player in the school."

Ruth already looked a little sorry she had asked her question.

"When he became a lawyer, his first case was a family that was expelled from their apartment. He defended them . . ."

It was the mythology of bedtime stories, adorning a modern, living leader. But it didn't stop at that. There was the whole doublespeak arsenal, from words sapped of meaning—"in 1993, after the collapse of the Soviet Union, we had to find another way to advance"—to the incomplete explanation: "You see our police in Cuba? None of them are using pistols. We don't have anti-demonstration troops. We don't need them.

"There was a plan to build a thermo-nuclear plant near Havana. A big discussion. Fidel, having heard everything, said: 'I think the best thing is to follow the advice of the ecologists.'"

Out of utter exasperation I almost raised my hand and asked: "Could you please speak a little on the best way to prepare black beans?"

"Cuba," the boss concluded, "is not a paradise. It is not perfect. Who in the world is perfect?"

"A lot of people in the United States," Alice from California said, "are ignorant of the benefits of the Cuban government. How did you get into this line of work?"

He spoke, with obvious relief, about his own life. Then he excused himself, saying, "I have some friends from Chicago here—I want to say something to them."

After the meeting, Tamara, Ruth's granddaughter, went up to Carlos and said: "I want to know, when I get back to New York, what I can do to be a friend of Cuba."

There had been a man at the meeting I hadn't seen before. Sonia told me that this was the famous Randy. Whenever certain members wanted to give an utterance a ring of authority, they would preface it with: "Randy says . . ." Randy was their prophet, their resident authority. According to Sonia, he came here routinely to visit the various families he had "adopted." He spent most of his time with them, using the tour chiefly as a visa vehicle for getting into the country.

Parker, too, had been here once before, and was now seriously looking into renting an apartment for his next visit. His room at the Nacional was costing him a few hundred dollars a night. And with all that late-night salsa dancing, how much time does one spend in a hotel room?

On our way to dinner that night, we swung by the Nacional and stopped on the street outside. When the door opened, Parker stepped up, reached around to the refrigerated case, grabbed a bottle of mineral water, and then stepped out. It took only a few seconds, but consumed minutes of subsequent thought by me. Had he requested we come by just so he could pick up some water? Or had he been planning to join us, then all of a sudden decided he only needed a drink? And why couldn't he have paid for a bottle in the hotel gift shop?

It was interesting to me as well, that the two people who passed the least amount of time with us were the most dissimilar—the Good Samaritan and the Party Animal. But there appeared to be a vast array of reasons for coming to Cuba, which made sense, since Cuba has long been, in Americans' minds, more than a country. There are those who come to help, and those who come to play. Those who come out of curiosity, and those who come to confirm preconceptions. There are those who see a tour of Cuba as an endorsement, by contrast, of democratic capitalism, and others who look at it as an act of ideological homage, a kind of political pilgrimage. Some from this crowd go even further, viewing the journey as a protest against their own country and its policies, a kind of subversive tourism.

We had a few of these. An afternoon trip to a Women and Family Orientation House had prompted, among some in our group, numerous unfavorable comparisons to the United States, and the miserable condition of American women. It didn't seem to dawn on any of the female admirers that in their backward state they had nevertheless managed to scrape together enough money for a vacation abroad, an achievement that was far beyond the dreams of most of their privileged Cuban "sisters."

And we had others. The Holy Grail for some people was nothing more than a dinner in a *paladar,* a restaurant in a private house. And Sonia had a passing interest in seeing a *santaría* ceremony, which she expressed to Gustavo that evening in the van. He said that he knew of a *babalao* (priest), but that he lived quite far away.

"Have him meet us at the *parador,*" said Chip, the Spanish butcher.

"You can't do that!" said the heretofore silent Andrew, laughing hysterically. "Take the *babalao* to a restaurant!?! He'll bring all his stuff, his chicken, his goat . . ."

We swept through a tunnel and then up a hill, to yet another empty restaurant, with the same multiple choice of pork, chicken, or fish, and the now familiar serenade, an infusion of forced gaiety, like a glee club visit to a nursing home. Except that here in Cuba the vital visitors were always entertained by the prospectless patients. As usual, the musicianship was excellent. Tonight we got not only "Guantanamera" but also "Dos Gardenias." It occurred to me that the ideal Latin American country would have the food of Mexico and the music of Cuba.

La Fortaleza de San Carlos de la Cabana sat a short walk up a crowded path. Visitors, most of them Cuban, were heading to the nightly cannon blast from the second-largest fort in the Western Hemisphere. No sooner had the shots been "fired," by solemn men in period garb, than Afro-Cuban dances broke out. Women in bright headscarves writhed alarmingly across the cobblestones, as delighted spectators followed behind. A circle then formed, the dancers creating a feverish blur in the middle. It was all part of the show, and what seemed a national talent—I thought back to the Camilo remembrance—for turning the ceremonial into the celebratory.

The city fell away quickly, replaced by a rich, uncomplicated greenness. We could feel at last, as our van sailed east toward Santa Clara, that we were in the Caribbean.

Havana, for all its humid decay, still seemed more like a major metropolis than an island capital. The countryside also had something of this grand scale: endless rows of sugar cane, men on horseback under a spacious sky, ranges instead of mere mountains. But there were familiar, tropical touches as well: straw hats, tiki huts, people with bundles waiting patiently for lifts, though often their numbers grew so high that they formed the equivalent of a big city bus stop.

It was hard to place Cuba. When you arrived you saw the conditions and thought that things were much worse than anything you'd seen in other communist countries—though that was in Europe. So you moved your field of comparison, and decided: It's not so bad when you look at many other parts of the Caribbean. But then you realized that that was not quite fair either: Cuba is not just an island, it is a country the size of Florida. It once possessed a technologically sophisticated society, though one with a brutal divide between rich and poor. By the end of the nineteenth century, Cuba had more railroad lines, for its land mass, than any country in Latin America; in 1921 it also claimed more telephones per capita. As the 1950s arrived, urban households gleamed with modern appliances. Wormold, the hero of Graham Greene's *Our Man in Havana,* sold vacuum cleaners on Lamparilla Street.

We stopped for lunch at a roadside restaurant. It looked to be in the middle of nowhere; however, a band appeared, with CDs for sale.

"Things aren't as bad here as in some places I've been," said Ruth. "Like Botswana."

"Or Nepal," said Vera.

I whispered to Sonia. "And they don't read the travel section."

"I find the people very nice," someone commented. "Not depressed."

I took issue with the second part, mentioning my visit to the librarian Juan.

"Well, he's doing better than me," Wanda said brusquely.

"Wanda," I said, "you're HERE! On VACATION! You paid over $2,000 for this trip!"

"You need to talk to a wider range of people," she said. "I think as a reporter you should get a more balanced view."

I remembered my care package—aspirin, soaps, pens, shampoos, Band-Aids, a couple of baseballs. I had been saving it for Juan, but now I was tempted to give it to Wanda.

"Wanda, I'm sorry, I didn't realize things were so bad for you in San Jose."

After lunch, Ruth approached me. "I'm going to read your article and then I'm going to write a letter to your editor and tell him that I had a completely different impression."

A light drizzle was falling when we stopped at the Vocational School for the Arts for a subdued performance by expressionless students in an auditorium that smelled of gasoline.

Our hotel was just down the road, a leafy complex of thatch bungalows reminiscent of a Yucatan resort. I ended up in one of the more modern dwellings, but with a window looking out on dripping vegetation. I missed the *Sturm und Drang* view from the Hotel Presidente.

A kindly bus driver gave me a lift into town. It too reminded me of Mexico, with its low, faded buildings framing a central plaza. Through the wide open windows and door of the library I could see students reading at large desks under high fluorescent bulbs and a portrait of Che.

In front of the Teatro La Caridad, I ran into Sonia, Ellen, and Chip. We piled into La Marquesina bar next door and ordered beers. A weathered farmer offered us each a potato chip from his bag, and then recited a poem to Ellen. Outside she said:

"He told me I was the first American he had ever spoken to."

We washed a bad dinner down with delicious *mojitos* and then took a stroll. Popping into a bookstore, Sonia asked the clerk if he had anything by Reinaldo Arenas. She had read *Before Night Falls,* and seen the movie. The clerk said he didn't know the name. I remembered that the Argentine journalist Jacobo Timerman, on a visit in the 1980s, had described Cuba as a country with 99-percent literacy and nothing worth reading. The flimsy daily *Granma* was an embarrassment even in the half-light world of party organs.

Just as we were about to look for a taxi, a Valentino appeared in a black leather jacket.

"Los Caneyes?" he asked, saying the name of our hotel.

"How much?"

"Three dollars."

His ancient Lada stalled three times before we reached the corner.

"My girlfriend," he said in Spanish, "she plays the violin at your hotel." He also said he had a brother in Miami. Then he pushed in a cassette; it was not her, it was someone other than the Righteous Brothers doing "Unchained Melody." And within two seconds, we were all singing along loudly, passionately, unabashedly. "*Are you . . . still miiiiiiiiinnee?*"

It was totally spontaneous, and strangely beautiful, belting out this song from our youths in an antique Russian car driven by a black-haired Adonis in the Cuban interior. It was like a scene from a movie, an unexpected moment of lightness, and connection, the first real one of the trip. (Only later did it occur to me how fitting, from an exile's perspective, that song's lyrics are.)

"Cuban people don't like vegetables," Gustavo said.

"I can't imagine," said Tamara, "a whole country that doesn't like vegetables."

But when we arrived at the office of the model family practitioner the next morning, we were told that the biggest health problem in Cuba was hypertension, due to the poor lifestyle. We were enlightened regarding the successes in responding to emergencies and in preventing teenage pregnancies. (The news that teenagers don't need parental permission to obtain contraceptives, which are free, won applause from the two Tamarac ladies.)

Someone asked about AIDS. Silvia, interpreting, said that a person who tests positive for HIV is taken to a place—"a sanitarium, and is treated, and taught to be responsible. And when he is responsible, he leaves."

Outside, Michael, the only member of our group fluent in Spanish, said: "The doctor was less clear on the leaving part."

We then traveled to the model policlinic. Four beds with scratched metal posts filled one room. Sheets were worn thin and dotted with holes. A lone patient grimaced with pain while his wife shooed a pesky fly from his face. The windows were open wide to the street.

Out in the corridor, Sonia whispered: "Tom, if anything happens to me on this trip, promise you'll make sure I get sent home."

Bernie said: "Very impressive. For a low-tech system, very impressive."

(After the trip, I got a message from Bernie informing me that he had sent the clinic some costly and badly needed equipment.)

In the afternoon we visited the Che memorial and museum. (When I had told Juan that I was coming to Santa Clara, he said he'd been to the town, but had never visited either.) We parked to the side of an empty expanse fronting a large statue of the revolutionary. The words "*Hasta La Victoria Siempre*" (Ever Onwards to Victory) blazed underneath. It was in Santa Clara that rebels led by Che had won one of the last battles in the war against Batista.

From the memorial—with its tablets to those killed with Che in Bolivia—we entered the museum. Here, captioned pictures stretched back to his seminal motorbike journey around South America, his medical school years, his comfortable, middle-class childhood in Argentina. There was an arresting photograph of him, shortly after the revolution, sitting with his mother and brother at José Martí airport, the three of them sharing a laugh as if in some student center during Parents' Weekend. Pale, soft, almost pudgy, he rarely resembled the iconic poster boy.

"Only two people could go in his office without knocking," Gustavo said. "Not Castro. Camilo and Ochoa." Ochoa, he explained, was the general convicted in the drug trafficking scandal in 1989 and executed. Wrongly, Gustavo thought. "He did some great things for the revolution."

We moved to a video of rebels singing a revolutionary song. Gustavo sang along softly; not for us, I sensed, but out of true conviction.

Alice, who had taken to wearing an "I ♥ Cuba" button, was red with tears.

Back in the van, Gustavo asked if we'd enjoyed the museum.

"Yes, it was very educational," said Wanda. "It's so nice to be in a place where you can learn about history. In our country they just want to keep everybody ignorant."

The tour was winding down. Evening showers kept us captive at the hotel. I found Ellen and Tamara in the open-air bar drinking sodas with Gustavo.

"People think we hate the Cubans in Miami," he said. "But we have friends and family there." He claimed that, of his high school class, he was the only one still living in Cuba. "I have an uncle in Miami. He went over in a raft. He stole the car of a colonel and then used the engine for the raft."

He took a sip of his soda. "With the Soviet Union, we were spoiled. We lived in a glass bubble. We got aid, and many supplies for free . . ."

It was all so obvious, but somehow startling coming from our guide. "Cuba has to move forward," he said. "We have been the same . . . while the rest of the world has moved on. We have to move too."

He added that he had plans to attend business school; he wanted to be prepared for whatever came next.

After dinner we dashed through the rain to the bar again. Cuban music was playing, and we watched Gustavo dance with the souvenir saleswoman. They looked like professionals, executing complicated footwork and synchronized spins. They were all grace and sensuousness. Then she left and American music came on. We all got up, joining our guides, bumping and grinding, the smooth and sensual now reduced to the inane and suggestive. A few couples formed, youth with youth. It was the wet tropics, and the last night away from the capital . . .

Friday we returned to Havana for our farewell meeting, complete with hors d'oeuvres. (Of course—the evening we had reservations at a *paladar.*) Carlos, from the Cuban Institute of Friendship with the Peoples, wanted to know our thoughts.

"First, I want to thank the guides and the drivers," said Alice. "This has been a wonderful tour. Let's hope that we can have peace in our world."

Carlos looked pleased, then asked what suggestions we had for improving the tour.

"More time at the Che museum," said Alice.

"It would be nice to stay with families," said Phyllis. "I don't like staying in fancy hotels in poor countries."

"I would like to meet musicians in the street," Michael said.

"See a nice small town," added his wife, "with a church."

"Meet Fidel," said Chip.

"*I* would like to meet Fidel," said Carlos. "I would like to shake his hand. But did you feel that you were hearing the truth?"

"Not everybody has answered us as truthfully as we would have liked," said Vera. "Let them know that we know that they were not up-front with us."

"I felt that people were very up-front," said Alice. "I'm not a naïve person. I worked in L.A. I think people were being polite."

"It's not a perfect world," said Chip.

"Chip the peacemaker," Sonia whispered to me. "It's beautiful."

"You're never going to get all the answers to your questions," he said. "That's why you go on."

Back at the hotel, after a lobster dinner, I packed my bags and stared out the window. Lights speckled a dark thicket of dwellings while, off to the right, a black void sent waves billowing over the seawall. At night, too, the city loomed like a ghostly vessel, fighting through squalls, and going nowhere.